KV-030-458

WHAT FUTURE FOR SOCIAL SECURITY?

First published in Great Britain in July 2002 by

The Policy Press
34 Tyndall's Park Road
Bristol BS8 1PY
UK

Tel +44 (0)117 954 6800
Fax +44 (0)117 973 7308
e-mail tpp@bristol.ac.uk
www.policypress.org.uk

First published in 2001

Hardback edition of this book available from Kluwer Law International,
PO Box 85889, CN The Hague, The Netherlands

British Library Cataloguing in Publication Data

A catalogue record for this book is available from the British Library

ISBN 1 86134 410 4 paperback

Jochen Clasen is Professor of Comparative Social Research, Department of
Applied Social Science, University of Stirling.

Cover design by Qube Design Associates, Bristol.

Front cover: photograph kindly supplied by www.johnbirdsall.co.uk

Printed and bound in Great Britain by Hobbs the Printers Ltd, Southampton.

WHAT FUTURE FOR SOCIAL SECURITY?

Debates and reforms in national and cross-national perspective

Edited by Jochen Clasen

The POLICY PRESS

ACKNOWLEDGEMENT

The book originates form an international conference on the 'Future of Social Security' which was held at Stirling University in June 2000. I would like to thank Alistair Baker, Jacqueline Davidson, Kate Thomson and Sharon Wright for their help with the organisation and the smooth running of the conference. I would also like to thank the University of Stirling, the Faculty of Human Sciences, the Department of Applied Social Science, Kluwer Law International, the Anglo-German Foundation, the British Social Policy Association, the Joseph Rowntree Foundation and Cambridge University Press for financial support. Finally, I am particularly grateful to Heike Böltzig and Fiona Clasen for their help with the production of this volume.

Jochen Clasen
Stirling University

CONTENTS

B. REFORMING PENSION SYSTEMS

C.   ACTIVATION REFORMS

LIST OF FIGURES

LIST OF TABLES

NOTES ON THE CONTRIBUTORS

Helen Bolderson
is Associate Reader in Social Policy in the Department of Government at Brunel University, where, prior to reaching retirement age in 1995, she held the post of full-time Reader. She works at Brunel as an associate researcher and supervisor of doctoral students and is currently conducting two research projects, funded by the European Union and the Nuffield Foundation. Her research interests include the history of the concept of disability, disability policies in the Member States of the European Union, Australia and the USA; the social policy of the European Union and cross-national comparisons of social policies and their delivery and comparative methodologies. Recent publications include (with D Mabbett) (1997) *Delivering Social Security: A Cross-National Study*, HMSO, London and (1999) 'Theories and Methods of Comparative Research' in Clasen J. (ed*)* *Comparative Social Policy*, Blackwell, Oxford; (with S. Roberts) (1997) 'Social Security across Frontiers' *Journal of International and Comparative Social Welfare* XIII: XIV; (with D. Mabbett) (1999) 'Devolved Social Security Systems: Principal-agent versus multi-level governance' *Journal of Public Policy* 18: 2

Francis G. Castles
is Professor of Social and Public Policy at the University of Edinburgh. Until recently he was Professor of Political Science in the Research School of Social Sciences at the Australian National University. His most recent books are *Comparative Public Policy: Patterns of Post-war Transformation* (Edward Elgar, 1998) and *The Welfare State Reader* (co-edited with Christopher Pierson for Polity Press, 2000). He has written extensively on comparative social policy and on social policy development in Scandinavia and Australia.

Jochen Clasen
is Professor of Comparative Social Research and Director of the Centre of Comparative Research in Social Welfare at the University of Stirling. His research interests include comparative social policy, social security policy, unemployment and employment policy in cross-national European contexts. Recent publications include *Comparative Social Policy. Concepts, theories and methods* (ed) (Blackwell, 1999); 'Beyond Social Security: the economic value of giving money to unemployed people', *European Journal of Social Security*, 1, 2, 1999; 'Motives, means and opportunities. Reforming unemployment compensation in the 1990s', *West European Politics*, 23, 2, 2000 and 'Social Insurance and the Contributory Principle. A paradox in contemporary British social policy', *Social Policy and Administration*, 35, 6, 2001.

Martin Evans
is a Research Fellow at the Centre for the Analysis of Social Exclusion, London School of Economics. His current research is on European social exclusion policy, welfare to work programmes and on small area analysis of social policy in Britain. Recent

publications include 'Change and Choice in Social Protection: The Experience of Central and Eastern Europe' - Volume 2 , Phare Consensus Programme European Commission, ADECRI, Paris, 1999; 'Poor Show: America's welfare reforms have changed attitudes but we should be aware of the potentially negative impact of the work-first approach?' *The Guardian*, 6th March 2000; 'Getting the Smaller Picture', with Bramley G, *Fiscal Studies*, June 2000; '21st Century Pensions - A Partnership or a marriage to the means-test?', with K. Rake K and J. Falkingham, *Social Policy and Administration*, October 2000, and 'The British New Deals', *International Journal of Social Welfare*, Spring 2001.

Jørgen Goul Andersen
is Professor of Political Sociology, Department of Economics, Politics and Public Administration at Aalborg University. He is Director of the Centre for Comparative Welfare State Studies, Aalborg University and Management Committee Member of COST Action A13, Working Group on Unemployment. He is also Co-director of the Danish Election Programme (with Ole Borre) and Director of the Danish ISSP Programme. His publications include 'Welfare Crisis and Beyond', in S. Kuhnle (ed) *The Survival of the Welfare State*, Routledge, 2000; 'Changing Labour Markets, New Social Divisions and Welfare State Support: Denmark in the 1990s', in S. Svallfors and P. Taylor-Gooby (eds) *The End of the Welfare State? Responses to state retrenchment*. Routledge, 1999; 'The Legitimacy of the Nordic Welfare States', in M. Kautto et al. (eds) *Nordic Social Policy. Changing Welfare States*, London, Routledge; 'The Scandinavian Welfare Model in Crisis?', *Scandinavian Political Studies*, vol 20(1), 1996. 'Marginalisation, Citizenship and the Economy: The Capacity of the Universalist Welfare State in Denmark', in E.O. Eriksen and J. Loftager (eds) *The Rationality of the Welfare State*, Scandinavian University Press, 1996.

Karl Hinrichs
works as a Research Associate at the Centre for Social Policy Research at the University of Bremen (since 1990) and teaches political science at Humboldt-University in Berlin. In 1989/90 he was a John F. Kennedy Fellow at the Center for European Studies, Harvard University, and in 1999 Visiting Professor at Berlin's Humboldt-University. His main area of research is the German welfare state in comparative perspective. Recent publications include: 'Health Care Policy in the German Social Insurance State: From Solidarity to Privatization?' in *Policy Studies Review* 17 (2000); and *Kontingenz und Krise. Institutionenpolitik in kapitalistischen und postsozialistischen Gesellschaften*, Frankfurt/New York: Campus, 2000 (co-edited with H. Kitschelt and H. Wiesenthal).

Olli Kangas
is Professor of Social Policy and the Head of the Department of Social Policy at the University of Turku, Finland. His PhD thesis 'The Politics of Social Rights' dealt with the historical development of sickness insurance in 18 OECD countries. The study revolved around various structural and political prerequisites that explain cross-national differences and similarities in the timing and institutional forms of the scheme. Thereafter he studied insitutional set-ups of other social insurance programmes, especially pensions. The main research issue has been how various institutional solutions

manage to guarantee livelihood in the case of unemployment, sickness, old-age and work incapacity. The topics in these studies has been to evaluate the effectiveness of various social policy solutions to combat poverty. In addition, he has studied the ramifications of various social policy institutions on public opinion and the legitimacy of social policy in different countries.

Jon Kvist,
is Senior Researcher at The Danish National Institute of Social Research and is affiliated with Copenhagen Business School and Copenhagen University. He is Chair of the working group 'Outcomes, Outputs, and Trajectories of Social Protection Reform' which is part of the COST A15 programme 'Reforming Social Protection Systems in Europe'. His main research interests are comparative social policy and welfare state research, encompassing labour markets, methodology, and social divisions of welfare. Recent publications in English include 'Welfare Reform in the Nordic Countries in the 1990s: Using Fuzzy-Set Theory to Assess Conformity to Ideal Types', *Journal of European Social Policy*, 9 (3), and 'Complexities in assessing unemployment benefits and policies', *International Social Security Review*, 51 (4).

Deborah Mabbett
is a Lecturer in the Department of Government at Brunel University. Her main area of research is social security, with a particular focus on institutional issues, such as relations between public and private providers and between different levels of government. She is currently working on a project financed by the European Commission on disability policy in the member states of the EU. Recent publications include (with H Bolderson) 'Theories and Methods of Comparative Research' in J. Clasen (ed) *Comparative Social Policy*, Blackwell, Oxford (1999) and (with H. Bolderson) 'Devolved Social Security Systems: Principal-agent versus multi-level governance' *Journal of Public Policy* 18: 2 (1999), and 'Social Regulation and the Social Dimension in Europe: The Example of Insurance', *European Journal of Social Security*, 2, 4 (2000).

Luis Moreno
is Professor of Sociology and Political Science and Senior Research Fellow at the Spanish National Research Council (Consejo Superior de Investigaciones Científicas). His main fields of research are territorial distribution of power (federalism, nationalism, and political decentralization) and social policy and welfare state. His publications include: *La federalización de España: poder político y territorio,* Madrid: Siglo XXI, 1997 (English version: *The federalization of Spain*, London: Frank Cass, 2000); *Unión Europea y Estado del Bienestar* (ed.), Madrid: CSIC,1997; *Social exchange and welfare development* (ed.), Madrid: CSIC, 1993. He has completed the Spanish version of the book *Precarious Citizens. The 'safety net' of social protection* (Barcelona, Ariel, 2000). He is director of the book series *Politeya* (Studies on Politics and Society), and is a member of the editorial board of *Nationalism & Ethnic Politics*, and of of *Revista Internacional de Sociología*. He is a collaborator within the European project 'Welfare reform and the management of the societal change' (Framework V, 2001-04).

Einar Overbye
is Senior Researcher at NOVA in Oslo. He has a PhD in political science from Oslo University. His research interests include the public/private mix in welfare policies, studies in pre-retirement, disability and family policy, and more generally the crossover between game theory and social psychology - applied to politics. Publications include 'Convergence in policy outcomes?', *Journal of Public Policy*, 1994; 'Explaining welfare spending', *Public Choice*, 1995; 'Making a case for the rational, self-regarding, "ethical" voter', *European Journal of Political Research*, 1995 and 'Risk and welfare' (PhD/NOVA report 5/1998). Ongoing research projects include cross-national studies in private and public pensions, determinants of pre-retirement, social integration and disability.

Ann Shola Orloff
is Professor of Sociology at Northwestern University, where she is also affiliated with the Departments of Political Science and Women's Studies, and the Institute for Policy Research. Her areas of interests include political sociology, historical and comparative methods in the social sciences, sociology of gender, and social (including feminist) theory. Her research has focused on the relationship of state-building processes, state capacities and structures, and policy legacies to the making of social policies, and on the ways in which states affect and are affected by social relations across a range of institutions. Her publications include 'Gender and the Social Rights of Citizenship: The Analysis of Gender Relations and Welfare States', in *American Sociological Review*, 1993 and *Markets, Families: Gender, Liberalism and Social Policy in Australia, Canada, Great Britain and the United States* (co-authored with J. O'Connor and S. Shaver), Cambridge University Press, 1999. She is also the author of *The Politics of Pensions: A Comparative Analysis of Britain, Canada and the United States, 1880s-1940* (Wisconsin, 1993) and the co-editor (with M. Weir and T. Skocpol) of *The Politics of Social Policy in the United States* (Princeton, 1988). Other articles have appeared in *American Sociological Review*, *Annual Review of Sociology*, *Political Power and Social Theory*.

Bruno Palier
is chargé de recherches CNRS in Centre d'études de la vie politique française (CEVIPOF), Paris. He is a member of the Management Committee of Cost A15, 'Reforming the Welfare Systems in Europe' and was responsible for the MIRE programme 'Comparing social welfare systems in Europe'. He has recently published 'Defrosting the French Welfare State, *West European Politics*, 2000, 23, 2; and with G. Bonoli 'How Do Welfare States Change? Institutions and their Impact on the Politics of Welfare State Reform', *European Review*, vol. 8, no. 2.; and 'Changing the politics of social programmes. Innovative change in British and French welfare reforms', *Journal of European Social Policy*, 8, 4, 1998. He co-edited (with R. S. Sykes and P. Prior) *Globalization and European welfare states: challenges and changes*, London: Palgrave, 2001.

Wim van Oorschot
is Associate Professor of Sociology, specialising on social security. He has published widely on the take up of benefits, poverty, local social policy, the history of social security, client satisfaction in social security administration, disability benefits and reintegration measures, activation of unemployed people and on occupational welfare arrangements. He is currently involved in (international comparative) studies of welfare solidarity (using e.g. data from the European Values Survey), work-conditionality of unemployment benefit schemes, labour market (re-)integration of disabled workers, and of care arrangements in social security schemes and labour law.

Sharon Wright
is lecturer in Social Policy at the University of Warwick. Her research interests are in policy making, service delivery and implementation, the relationship between citizen and state, social security, unemployment, welfare to work and poverty. Her doctoral work is an ethnographic study of the interaction between staff and clients in a Jobcentre office. She has also worked in collaboration with voluntary organisations and is an active anti-poverty campaigner. She is a co-author of 'Towards "single gateways"? A cross-national review of the changing roles of employment offices in seven countries', *Zeitschrift für ausländisches und internationales Arbeits- und Sozialrecht,* 1, 2001.

Chapter 1

Social Security in the New Millennium

Jochen Clasen

Looking back over the last century, the expansion and maturation of statutory social security systems can be seen as a key characteristic in the development of industrial societies. Social scientists have a tendency to emphasise change, yet it is difficult to ignore the feeling that, at the start of the new century, the socio-economic, political and also cultural contexts within which social security programmes operate are in a state of flux. As a result, debates about social security are currently more intensive than they have been for some time. From different angles and preoccupied with somewhat different concerns, sociologists, economists, political scientists and social policy analysts are discussing the normative foundations of established and new principles of social protection, the capability of traditional schemes to adapt to changing environments, the options for and barriers to reform, the merits and the problems of current systems, their impact on citizenship, labour market behaviour, family life and individual choice – in short, the future of social security.

The improved knowledge of, and interest in, social security programmes in different countries has made this debate more complex, but has also enriched it. Compared with

20 or even 10 years ago, social security debates have become much more international, cross-national and comparative in character. At the same time, there appears to be more frequent contact and exchange between social scientists and non-academic institutions and individuals.

The chapters in this volume were first presented at an international conference on social security at the University of Stirling in June 2000. The idea for the conference was inspired by an event at Edinburgh University which was held ten years previously and concentrated on 'The Sociology of Social Security' (Adler et al. 1991). The Edinburgh conference revolved around four themes: conceptual and analytical issues of social security; the relationship between social security systems and labour markets, the impact of social security on the role of women and aspects of social security administration. Some of these issues remained sufficiently relevant to become major streams within the Stirling conference, others acquired even more prominence which is not surprising if the time period between the two conferences is taken into account. Despite many similarities in the context within which social security was discussed at the end of the 1980s and the beginning of the new millennium, substantial changes have also occurred. Briefly, the Berlin Wall was still standing and the process of economic and social transition in Central and Eastern European countries was yet to happen. Demographic pressures on social security systems (and retirement pensions in particular) were matters of debate – yet the so-called and misleading term 'demographic time bomb' had yet to enter and dominate the policy debate as the central context for discussions about the future of public pension systems. The state of labour markets was in many countries bleak – and the erosion of the so-called 'standard employment relationship' was a central context for the need to change social security programmes. Ten years on, this debate has intensified and the need for a more flexible labour market has become a mantra in many public debates. As a consequence, social security programmes and principles which were designed around the standard form of male participation in employment are being questioned. This applies to the principle of social insurance in particular which many deem to be outmoded - and yet it remains paramount in many countries. Over the past ten years or so some countries have improved labour market performance considerably – but others have not. Success has been partly attributed to new forms of labour market policies – including changes to social security systems which involve a new balance between rights and responsibilities – and a so-called activation of benefits for the unemployed.

In a wider context, the labour market has become much more central to the debate about social security than it was in the 1980s; to the point that it is labour markets (rather than social rights) which are the principal means for conferring citizenship and paid employment proclaimed as the best way to tackle poverty and social exclusion – this has implications for social security systems. Ten years ago, family and household patterns were already in a process of change. If anything, this change has continued, fuelling further the debate about the adequacy of current social security systems. Finally, the political options to respond to the above changes seem more constrained now than they were before – due to economic change (globalisation; post-industrialisation), political developments (European integration) and demographic shifts (low birth rates). To which extent those pressures are real and how constraining they really are, might be a matter of debate – but unlike 10 years ago they figure strongly in public debates about the future for social security.

From a social scientific perspective, the analysis of welfare programmes generally, and social security systems in particular, which represent by far the largest share of social expenditure in any mature welfare state, the character of research has become even more international and comparative, perhaps corresponding with an increasingly strong international focus on social security and social security reform, not least due to the influence of diverse supra-national organisations such as the OECD, the EU, the ILO and also the World Bank. There appears to be a much greater interest in what goes on in other countries, either motivated by interests in gaining knowledge, lesson learning, testing theories, or making policy recommendations. As a result, the debate is more complex – but also richer, than it was 10 years ago.

Social security in academia has never been a topic merely for sociologists or economists. A few eminent political scientists have always shown an interest in the welfare state. Yet recent publications and research initiatives give the impression that political scientists have become increasingly interested in social security, and particularly in the ways in which social security systems change, or are resistant to change. This should not be a surprise given the intensity of national discussions about ways of reforming social security (and particularly pension systems), the interest in countries which appear to have found some solutions to problems of reconciling 'work and welfare', and the impression that social security programmes seem to be easier to change in some but not in other countries. These seemed sufficient reasons to devote half of this book to the issue of reform, with reflections on theoretical issues of improving our understanding of stability and change in welfare states, followed by reforms within two fields of social security: pensions and unemployment policy (nowadays referred to as 'activation' policies). These two areas are very much in the centre of national and international debates about the future of social security. The former because it represents the most substantial aspect of welfare states in terms of expenditure and (current and future) claimants and is thus an extremely sensitive area in economic and political respects. The latter, because of the continuously significant task of improving labour market integration for economic and social reasons on the one hand, and as the area where the balance between 'rights and responsibilities' within modern social security systems appear to be significantly readjusted in many countries.

The future of social security

Broadly the book deals social security debates and change. The first part is concerned with discussions which revolve around principles, contexts, and concepts. The second focuses on attempts to understand the nature of change and development in social security and consists of three aspects: the theoretical underpinning of social security reform; public pensions and reforms herein and finally activation and 'welfare to work' programmes.

A word about the book's title might seem appropriate. The book is not an attempt to evaluate, or even predict, the future shape of social security based on an extrapolation of economic, demographic and political development. Instead, an underlying theme for the book is to question and reflect on widely held assumptions about the future of social security in terms of a need for reform, the directions of reform and the impacts of reform. The starting point is the recognition that social security systems have indeed been subjected to much reform activity and policy change in the 1990s, and that some reforms might (potentially) bring about substantial (systemic, third order, path-breaking) change rather than merely adjusting and thus maintaining current structures. However, many commentators have linked this readily to, by now, commonly referred to economic, demographic and political challenges which welfare states have been faced with in recent times. At times these challenges have been too readily accepted as 'irresistible forces' (Pierson, 1998) which inevitably will lead to change, and to a particular kind of change. This is a notion which the book will take issue with, for two reasons.

First, within public debates there are widely held assumptions about (waning) public support for social security, or the inevitable direction of change. In fact, these are problematic conjectures which need reflection. For example, rising average living standards and economic growth, it has been argued, have made redistributive social security policies increasingly superfluous. Although still popular, another widely held assumption is that tax increases for social security programmes would not be acceptable to a majority of the population which is suspicious about public income maintenance, or that European integration will have a strong impact on the shape of national social security. Other chapters deal with the problem of how social security systems could be adjusted in order to become more efficient, encompassing or to correspond better with new conceptions about public policy aiming to achieve a more equal distribution of life chances and guarantee access to income security. All these aspects are covered in Part I of the book.

The second reason why commonly held assumptions about the future of social security need questioning relates to the link which is often made between challenges and reforms, and about the causes and impact of reforms for national social security systems. This basic view of reform activities ignores the fact that (some) policy changes might have occurred without having been prompted by any identifiable challenge. Indeed, instead of a simple model of cause and effect, recent social security reforms require theoretically complex and ambitious explanations, not least since they are often difficult to classify simply as retrenchment or cutbacks. As to the scope of challenges, there has been a tendency to overstate the pressure which they exert. For example, there is a widely held assumption that public pension systems need to be substantially reformed due to population ageing, that demographic ageing will have largely similar effects across countries and that, as a consequence, pension systems have already become more alike and will converge even more in the future. As a response, non-governmental organisations, not least the World Bank, have been very active in recommending certain types of pension reform. Here, commonly shared perceptions about the merits and, more often, the problematic nature of pension system which would heed the World Bank proposals have been quickly introduced in public debates without much consideration of cross-national differences.

Another widely held assumption about social security, and the way in which it should progress, is the notion that benefits should become less 'passive' and more 'active'. Indeed, 'activation' is a term which has left the confines of Scandinavian (and particular Swedish) welfare state policy and entered the vocabulary of social security debates on a much broader scale. While it is sometimes difficult and problematic to clearly distinguish which policies are 'active' and which 'passive' (Sinfield 1997), in popular debates activation policies often refer to cutting back the generosity of benefits available to the unemployed, introducing tougher work tests, mandatory participation in labour market or even workfare programmes (Lødemel and Trickey 2001). Yet activation can be understood much more broadly, there are crucial cross-national differences in 'welfare to work' programmes in terms of the social groups which are targeted and, at times, the introduction of new 'activation' programmes can be little more than policy rhetoric because policy implementation has not changed that much. These are important qualifications which are rarely considered within the current drive to reform unemployment policies and thus deserve to be subjected to detailed reflection in order to arrive at a more cautious deliberation about possible futures for social security. The remainder of this introductory chapter provides a brief overview of the chapters in the two parts of the book.

Debates

Most, but not all chapters in this volume are comparative. Some have a decidedly conceptual focus or deal with a matter which is relevant beyond the particular country they are dealing with. The contribution by Olli Kangas is both cross-national and conceptual. It deals with the interaction between economic growth, inequality and poverty and reflects on the often stated idea of 'trickle down'. This can be linked to Rawlsian theories of distributive justice, justifies (growing) income inequality if it benefits (also) poorer sections in society. Kangas shows however that, from a comparative perspective, the poor are not better off in countries with higher income inequalities. He demonstrates that economic growth has an effect on the number of the poor and the economic well-being of the worse-off in society. However, the fact that there are substantial national variations in the capacity of increasing economic prosperity reaching the poor gives distributional policies an important role since the capacity is mediated by specific configuations of national social security systems.

In parliamentary democracies, such an economic justification for more than a residual social security system requires the sustained support of those who actively contribute to income transfer systems. Yet public discourses in many countries seem to indicate a declining motivation to pay for social security programmes, even if attitude surveys register continuous support for the welfare state. Wim van Oorschot's analysis of the motivation for paying for social security indicates that there are several reasons why people continue to be willing to contribute, such as feelings of moral obligations and emotional ties with benefit claimants. However, he also shows that 'self-interest' seems to be a crucial factor, at least in the Dutch welfare state which he uses as a case study in his empirical investigation. Given the encompassing nature of the Dutch social security system which makes it appear relevant to the vast majority of the population, Van Oorschot is in a strong position to argue that comprehensive, rather than residual, systems seem to generate a broad basis of legitimacy supported by self-interest as a strong motivator, in addition to other types of reasons.

Particularly in the Dutch welfare state, but also in many others, there has been a rise in the number of people classified as disabled and thus eligible for social security support. Helen Bolderson and Deborah Mabbett concentrate on this particular type of benefit in order to reflect on current ways of the apparent need to draw boundaries and to classify social groups in order to establish benefit entitlement. The authors speculate about the implications of alternative options of identifying needs in a future system of social security which would correspond with an improvement in social knowledge and developments in social research. Would a social security system be possible which avoids categorising groups and yet provides income security adequately and fairly? After detailed considerations, Boldersen and Mabbett remain sceptical and argue that, since the discriminatory function of social security cannot be eliminated if a just distribution of resources is to remain a central aim for social security, categorisation should be done in an unobstrusive unstigmatising fashion.

One motivation for the search for alternatives to meeting needs which does not rely on categorisations is the notion of equality. This is also the focus in Ann Orloff's contribution which puts social security in a broader context of male and female participation in paid and unpaid work and asks how social security systems can be assessed in the light of their promotion of gender equality. Clearly, any reforms and designs of future social security systems should recognise that there are new risks which need to be included as giving rise to support, such as of income disruption due to maternity and participation in caregiving activities or single parenthood. Adopting a comparative perspective, Orloff shows that problems and policy issues such as the threat of poverty, the ability to form autonomous households and access to care and employment are not only 'gendered', but also manifest themselves differently in different welfare regimes and partly within different countries within the same regime. Depending on their construction, social security provisions such as maternity leave and benefit programmes play an important role in allowing women to take up employment on more or less equitable forms. But there are other policies (tax subsidies, wage policy, service provision) adopted by different countries in order to achieve similar outcomes (e.g. high levels of women's employment or economic security) in different ways. In turn, the lack of some of those policies indicates regime- or country-specific problems if the aim is to improve gender equality.

The final chapter of the first part of this volume takes as its background the role of the European Union for the future of national social protection systems. This is an issue which has been increasingly discussed in recent years. This discussion however seems unnecessarily polarised between those who assume that the EU will (continue to) have little impact on direction of national social security policy, at least as far as the major programmes (in terms of expenditure and coverage) are concerned. On the other side of the spectrum are those who identify a number of current direct and indirect influences and point to further inroads which the EU will make into previously national sovereignty which, it is predicted, will seriously undermined. Luis Moreno agrees with those who see a growing role for the EU, not least via the European Court of Justice. However he breaks out of this debate by reflecting on levels of governance beyond which the EU or central states could play. Indeed, he detects and welcomes an increasing role of meso-governments in the area of social protection, a process which appears to be particularly advanced in Southern Europe. In fact, the planned intergovernmental conference in 2004, he argues, gives a further indication of an important strand of thinking within the EU which favours strengthening regional policy input and processes of decentralisation and territorial subsidiarity in establishing 'safety nets', integrating, for example, social assistance and welfare services. Much provision of social protection, Moreno argues, is indeed better placed at sub-state intermediate levels since this would facilitate processes of policy innovation, strengthen democratic accountability and facilitate a form of 'bottom-up' policy participation. It would thus lend legitimacy to the process of Europeanisation.

Reforms

The appearance of a number of recent publications on policy change within welfare states bears witness to the fact that comparative welfare state research has not only been revitalised in recent years. It also indicates a welcome shift from the previously somewhat static discourse on regime boundaries towards an interest in more dynamic understanding of regimes as a way to help understand welfare state change and stability. Perhaps it was two seminal works which sparked off this interest: Pierson's (1994) thesis on the need to search for a new theoretical understanding which helps to explain recent current welfare reforms and Esping-Andersen's (1996a) collection of studies which argued that the options to change and, accordingly, the routes of reforms adopted in different countries seemed regime specific. In any case, these two publications figure prominently in recent efforts which have tried to make sense of what has been going on in mature welfare states (Ferrera and Rhodes 2000b; Scharpf and Schmidt 2000; Kuhnle 2000a; Leibfried 2000; Pierson 2001a). One thing which these studies have in common is an interest in analysing change rather than merely pointing out that welfare states seem broadly stable. The widespread perception that welfare states, with the odd exception, have shown to be largely resistant to change has been superseded by a view which recognises that in some countries, substantial reforms were introduced during the 1990s; that in others seemingly small and incremental changes can potentially have far-reaching impacts and that, thirdly, not all change can be classified as welfare state contraction or retrenchment.

The latter point is the central premise in Bruno Palier's contribution which reviews recent theoretical attempts to account for social policy change and argues for the need to recognise that more policy changes can be identified than have often been acknowledged (even in supposedly inert welfare states in continental Europe) and that different welfare states appear to change differently. The latter point acknowledges the contributions which were made by regime theory and the notion of path dependency. Palier argues that different welfare state logics combined with the specific configuration of welfare institutions serve a useful framework for analysing change, and draws on Hall (1993) in order to differentiate between types of change. What is more, social policy research should make use of analytic tools developed within public policy in order to arrive at a better understanding of stability and change in contemporary welfare states.

There is a considerable degree of common ground between Palier's and Jørgen Goul Andersen's contributions to this volume, regarding the notion of the relevance of ideas, for example, or their criticism against common understandings of path dependent change. Goul Andersen argues that path dependency has been wrongly associated with the notion of institutional inertia. Instead, with reference to the notion of 'policy martingales' (March and Olsen 1984), and reiterating Palier's point, he argues in favour of a dynamic understanding of institutionalism which allows for what at times are small initial changes but over time have the potential of leading to path-breaking changes of previously entrenched welfare policies and principles. However, to some extent Goul Andersen goes further in his criticism against much recent theoretical interpretations on welfare state reform which he accuses of adopting an inappropriate degree of functionalism. In particular, he questions the link which has often too readily been made between 'challenges' (be they of an economic, demographic or political nature) and welfare state responses or adaptations. To reduce all welfare reforms to such a model of 'stimulus-response' underestimates the roles played by the interests and ideas of actors involved in policy making and the social construction of policy problems and solutions. He illustrates this point with the example of Danish social security reforms and pension policy in particular. During the 1980s when the Danish social protection system was faced with strong challenges hardly any reforms of significance were introduced. By contrast, the level of economic pressure on the system had considerably subsided in the 1990s and yet this was a decade which introduced, as Goul Andersen argues, a 'silent revolution' in the Danish welfare system, including some changes with potentially profound impacts.

One predominant challenge which Goul Andersen refers to is of a demographic nature. The extent of population ageing, it is often argued, implies the detonation of a 'demographic time bomb' and thus depleted public coffers and bankrupt welfare states, unless substantial policy changes are introduced across all advanced welfare states with mature public pension systems. As a result of these policy changes, national pension profiles will become increasingly similar over the forthcoming decades. Acknowledging the effect of ageing on pension finance, Francis G. Castles questions a scenario of democratic decision making becoming inevitably determined by demographic challenges. Instead, the threat of population ageing for public expenditure needs to be disaggregated and put in national contexts. Even those countries with the most expensive pension systems maintain ample scope for policy manipulation of pension coverage and generosity. What is more, population ageing presents the English-speaking 'family of nations' with problems which are of a much lesser magnitude than elsewhere and should therefore be much more manageable than often argued in debates about the future of social security.

But even countries with mature pay-as-you-go pension systems which are wedded to the wage-replacement notion of public retirement income, the so-called 'social insurance' countries, have shown that policy making has not become paralysed in the face of demographic change. Karl Hinrichs carefully analyses the different types of reforms which are available to those countries, discusses the strategies which have actually been pursued and reflects on their implications. In order to be successful, he demonstrates, reform plans need good timing and to rely on broad support which often reaches beyond parliamentary majorities to opposition parties or trade unions. In order to attain such broad alliances, the involvement of all actors committed to reform in specially set-up commissions which have the task of forging compromise reform packages and their (re)distributional consequences seems a strategy which has been proven in many countries.

Einar Overbye is also concerned with pension policy and the issue of redistribution. He asks whether the World Bank pension recommendations in favour of defined-contribution arrangements could be beneficial for lower income groups. The answer depends, he rightly points out, on existing schemes which would be replaced. Many national pension schemes tend to redistribute from higher but also from lower income groups towards middle income groups. This is the case particularly where minimum contribution periods are required before entitlement is established. The World Bank proposal has been criticised as inequitable particularly within countries which are part of the OECD. Beyond the OECD the reception was often somewhat less hostile and this might be because the system could actually be more redistributive, particularly if coupled with a minimum tax-funded system. In other words, the assessment of the redistributive impact of the World Bank proposal is contingent on existing national schemes, a point which has often been ignored or neglected.

The final three chapters are concerned with the trend towards 'making benefits more employment friendly' or 'activation'. This term has been applied particularly in Sweden in conjunction with labour market policies. Since the 1990s it has both left the Nordic confines and is more widely applied nowadays, but at the same time has become more limited in public debates, referring to benefits for (some groups of) unemployed people which should be replaced with participation in labour market integration schemes, such as training, work experience or education. However, much wider concepts of activation could be applied, as is the case in Scandinavian countries, which link social security with other policies (such as child care and education) and thus see unemployment benefits as but one aspect of 'activating welfare states'. Thus, as Jon Kvist points out, welfare states can adopt three types of policies which in combination potentially enhance labour market integration particularly for women and less skilled people. Taking over caring tasks from families (de-familialisation) can be coupled with relatively generous and easily accessible benefits for the unemployed (de-commodification) and targted labour market proframmes aimed at increasing skill levels and reducing work disincentives (re-commodification). With the premise that access to paid work is the major route to poverty prevention and social inclusion, such a broad strategy has been adopted in Denmark, Sweden and Finland and constitutes the major distinction in policy profile between these Nordic and other European countries.

However, even beyond Scandinavia, there are substantial cross-national differences in 'welfare to work' policies, as Martin Evans shows by comparing the UK with France, Germany, the Netherlands and the USA. Beginning with a careful analysis of who has access to what kind of activation programmes in those countries, Evans is able to identify the size and profile of national 'claimant reservoirs', i.e. the target or welfare population for 'welfare to work' efforts. His analysis continues by tracing the various policies aimed at moving benefit claimants into paid work. Finally, policies which address the 'work' aspect of activation policies (such as tax credits, employer subsidies and public work schemes) are compared. From such a broad perspective, the British 'welfare to work' policy profile is distinctive in two ways: a disproportionate focus on some groups of the unemployed within a claimant reservoir which covers many other benefit groups, and a weak employment element.

The latter comes as no surprise in a country which for decades has been reluctant to adopt job creation schemes on any significant scale or to promote intermediary labour markets. Against this background, the implementation of 'activation' and other types of New Deal policies since 1998 has certainly broken new ground. The New Deal has introduced new principles and shifted the balance between rights and responsibilities within social security, particularly for younger benefit claimants. However, Sharon Wright demonstrates that administrative practices have not always kept up. Pressures of time, a reluctance to change work routines and the need to meet performance targets seem to influence street-level workers more than official policy guidelines. As a result, employment office staff re-formulate and redefine policies on the ground, making policy implementation of supposedly new policies much less 'active' than they appear at policy formulation stage. Wright's contribution concentrates on the UK only, but it serves as a useful reminder that issues such as policy change or stability, path dependency or path dynamic etc., require to be analysed not only by concentrating on pressures and challenges impacting on policy makers, but also by taking account of policy implementation and policy 'takers', i.e. where social security ultimately really matters.

PART I

DEBATES

Chapter 2

Rising Tides and Rusty Boats: Economic position of the poor in 1985-1995[1]

Olli Kangas

Introduction

In the marital vow the bridge and groom promise to love each other throughout their lives, for better or for worse. In principle, one can presume that a similar contract has been signed between citizens and the state. In that contract, the state has promised to 'love' her citizens when they are ill, unemployed, young or old, and that love should be fair in the sense that all are entitled to social security on similar terms. However, the validity of that contract has been questioned. It has been argued that the contract was

1 This chapter was written while I was a visiting professor at Zentrum für Sozialpolitik at the University of Bremen. I would like to thank Antti Parpo for his excellent research assistance and Frank Castles, Jochen Clasen, Karl Hinrichs, Leif Nordberg, Veli-Matti Ritakallio, and Wim van Oorschot for their valuable comments.

written during the golden age of prosperity and that slackening economic growth will negate earlier promises. The state is losing both its capacity and willingness to help all its citizens. Because of fiscal and economic constraints it is more likely that the welfare state has grown to its limit (Flora 1986) and instead of continuous expansion we are likely to see a 're-period', i.e. a period of retrenchment, reorientation and programmatic reformulation in social policy.

Economic factors also play an important role when it comes to the ebbing willingness to expand social policy programmes. Instead of emphasising social rights and redistribution, the prevailing political discourse nowadays stresses more social duties and obligations. Consequently, the conceptualisation of the relationship between social policy and economic growth has essentially changed. During the Keynesian period of economic policy-making, social policy and redistribution through social policy measures were regarded as an important factor in enhancing stable economic growth. Now, equality and redistribution are often seen as obstacles to economic growth, especially in Europe, where the high level of social protection is regarded as one important reason why the European economic and employment performance is lagging behind its American counterpart. Instead of income equality, there are more demands for income inequality in order to increase incentives to work and thereby to enhance economic growth, and when the economy is booming the worst-off sections in society will also get their share of the rising economic tide.

In economic discourse, this idea is presented in the form of the so-called trickle-down theory. According to this theory, we must create incentive structures that encourage people to take individual responsibility, to work harder and to contribute to economic growth as much as they can. In societies where people have such incentives, i.e. where there are real income differences and a threat of poverty, where the welfare state has not taken away individual responsibility and weakened the incentive structure, the economy will grow more rapidly and the economic tide will also lift the worst-off boats (for a discussion, see e.g. Saunders 1994; Schmidtz 1998; and for empirical analyses see e.g. Gottschalk and Smeeding 1997; Bradbury and Jäntti 1999). Thus, the theory predicts growing inequalities which at the first glance seem to be harmful to the poor, but in the long run are the best medicine to help the poor.

The central idea in the trickle-down theory has certain similarities with John Rawls's (1972 and 1996) ideas of distributive justice. The so-called Rawlsian difference principle states that the division of all primary goods, including income and wealth, should be equal unless there are reasons why an unequal distribution will help the worse-off. Since there are severe incentive problems in strictly equal distribution, it is unreasonable to stop at absolute equality (Rawls 1996:282-283). Social institutions responsible for the distribution of societal goods must be designed to create incentives and gradually these incentives will also help the worse-off.

This principle of justice would allow economic inequalities as long as these differences improve everyone's situation. Special care must be taken of the lot of the worse-off. Income differences, for example, are acceptable on condition that they cause people to work harder, and because of this hard work national wealth is increased more rapidly and the increase will gradually diffuse also to the worse-off. Thus inequalities generate growth and improve the circumstances of the poor. According to Rawls, inequalities are therefore permissible if they make a functional contribution to the situation of the poorest.

These two interlinked theories have been used to different degrees in different disciplines. Economists have been more inclined to emphasise, in line with the trickle-down theory, the role of economic growth, whereas sociologists and social-policy analysts have been more interested in aspects of distributive justice (see e.g. Arthur and Shaw 1991).

The central ideas presented in the two aforementioned approaches serve as a heuristic starting point for this chapter on income distribution in a handful of advanced countries. The purpose of the chapter is to present preliminary considerations of how Rawls's ideas and trickle-down theory could be used in empirical comparisons of the distribution of financial rewards in Western countries between 1985 and 1995. The first part of this period, the late 1980s, was characterised by high economic growth, while slackening economic performance cast a shadow on the early 1990s. A comparison of these periods is therefore an interesting way to examine how the blessings of prosperity and the burdens of the recession were distributed among population groups in different countries. At a more general level the two questions the chapter seeks to answer are as follows:

1.   To what extent does the difference principle apply in different countries as measured by cross-sectional analyses of poverty? To justify higher poverty levels we should find a positive relationship between the incidence of poverty and the economic well-being of the poor.

2.   To what extent did the economic tide lift, or economic ebb lower all boats? Here we could justify higher income levels for the rich provided that in countries where the rich are considerably richer than the poor, the position of the poor is better or has been improved more than in countries with smaller income disparities.

The first research task maps the cross-sectional situation, while the second one is more dynamic and concentrates on changes. At a more precise level we study the extent to which economic growth and decline have affected the income level of the poor (those whose OECD equivalent income is less than 50 per cent of the median), the median income and income of the rich (those whose income is more than three times the median). Moreover, the study seeks to give a general picture of how economic growth, the distribution of 'richness' and poverty, either improve or worsen the lot of the worst-off in OECD countries.

The data is from the Luxembourg Income Study (LIS). The selection of countries is partially determined by the availability of data. Despite the fact that more than 30 countries are included in the LIS, data for several points in time is available only for a limited number of nations. These countries are included in our sample. There is also a socio-political motive: the countries represent different kinds of welfare states or welfare regimes. Therefore, it is interesting to see how the economic tide or ebb has affected the poor and the rich in different types of welfare state.

In the first section of the chapter, we analyse the cross-sectional relationship between poverty rates and the income level of the poor. Thereafter, we take a close look at changes in time: how poverty and 'richness' rates and changes in the income of the poor and the rich are related to each other. Unfortunately in this section, we must restrict our analyses to a smaller number of countries for which data for 1985, 1990 and 1995 is available. To be more precise, since observation years in the LIS data base vary from country to country, observations from the mid-1980s, late 1980s/early 1990s and mid 1990 have been adjusted to 1985, 1991 or 1995 values, respectively, by using national consumer price indices. Thereafter national figures for each of the three years have been changed to US Dollars by using purchasing power parities (PPP) and exchange rates. To start off, the first part of the study is a cross-sectional inspection of the situation in 1991. Both PPPs and exchange rates are used.

The second part of the chapter illustrates how the economic tide has improved the lot of the middle-income earners, the worse-off and the best-off. Have the rich taken all the money and run? Is there anything left for the poor? For space considerations and for the sake of clarity, we will only use PPP-based income data in this section. The last section of the chapter discusses the fairness of income distribution and presents some tasks for future research on the topics.

Relative poverty rates and the absolute income level of the poor

The Rawlsian difference principle as well as the trickle-down theory allow inequalities if those inequalities improve the lot of the worse-off. In other words, the difference principle would allow higher relative poverty rates for a country if the real income level of the poor in that country is higher than in a country with lower relative poverty.

The same idea is expressed from another perspective in the trickle-down theory. It argues that the economic tide is not an external and independent force but people themselves form and contribute to the tide. In countries where there are real incentives to work, economic growth will be stronger, and in the long run, the standard of living of the poor will be higher than in those countries where such incentives are weakened or totally destroyed by redistributive policies. Therefore, it is just to let income differences grow, and in fact, this expansion is also the most effective way to help the poor (Schmidtz 1998:6).

We can try to operationalise these statements in a couple of different ways.

(1) We can think that the fulfilment of these criteria demands that income levels of the poor should be higher in countries with high relative poverty rates, or to put it more technically, the correlation between poverty rates and the absolute income levels of the poor should be positive. The higher the poverty rates the higher the level of income of the worse-off. Only then can we accept higher relative poverty rates as just.

(2) Alternatively we can approach the situation from the other end of the income ladder and take the rich as our starting point. Let us suppose that there are two societies, A and B. In society A there are many rich and poor people, and all income distribution indices display high levels of inequality. Due to a strong incentive to work, the average income levels both for the rich and the poor are high. In society B income distribution is very egalitarian and differences are very small but the average income level is low (no incentive to work). According to our ideas, we can say that society A is just, it fulfils the difference principle and proves the validity of the trickle-down theory.

The issue is tentatively assessed in Table 2.1 (see end of chapter). The table presents both relative poverty rates (the poor are defined as all those people whose OECD-equivalent incomes are below 50 per cent of the national median) and absolute income levels of the poor (measured as the median income for those persons who are classified as poor according to the aforementioned criteria) in 18 OECD countries.[2] Moreover, we have also calculated 'richness' rates (percentage of those whose income is more than 300 per cent of the national median) and the median income for those classified as rich. The absolute income levels are converted into a common currency – US Dollars – by using two different methods: current exchange rates and purchasing power parities (PPP). To put the rich, the middle-income earners and the poor in a wider context we also display the Gross Domestic Products per capita for each country. Also GDP figures for 1991 are converted to US Dollars both using exchange rates and purchasing power parities.

There are substantial variations both in the poverty rates between nations – the rates vary from 3.3 per cent in Luxembourg to 17.3 per cent in the US – and in the absolute income levels of the poor. As can be seen in Table 2.1, the picture of the absolute level of income depends heavily on the method of converting national currencies into US dollars.

---

2 Another possibility has been to use income deciles and calculate the medians for the lowest, middle and the highest deciles (see e.g. in Rainwater and Smeeding 1995). Since we are here also interested in changes in the shares of the best and the worst-off, the approach used here serves our purposes better than the decile approach used in previous studies.

As a rule, all other countries will lose in comparison to the US if PPPs are used instead of exchange rates. PPP-transformations also reduce cross-national differences.

In some cases, the PPP and exchange rate calculations give substantially and strikingly different results. For example, according to the exchange rates, the income of the poor in the Nordic countries is 1.5 times higher than that of the poor in the United States, whereas in the PPP comparisons the American poor perform as well as their Nordic counterparts.[3] In other words, in PPP comparisons the difference between Scandinavia and the US is expressed in the prevalence of poverty instead of the depth of poverty. According to both absolute measures the situation of the Canadian and Luxembourgeois poor is very good in comparison to the other countries, and these results are not sensitive to currency transformations. Indeed, the poor in Luxembourg seem to be very bourgeois!

This 'embourgeoisment' also applies to rich people living in Luxembourg: comparatively speaking they are rich on all measures. The same goes for the Northern Americans and Norwegians, whereas the heavy purses of the Finnish and Swedish rich are much lighter if we use PPPs comparisons.

Table 2.1 also presents bivariate correlations between various indicators.[4] In order to validate the trickle-down theory we should find negative relationships between poverty and richness and between poverty and GDP levels. The idea gets qualified support. The GDP measures ($r = -.40$ for GDP in US\$ and $-.10$ for GDP in PPPs), the median income ($r = -.38$ for medians in US\$ and $-.15$ for medians in PPPs) and the income levels for the rich ($r = -.40$ for the US\$ and $-.20$ for the PPPs) are negatively related to the incidence of poverty. Amongst plenty, poverty is an uncommon phenomenon. Due to the rising tide all boats float. However, the validity of our interpretation depends heavily on two factors. First, the method to convert national currencies to the US Dollars plays a decisive role. According to current exchange rates, rich countries, especially Sweden, Norway, Finland and Luxembourg, have eradicated poverty, whereas PPP inspections clearly suggest a non-significant – yet negative – relationship. Second, our results are sensitive to the sample of countries. If we omit such poor countries as Hungary, Poland

---

3 Obviously the exchange rate conversion tends to neglect high costs of living and exaggerate the material well-being in the Scandinavian countries, while PPPs tend to work in the other direction. Moreover, PPPs are based on a certain basket of goods and the underlying assumption is that the consumption of the basket is evenly distributed in society and between nations. In reality this is seldom true. The more uneven the income distribution, the more inaccurate the basket procedure is to describe the situation of the worst-off. The true picture of purchasing power is probably found somewhere in between the two currency conversions (for a more detailed discussion, see Bradbury and Jäntti 1999).

4 Since the number of countries is small, correlation coefficients are used as a heuristic device to get the most out of the data. An alternative, and perhaps a better and clearer option, is to use bivariate scatterplots, but due to space considerations we will only use correlation coefficients (the story told by these two methods is exactly the same).

and Spain our results produce a slightly different conclusion. Exchange rates still confirm our previous interpretation: the richer the country, the less poverty, but now the PPP evidence is more ambiguous. The wealth of a nation seems to have nothing to do with the prevalence of relative poverty. Some boats float, some boats sink, and the high tide is not that important.

In the Rawlsian spirit, it is very hard to justify our first statement that we could forgive a high incidence of poverty if the absolute income level of the poor is high enough. Correlation coefficients point in the opposite direction to the anticipated one and instead of a positive we find a negative relationship: the correlation coefficient between the poverty rate and exchange-rate-based income levels for the poor (POORUD) is -.45, and -.57 without Poland, Hungary and Spain. Neither does the inspection of the PPP-based correlations improve the fit of the theory (r = -.28 or -.21 if we exclude the three outliers). The trickle-down theory does not seem to work that well in a cross-sectional analysis of poverty. The absolute income level of the poor is not improved if the poverty rate is high; on the contrary, the results indicate that the lower the poverty rates the better the absolute position of the poor. Moreover, the incidence of poverty and 'richness' goes hand in hand (correlation between 'richness' and poverty rates is .89). Thus, on the basis of cross-sectional data we must reject our first hypothesis.

An alternative way to look at the same situation would be to study the relationship between the income of the poor and the general affluence of society e.g. as measured by the GDP or the median income for the total population. Furthermore, the prevalence of 'richness' in a society provides opportunities to assess the validity of the trickle-down theory. Increases in GDP, and in the medians for the total population and the rich are supposed to lift the poor out of their destitution. Therefore, we should expect a positive relationship between the various indicators of affluence (GDP, medians for the total population and medians of the rich) and the income level of the poor. Indeed, this is precisely what we find. The higher the GDP and the more affluent the median population and the richer the rich, the more affluent the poor. So far so good. Our results seem to give qualified support to the trickle-down theory and they also seem to fulfil the Rawlsian criteria for just distribution.

The only problem is how to put our results together. On the one hand, economic prosperity does not eradicate poverty but on the other hand prosperity is strongly associated with the income level of the poor. The solution is pretty simple and obvious. The high absolute income levels of the rich and the poor are overall indications of high prosperity in a country (here our hypothesis 2 is true), but the overall high-income level does not automatically guarantee high economic well-being to the poor. Qualifications apply: a closer inspection of Table 2.1 reveals that the path to secure high absolute incomes for the poor combines the overall wealth of the population with a low incidence of relative poverty and 'richness'. Table 2.2 which presents results from regression models based on cross-sectional data for 1991 tells the same story. Models (which are only tentative and due to a small number of cases very sensitive to sampling) have been used as heuristic devices to visualise relationships between different indicators.

Table 2.2. The relationships between the absolute level of the poor and some indicators of richness, regression coefficients.

Variable	U.S. Dollar Convertions				PPP Convertions			
	18 OECD countries		15 OECD countries		18 OECD countries		15 OECD countries	
	Coeff.	T-statistics	Coeff.	T-statistics	Coeff.	T-statistics	Coeff.	T-statistics
Constant	460	1.48	907	1.52	92	.26	116	.167
Median for the total	.55	6.04***	.52	4.76***	.54	4.08***	.57	3.50**
Poverty rate	-49.30	-2.28*	-56.50	-2.28*	-51.67	-2.28*	-53.19	-2.11
Median for the rich	-.04	-1.81	-.04	-1.56	-.03	-1.00	-.04	-.97
Adj. R sq	.97		.91		.93		.77	

In our equations, median income for the total population has been used as a measure of the overall prosperity of a nation. In addition, we have included the poverty rate and the absolute income level for the rich in regression models. The significant and positive coefficients for the median income indicate that a high national income level is a decisive factor determining the level of economic well-being of the worst-off.[5] This is the main but not the entire story. The relative poverty level has some impact upon results. The higher the incidence of poverty the lower the absolute income level of the poor. To use the tide metaphor: the rising tide is necessary to lift the boats but the worst boats must be in such a condition that they can float.

The cross-sectional analyses presented above are static in the sense that they only map the situation at one point in time, whereas the Rawlsian idea and the trickle-down theory are more dynamic in their orientation. We should also concentrate on changes of economic well-being and not only study a static cross-sectional picture of one point in time. Therefore, it is interesting to take a short look at the correlation between poverty rates/changes in poverty rates and changes in the economic well-being of the poor in different countries at different periods in time (Figure 2.1). The time period studied is from the mid-1980s to the mid-1990s, but due to the limited availability of data, unfortunately we must restrict the number of countries to ten: Australia (AUS), Canada (CN), Finland (FI), Germany (GE), Italy (IT), Luxembourg (LUX), Norway (NO),

---

5 A tentative path analysis showed that the volume of social transfers (as a percentage of the GDP) is significantly associated with the incidence of poverty (the bigger the transfer budget, the lower the poverty rate) but transfers had no direct association with the absolute income of the poor.

Sweden (SE), the UK and the US Numbers after country labels refer to the period under inspection, e.g. LUX85-91 pertain to changes that took place in Luxembourg from 1985 to 1991. Because of space limitations and our 30 observations being so close together country labels unfortunately overlap and in some cases it is hard to separate individual countries and time periods. Since we are here more interested in inspecting general trends than country-specific patterns, this overlapping is not a major problem. In principle, all country names could be dropped and instead, we could inspect general trends expressed in regression lines in each figure.

Again, as previously, we would expect a positive correlation between the poverty indicators and the improvement in the income level: the higher the poverty rate and the bigger the increase in poverty, the bigger the increase in the income of the poor. Otherwise, it is hard to justify higher poverty rates by reference to the difference principle. However, Figure 2.1 does not lend much support to the hypothesis that a higher incidence of poverty is linked to bigger improvements in the standard of living of the poor. Correlation between changes in the PPP adjusted median income of the poor and poverty levels is negligible ($r = -.24$). As is evident from upper panel of the figure, Luxembourg is a deviant case that may determine the direction of the relationship. The exclusion of Luxembourg changes the relationship close to zero ($-.03$). But, if we exclude the Luxembourgeois case, Italy, the US, the UK and, due to their developments in the 1990s, also Finland and Sweden become outliers, and the simultaneous removal of these influential observations with Luxembourg will turn the coefficients to be clearly negative ($-.50$).

In the lower panel we are interested in the relationship between changes in poverty levels and changes in the economic position of the poor. The story told by this inspection is very much in accordance with the testimony presented above. However, the correlations are more strongly negative: $r = -.27$ among the total sample, $r = -29$ if the deviant cases Luxembourg, Italy and the UK are excluded, and finally, if we additionally omit Sweden and Finland, the association turns out to be significantly negative ($r = -.48$). In sum, our results seem to be sensitive to the choice of countries included in the analysis but we may nonetheless conclude that it is hard to apply the difference principle to motivate higher poverty levels.

Economic tide and the position of the poor

The emphasis in the trickle-down theory and the difference principle is on dynamic changes or increases that economic growth causes in the income level of the poor. The former, in particular, emphasises the decisive role of growth. In order to evaluate the validity of the theory, in the subsequent section we will concentrate on the impact of economic growth upon the economic well-being of the poor. The economic tide is operationalised as the GDP growth in a given period of time (economic indicators are derived from OECD 1997a). The effects of the tide are measured by changes in the median income of the poor, the rich and the total population. These analyses are based on absolute changes when it comes to the income of the poor and percentile changes for the GDP growth. Numbers after country labels again pertain to the period under inspection for each individual country.

Figure 2.2 clearly indicates that the improvement in the position of the poor is highly dependent on overall economic growth (r = .70). This is true for both absolute (in PPPs) and relative (in percentiles) changes. Economic development has been impressive in Luxembourg and consequently, the poor there have improved their lot much more than in any other country included in our study. At the other end of the continuum, we find Finland (91-95) and Sweden (92-95), where economic performance was very bad and the deterioration of the lot of the worst-off was most severe.

Because of its extreme values, Luxembourg again is an outlier that determines the strength and the direction of the relationship between the variables. Indeed, the exclusion of Luxembourg will weaken the correlation but the exclusion does not change the direction of the relationship (r = .31). As in the previous correlations, the exclusion of Luxembourg indicates that we also have to omit Finland and Sweden because of their exceptionalism in the 1990s. If these two cases are excluded from the analysis, the correlation turns out to be non-significant, yet positive (.10).

We could then read at least two contradictory stories from Figure 2.2. The first one, based on the sample of all countries, speaks strongly in favour of the tide hypothesis. The flow is necessary to lift the poor boats, while the second story, based on a smaller sample, hints that economic growth is not that important. National experiences, especially from Finland and Sweden, provide more evidence for the former hypothesis: the economic ebb will also lower the poor boats. The results are very much in accordance with cross-sectional results from Tables 2.1 and 2.2. Economic growth is necessary but insufficient to improve the income level of the poor. The lifting capacity of the tide may vary between nations. In some countries, economic growth may benefit all sections of the population, whereas in other countries some social groups reap all the benefits of growth. In Figure 2.3 we try to visualise the increase of the income level of the poor and rich, and the median income of the total population. The countries included in the analysis represent different types of welfare state regimes.

The bars in the figure represent changes in these three variables. The higher the bar rises above the zero-line, the more rapidly the median income or the GDP have improved, and similarly, the further the bar descends below the zero-line the more severe the decline in median incomes. The first group of bars for each country represents growth in the late 1980s, the second one in the early 1990s and the last one depicts changes over the whole period.

A couple of interesting patterns can be distinguished. First of all, the Luxembourgeois case is extraordinary – so extraordinary that it is omitted from the visual presentation (which is mainly for reasons of scale; if the high Luxembourg growth rates had been included in the figure, they would have flattened the bars for the other countries and the whole point of the bar presentation would have been missed). In Luxembourg, there is a slight tendency for the poor to lag behind the average, but nevertheless, the position of the poor both in relative and absolute terms has improved more rapidly than in any other country. Luxembourg, perhaps better than any other nation, lives up to the Rawlsian difference principle. GDP growth has increased economic well-being in all income groups and the improvement of the lot of the best-off has also improved the lot of the poor; in other countries this is not self-evident.

In Australia, USA, Norway and Germany, there are some disparities between GDP growth and changes in income of the population. Especially in Australia and Norway, economic growth has been strong but the boats have not been lifted to the same extent. It seems to be the case that smaller Norwegian fishing boats are lagging behind fancy cruisers. A similar pattern is present in Germany where economic growth has not improved the position of the poor, while the median income of the total population has increased somewhat. One explanation for these descrepancies is the unification of Germany and the lower income levels in the eastern part of the country.

In the North American countries increases in the GDP and the median income have been slow compared to the other countries. Only the improvement of the position of the richest stratum in Canada has been quite satisfactory. Since the Northern American countries have often been portrayed as 'American job machines' and examples of successful employment policy, the situation is somewhat surprising. To exaggerate somewhat: the Americans seem to work hard but their hard work does not create economic growth, whereas the Europeans have not been particularly successful in creating full employment but, nevertheless, the economic performance has been as good as in the US or even better. In Europe, there was growth without employment, whereas in the US there was employment without growth.

Finland and Sweden form their own interesting group. Economic recession hit these countries most severely and the effects of this recession can be seen in decreasing median incomes. Up to the early 1990s, the poor in these countries did pretty well in comparison to other groups and, during the recession, their relative position did not deteriorate that much. Here our findings contradict previous studies to some extent which argue that in Sweden the recession hit the poor more severely than in Finland (Kautto et al. 1999). In Sweden, the greatest losers seem to be the rich, but on average they had maintained, and from 1987 to 1995, they had even increased their lead compared to other population categories.

In Finland, despite the fact that the median for the poor decreased during the deepest recession of the early 1990s, the income level of the poor in 1995 was about the same as it had been ten years earlier (see also Kautto et al. 1999). Moreover, the poor managed to maintain their income level as well as the population on average, while the contrary is true for most of the other countries. However, by and large, the rich managed to weather the recession better than other groups and their income in 1995 was clearly higher than it was in 1987. There are also indications that the rapid economic growth during the latter part of the 1990s has changed the picture: now the tide has lifted the best boats, while the poor are left behind and, consequently, income differences in Finland have increased and are back at the level they were 25 years ago (Uusitalo 1999).

Conclusion

The aim of this chapter was to try to evaluate from the Rawlsian distributive justice perspective how just or unjust societal development in a number of OECD countries has been. Rawls's difference principle, which has many ideas in common with the economic trickle-down theory, states that we can accept higher inequalities providing that those inequalities benefit the worse-off. Consequently the economic trickle-down theory argues that by introducing stronger incentives, e.g. in the form of greater income inequalities, people are encouraged to be more enterprising and thus contribute more to economic growth, and that this economic high tide will gradually lift all boats. Thus the weaker boats will also be helped.

The main conclusion of our examination was that it is very hard to justify social inequalities with reference to their beneficial effects on the poor. The absolute level of the well-being of the poor is not higher in countries with higher poverty rates, neither is their position improving more rapidly than in countries with lower levels of inequality. In this respect the trickle-down theory is definitely refuted and the conditions for the Rawlsian difference principle are not fulfilled.

Previous discussions can be summarised in a form of 'qualitative path analysis' displayed in Figure 2.4. The thickness of the arrow indicates the hypothetical strength of the posited impact. As suggested by the figure, the position of the poor is heavily dependent on the median income level, which in turn is positively associated with the GDP and the income of the rich. In this instance, the trickle-down theory emphasising the priority and importance of economic growth in relation to distributional issues is definitely supported. However, our results indicated that the economic tide does not lift all income groups similarly, and it is here that distributional issues enter the picture. First, the proportion of the rich is positively linked with the poverty rate, which in turn tends to decrease the absolute income level of the poor. Second, social security transfers will decrease the proportion of the poor and hence indirectly increase the economic well-being of the worse-off. Third, interestingly enough, there is no significant connection between the poverty rates and the indicators of the absolute income levels (such as the GDP per capita, or the median income or the income of the rich). There are huge national variations in the lifting capacity of the tide and that capacity depends on the set-up of national social policy programmes (see, for example, Björklund and Freeman 1997; Korpi and Palme 1998). In the Western hemisphere the incidence of poverty is more associated with (socio-)political factors than with economic prosperity, and for this very reason, there is misery and want amongst plenty (for a fuller discussion see Nussbaum and Sen 1993; Sen 1999).

In the dispute between hard-boiled economists and soft-boiled social scientists, we must take a middle position. Economists are correct in arguing for the beneficial effects of economic growth for the poor, whereas social scientists are right in their arguments on distributive issues. In other words, the absolute income level of the poor is strongly dependent on what is happening in the national economy, while the incidence of poverty in advanced countries is less associated with economic factors but the result of national social policy solutions, which in turn are political artefacts, dependent on political will.

The survey presented above is very preliminary and tentative and it suffers from a number of problems. First, our comparisons say nothing about the composition of the poor in different countries. We do not know who the poor are. On the basis of previous studies (e.g. Jäntti and Ritakallio 2000; Kangas and Palme 2000) we know that the incidence of poverty in the Nordic countries is highest within the age bracket 18-25. In some countries (especially in the US and the UK) families with children and the elderly are most exposed to poverty. It is a task for future studies to figure out in what way the incidence of low income has changed during the ebb and flow of growth in different countries. Particularly from a perspective of social justice, it is important to study the extent to which poverty is only a transitional phase, e.g. for young people, or the fate of certain groups of people (Goodin et al. 1997 and 1999). In the former case an increase in the poverty rate could simply indicate that there are more young people studying and therefore on low incomes, whereas in the latter elements of social injustice may be involved. During the economic high tide some boats seem to float nicely, whereas some boats are desperately stuck in the mud and cannot be freed by the tide alone.

Figure 2.1a: Poverty rate (%) and the median income for the poor.

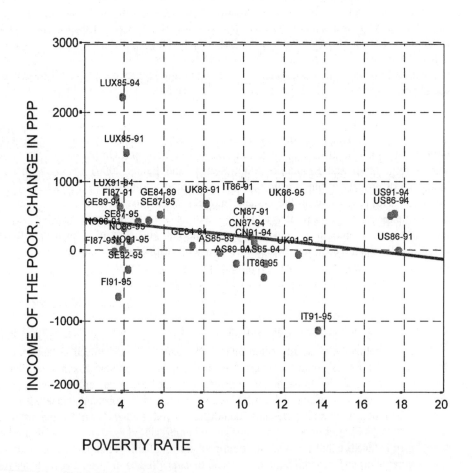

Figure 2.1b: Change in poverty rates (from the mid-1980s to the mid-1990s) and the median income for the poor.

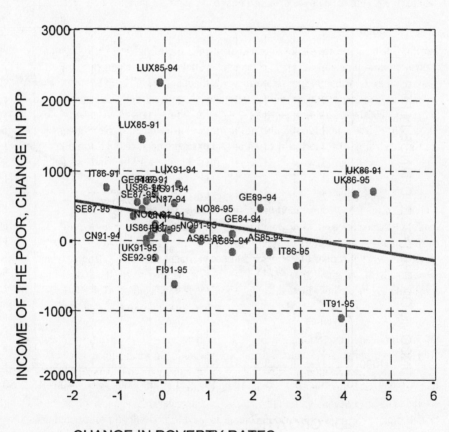

CHANGE IN POVERTY RATES

Figure 2.2: The growth of the GDP and the change of the median income for the poor 1985-95.

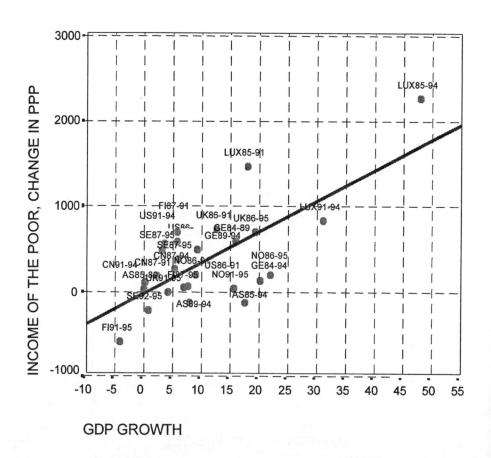

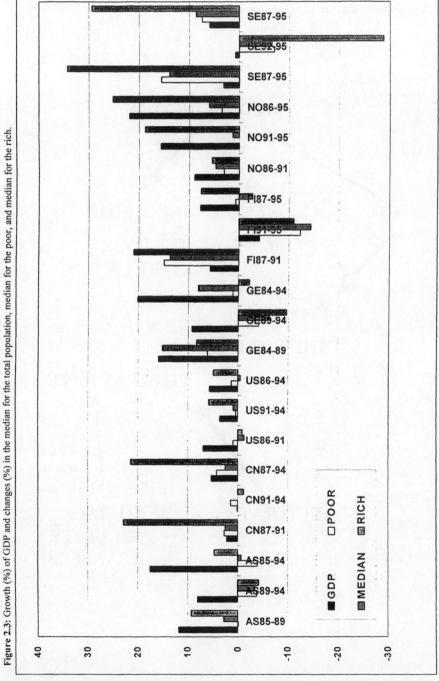

Figure 2.3: Growth (%) of GDP and changes (%) in the median for the total population, median for the poor, and median for the rich.

Figure 2.4: Hypothetical presentation of the determinants of the income level of the poor.

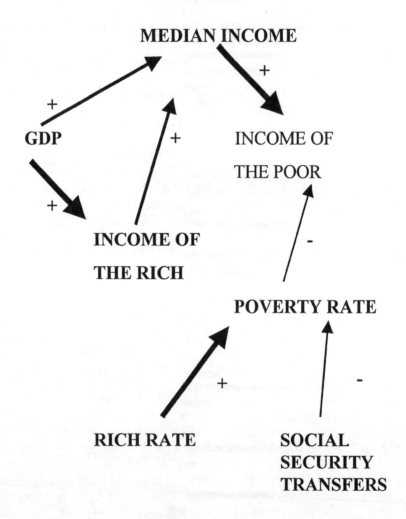

Chapter 3

Popular Support for Social Security.
A sociological perspective[1]

Wim van Oorschot

Introduction

From a sociological perspective the most critical variable for the future of social security lies in its societal legitimacy, that is, the degree to which individual citizens endorse its principles and operations and accept its requirements and outcomes. When post-war welfare states in the Western world began to reach the first stages of maturation sociologists began to express concern about their future in the light of potentially falling popular support as a result of certain political, cultural and structural developments in society. The early concerned prophets included Illich (1973) and Lasch (1978), who worried about the detrimental effects of the increasingly bureaucratic and statist aspects of welfare and social

---

1 A condensed article based on the data produced for this chapter will appear in *Policy and Politics* (Van Oorschot 2001).

security. From a political economy perspective, Rose and Peters (1978) claimed that support would decline to the degree that wage earners experience a drop in their real disposable income due to economic recession and a rising demand for social protection schemes. The 'abused taxpayer' would ultimately refuse to contribute. Crozier et al. (1975) feared the growing ungovernability of the broader welfare state due to 'rising expectations', i.e. if democratic processes led to an overload of demands on the government, exceeding its capacity to respond. Wilensky (1975) argued that the new 'middle mass', resulting from the ongoing differentiation of labour and social life and driven by economic individualism, would object to paying for social welfare, since they felt they would receive fewer or no benefits from it.

This 'middle mass' argument is still repeated regularly, e.g. in terms of the 'comfortable majority' who is reluctant to extend the welfare secured for itself to the minority of the poor (Galbraith 1992), or in terms of the notion of a 'one-third/two-thirds society' (Leisering and Leibfried 1998). From a cultural point of view Zijderveld (1979) argued that the comprehensive welfare state contributed to an immoral ethos among its citizens, where everybody tries to benefit much and contribute little, leading to a morally corrupting and economically unsustainable situation. Inglehart (1977) saw post-materialistic values becoming more important among post-war generations. Quality of life, rather material aspects of economic and physical social protection gained in significance, and Inglehart later added that welfare states had reached a point of 'diminishing returns', leading to withdrawal of popular support (Inglehart 1990). Recently a new argument has been introduced in the wake of the debate about the 'risk society', holding that 'manufactured uncertainty' reaches across all social groups, while at the same time people have become more suspicious of government's capability for offering solutions (Beck 1986, Giddens 1994, Beck, Giddens and Lash 1994).

Despite all these concerns, empirical studies into the legitimacy of welfare state programmes and social security have not detected any substantial decline in popular support. On the contrary, all comparative studies conclude that from the 1970s onwards it has remained high. A dip generally occurred in the recessive 1980s, but even then it was '...simply nonsense to speak of a crisis of legitimacy' (Ringen 1987:63). More recently, Pierson (1991:171) concludes from several public opinion studies that 'there is little evidence ... of large-scale popular backlash against the welfare state'. Comparing trends in various European countries on the basis of various data-sets, Pettersen (1995:229) concludes that '...there is no evidence that welfare states, or specific welfare programs, are generally losing support over time...'. Similar conclusions are drawn in the comparative studies by Ferrera (1993), Ploug (1996) and Abrahamson (1997).

Clearly, actual registered trends have defied theoretical expectations regarding developments in the legitimacy base of modern welfare states and social security systems. The obvious question, i.e. how this could be explained, has not yet been subjected to any systematic research. Most authors simply draw the conclusion that theories apparently do not explain actual developments. Pettersen (1995) goes a little further and suggests that in order to understand welfare support patterns, one should combine two sets of theories. The dominant one views support as based on people's self-interest, such as the theories formulated by Rose and Peters on the 'abused taxpayer', by Wilensky on the 'middle mass', and by Galbraith on the 'comfortable majority' (see also Esping-Andersen and Korpi 1984). The other set of theories assumes that people adhere to social values and norms regarding welfare contribution, (see Inglehart's notion of 'post-materialism'; but also Taylor-Gooby 1985; Coughlin 1991). Discussing the motivational basis for welfare support, other authors have come up with similar dichotomies. Kangas (1997) and Lindenberg (1990) refer in this respect to models of 'homo economicus' and 'homo sociologicus', Taylor- Gooby (1999) to 'instrumental rationality' versus 'normative' behaviour, Elster (1990) to 'selfishness' versus 'altruism' and Mansbridge (1990) to 'self-interest' versus. 'love and duty'. All of the above agree that people might be motivated to contribute to welfare by both types of considerations at the same time, and that social contexts condition the type and strength of their reasons for doing so.

This would suggest that a combination between self-interest and values, norms and beliefs would be a means to understand the observed mismatch between actual trends and theories. However, even if this notion has been accepted, questions remain as to what mixes actually exist, to what degree people differ in their reasons for acting as they do, and how these differences can be explained. A problem here is that thus far, people's reasons for contributing to welfare and social security have only been measured indirectly, making it impossible to adequately assess the relative importance of the two types of reasons and to analyse the structural and cultural determinants of people's motivational mixes. Usually, the prevalence of the two types of reasons are deduced from the influence on support exerted by 'interest indicators', such as age, household type, income and class position, and 'value indicators' like egalitarianism, left-right preferences, individualism, social ideologies and a range of welfare attitudes (see Coughlin 1980 and Peillon 1995 for reviews of empirical studies). We know of no empirical study that directly asked people what made them support welfare in general, and social security schemes in particular.

This chapter aims to contribute to a better theoretical and empirical understanding of people's reasons for supporting welfare schemes and the determinants behind those. For this purpose, an instrument for measuring reasons will be developed, and the results of a Dutch public opinion study applying the typology will be presented.

Reasons for supporting welfare schemes

Sociological theories on social solidarity address the issue of why and under what conditions people are willing to contribute to the common good, i.e. let collective interests prevail, even if this conflicts with their personal interests.[2] Such theories therefore help to identify the various reasons why people support welfare schemes.

---

2 See van Oorschot (1999b) for a more extended discussion of sociological theories of solidarity and

Durkheim (1966/1893) and Weber (in Henderson and Parsons 1964) conceived of social solidarity as a state of relations between individuals and groups enabling collective interests to be served. The essence and basis of these relations is that people experience a common fate. They do so either because they share the same identity as members of a collective and therefore feel a mutual sense of belonging and responsibility (which are the central ideas in Durkheim's concept of mechanic solidarity and Weber's 'communal' relations of solidarity), or because they share utility in the sense that people need each other to realise their life opportunities (which refers to social bonds of a type described by Durkheim as organic solidarity and by Weber as 'associative' relations of solidarity). The scope and strength of solidarity in a social system is a function of these shared identities and utilities, since they constitute the basis for motivations to contribute.

There are several types of reasons. First, Mayhew (19971) stresses the role of people's feelings and sentiments in this connection. In his view, the degree to which people feel attracted to one another and are loyal at the micro level, and the degree to which they perceive a collective identity and 'we-feeling' at the meso level are decisive for their willingness to contribute to the common good. A second reason for solidarity, which figures explicitly in the solidarity theories of Durkheim (1966/1893) and Parsons (1951), depends on culturally-based convictions which imply that the individual feels a moral obligation to serve the collective interest. Enlightened self-interest can be a third reason for solidarity. It is central in Hechter's rational choice approach to solidarity (Hechter 1987) and it underlies Durkheim's organic solidarity in a modern differentiated society, where people learn that they benefit from contributing to the collective interest (if not immediately then in the long run). The same reason is also the basis for Weber's associative relations, in which people agree to help one another either by exchanging goods or services or by co-operating to achieve a common goal. Clearly, solidarity does not need to be grounded in warm feelings of love and duty, but can be based on a rational calculation. Authors who argue that the legitimacy of the modern welfare state mainly stems from the fact that the middle and upper classes benefit from it most implicitly refer to this type of reason (see e.g. Baldwin 1990, Esping-Andersen 1990, Goodin and LeGrand 1987).

Fourth, support for solidarity is not necessarily spontaneous or completely voluntary. According to Parsons (1951), contributing to the collective interest is only an act of solidarity if it results from institutional role obligations. Enforcement figures even more explicitly in Hechter's theory. Ruling out free-riding necessitates coercion and control of contributions to the common good. Empirically, one can imagine situations where the first three reasons – emotional ties and identification, moral conviction, and self-interest - fail to provide sufficient support for solidarity. The identification with other group members may be low, moral obligations may be perceived as unrealistic or unjust, and people may not have a strong personal interest in the group's revenues. In these cases, solidarity will not be supported spontaneously, and enforcement by a higher authority is thus necessary. It can be the group, the neighbourhood or the public which exercises social control, but in many

their significance for understanding reasons to support welfare.

fields of modern society it will be the state. However, enforced solidarity can only be stable in the long run if it is legitimised. Of course it can be legitimised by the reasons mentioned above, but the situation under discussion here is one where they are not sufficiently strong. The remaining possibility is that the authority has a legitimacy of its own. For instance, the obligation to exhibit solidarity can be instilled by the state, and thus perceived as legitimate because the state itself is seen as a legitimate authority.

To conclude, the legitimacy of solidarity relations is generally stronger if they link up with existing emotional ties and identification, correspond with relevant moral convictions and perceived duties, correspond to the long-term self-interest of individuals and groups and to the degree that they are backed by a more legitimate authoritative body. Solidarity relations and arrangements legitimated by all four of these reasons are likely to be the strongest.[3] Consequently, the welfare arrangements and institutions that serve the collective interest of modern societies have a stronger legitimacy to the degree that more people are motivated to contribute to the arrangements and people have more reasons to contribute. Furthermore, to a certain extent, a positive correlation can be expected between the various reasons people have for solidarity. This is because people tend to be most dependent on the collectivities they belong to, implying that shared identities and shared utilities tend to go together.

Hypotheses

What follows is an analysis of the degree to which the Dutch population is motivated by the various reasons to support welfare, particularly to pay for social security benefits, whether there are individual differences, and if so, which factors determine an individual's motivational pattern. Two sets of explanatory factors are distinguished: a set of personal characteristics comprising sex, age, educational level, income level and welfare use (whether people receive social security benefit or not); and a set of variables which indicate people's opinions, perceptions and attitudes regarding the welfare state in general and social security in particular.

With respect to *gender* one might assume that women are more strongly motivated to support welfare schemes because there is some empirical evidence which indicates that women generally favour welfare more than men (Deitch 1988). This might be explained by cultural differences in the sense that women adhere more to values of caring and mutual responsibility (Deitch 1988), which in turn implies that women agree more with moral conviction and emotional reasons. However self-interest might equally be a strong factor,

---

3 Zsuzsa Ferge (1999) recently argued that the legitimacy of various types of social exchange contracts depends on the number of distributive principles that underlie them. 'Hazy contracts' like social insurance programmes are based on more of such principles than social assistance schemes, and therefore have a stronger legitimacy base.

given that women are believed generally to benefit more than men since welfare arrangements enhance female self-sufficiency and labour market chances (Hernes 1987, Wearnes 1987, Erie and Rein 1988). While this might be true in many welfare states, in the Netherlands the case could be different. Here social security rights have become strongly connected to labour market performance (Van Oorschot 1999a), the labour market participation of Dutch women is relatively low and most women work part-time, which gives them relatively less income protection than men. Child care facilities are grossly inadequate, which might be another factor which makes Dutch women receive less benefits from the welfare state than they might in other comparable countries.

As to *age,* younger people might be expected to be motivated to contribute to a lesser extent than older groups. One can argue that social protection is less significant for the young personally, since they generally have lower chances of falling ill or becoming disabled, and old age is still far away. Many young people do not yet have responsibilities to spouses or children, and have invested less in the welfare system than older people (see also Svallfors 1989). Cultural differences might also come in here. In Inglehart's terms (Van Deth 1984), Dutch younger people are more 'post-materialistic' than older people and such an attitude is expected to correlate with less welfare support (Pettersen1995). Dutch young people have also exhibited a shift towards more conservative political preferences, with the accompanying values of individual responsibility and stronger anti-welfare sentiment (Ter Bogt and Van Praag 1992). With regard to *educational level,* the expectations are less clear-cut. Since their chances of becoming unemployed, ill or disabled are generally smaller, one would assume that people with a higher educational level are less motivated to pay for welfare schemes. They also have higher incomes and thus more opportunities to provide for themselves. These are two reasons why they might feel like 'abused taxpayers' (Rose and Peters 1978). There are also more 'post-materialists' among people with higher educational levels, and if this kind of attitude correlates with higher anti-welfare sentiment, as Pettersen (1995) suggests, this would be another reason for better educated people to be less motivated to pay for welfare schemes. On the other hand, as a result of their better education they may have developed a clearer understanding of the functional and moral necessity of contributing to the common good. Ganzenboom (1988) refers to the higher degree of 'moral enlightenment' of the better educated, and Hasenfeld and Raferty (1989) argue that formal education evokes a greater commitment to social equality and social rights.

With regard to *income level,* the expectations are rather straightforward. One would expect people with lower incomes to have a stronger interest in the welfare state, and therefore be more willing to contribute to it. The reverse can be expected of people with higher incomes. However, income differentials might be relatively small in countries with a comprehensive welfare system such as the Netherlands, compared with countries with a more residual system. In the Netherlands even people with high incomes can benefit strongly from general welfare arrangements, and perhaps even more so than those with lower incomes (which, according to Muffels et al. 1986 and SCP 1994, is actually the case). Finally, *welfare use* can also be expected to be a clearly decisive variable. People who receive benefits will perceive the various reasons in favour of paying for welfare schemes more clearly than people who do not. However, since benefit dependency is a reality close to the personal lives of many Dutch people, the differences might not be that large. In fact, no fewer than 92 per cent of the Dutch population have either themselves received social security benefits in the past, are currently in benefit receipt, expect to be dependent on social security transfers in the future, or have relatives or friends who receive benefits (see Table 3.1 and Van Oorschot 1997; included here are unemployment assistance and insurance, and sickness and disability benefits).

In order to further explore the possible determinants of people's reasons for contributing to welfare schemes, a number of relevant opinions, perceptions and attitudes are included. These variables might have a direct effect on the motivational pattern of individuals and can play a mediating role in the total influence of personal characteristics. With the variables in our data-set, it can be hypothesised that people who are more positive or less negative about various aspects of welfare will perceive more reasons to pay for welfare and do so more strongly. This pertains to people who, more than others,
- evaluate the social security system less negatively;
- perceive the individual, social, moral and economic effects of social security more positively or less negatively;
- would prefer benefit levels to be higher;
- perceive the actual benefit levels as inadequate for recipients;
- believe less that people have a certain degree of personal control over social risks;
- have a more positive attitude towards income solidarity, i.e. the principle that higher incomes contribute relatively more to the costs of social protection;
- believe less in the abuse of social security;
- have a higher general trust in others, and
- have a stronger general sense of solidarity in life.

In addition, people's political preference and strength of religious beliefs can be expected to be important. Regarding political preferences, the expectation is that people on the political left agree more than those on the right with reasons pertaining to moral obligations and affection. Socialist and Social Democratic ideologies adhere more to equality and the social protection of vulnerable groups than liberal and conservative ideologies. Christian Democrats are expected to be close to the left-wing position in this respect because of the Christian values of charity and compassion. In many surveys, political left-right variables account for a large, and often even the largest, part of variance in various types of welfare attitudes (Coughlin 1980, Taylor-Gooby 1983, Whiteley 1981, Pettersen 1995, Papadakis and Bean 1993). With regard to religion, the available variable is frequency of church attendance. Since it is assumed that people who attend church more frequently adhere more to Christian values and norms, they can be expected to be more motivated to contribute to welfare schemes.

Data and Methods

Data

Our data are from the *TISSER Solidarity Study*, a national representative survey (N=1500) among the Dutch population above the age of 16 which was carried out in the autumn of 1995. The survey was specifically designed to measure people's opinions, perceptions and attitudes regarding the welfare state in general and the system of social security in particular (see Van Oorschot 1998 for a summary of the survey's full results).

Measurement of reasons for welfare scheme support

Respondents were asked about their reasons to contribute to the Dutch system of social security benefits. Three of the above-mentioned reasons were operationalised into separate answering categories. 'Accepted authority' could not be meaningfully operationalised, since contributing to social security is a legal obligation for everyone with an income. The survey question was:

> *Paying premiums for social insurances is a legal obligation. Apart from that, people may have other reasons for paying them. What about you? To what degree do you agree or disagree with the following statements?*

> *'For me paying premiums for social insurances is something I also do because:*
> a.   *This way I will receive a benefit myself if I need it.*
> b.   *I regard it as a moral duty towards the less well-off in society.*
> c.   *I personally sympathise with the beneficiaries and their situation.*

> *Response categories: (1) strongly agree (2) agree (3) neither agree nor disagree (4) disagree (5) strongly disagree*

The statements indicate perceived self-interest, moral convictions, mutual affection and identification. In the first instance, a separate bi-variate analysis was conducted. However, since the observed mismatch between the theoretical pessimism about welfare legitimacy and the generally observed high support levels specifically raised an interest in the degree and determinants of combinations of reasons, a scale variable was construed for a multivariate analysis of determining factors.[4] This scale variable MOTIVATION combines

---

4 Multi-variately analysing the three reasons separately would of course be very interesting in itself. I did so at a preparatory stage and found that self-interest is significantly differentiated by only two of all the explanatory variables from the two sub-sets: the non-welfare users mention it a bit less, as do the youngest age group (which mentions all the reasons less). This result demonstrates that there is very little variation in the dependent variable (82% of all Dutch citizens agree on it). I also found

the responses to the three statements as follows: (0) no reason mentioned (i.e. no 'agree' or 'strongly agree' on any of the statements, implying that legal obligation is the only reason for paying premiums); (1) only 'perceived self-interest'; (2) 'perceived self-interest' plus either 'moral duty' or 'mutual identification'; (3) 'perceived self-interest', plus 'moral duty' and 'mutual identification', as well as 'moral duty' and 'mutual identification' but not 'perceived self-interest' (the latter group represents less than 2 per cent of the respondents). The scale is not designed to measure whether individuals support welfare schemes or not (82 per cent do on the basis of a perceived interest and 87 per cent on the basis of any of the reasons). Instead, it measures the strength and nature of the support. Higher scores on the MOTIVATION scale imply stronger support for welfare schemes, since it means that people are motivated by several of the various reasons. Higher scores also indicate a stronger moral and emotional base of support in addition to self-interest. The scale correlates .40 with 'perceived self-interest', .75 with 'moral obligation' and .73 with 'affection' (all p<.000).

Explanatory variables

As indicated in the previous section, two distinct sets of relevant variables are available from our data: personal characteristics and a set of opinions, perceptions and attitudes. Their measurement and construction are shown in the Appendix.

Analysis

In a first step, the distribution of the reasons over the personal characteristics is presented for each reason separately. It shows which groups in society are the most or the least motivated to pay for welfare schemes. These bi-variate analyses also give an idea of the validity of the hypotheses formulated above.

In a second step, multivariate analyses of the motivation scale are carried out. Attention is paid to the direct effects of all the explanatory variables on the reason for welfare support and to the indirect effects of the personal characteristics which might influence opinions, perceptions and attitudes. Therefore an explorative, two-stage LISREL analysis is carried out. In the first stage, the reasons are regressed on all the explanatory variables from both sets, and at the same time all the variables of the set of opinions, perceptions and attitudes are regressed on all the variables of the set of personal characteristics. This analysis is repeated in the second stage, but only with those variables which have shown to have significant effects in the first stage.

---

that there is a relatively high Pearson correlation among the other two reasons of .58 (p<.000), so that the patterns of their determinants proved to be quite similar.

Results

Why pay for social security?

The first finding is that there is no evidence whatsoever that enforcement is the only way to motivate the Dutch to pay for welfare schemes. On the contrary, most Dutch people admit having other reasons besides merely fulfilling a legal obligation. Most notably, paying for welfare schemes is accepted on the grounds of a perceived self-interest: no less than 82 per cent of the Dutch willingly contribute to social security since they expect to be dependent upon it themselves at some point in the future. The comprehensive Dutch social security system, with its earnings-related benefits for the ill, the disabled and the unemployed, its non-means-tested old age pensions and child benefits, and its housing benefits for tenants and tax credits for home-owners is seemingly experienced as a beneficial institution by nearly the entire population. In contrast to the United States, there is no sign of a middle class perceiving welfare as reserved for the poor (Weir et al. 1988, Kluegel et al. 1995), or on the dependence on 'loyalties of the numerically weak, and often politically residual, social stratum', which is how Esping-Andersen (1990) typified the situation in residualist welfare states such as the United States and Canada. The relatively strong solidarity of the Dutch population corresponds with international comparative studies (Hofstede 1998, Stevens and Diederiks 1995). It is also reflected in the fact that as many as two-thirds of the respondents also claim that they are motivated to pay for social security on moral grounds, i.e. they perceive paying premiums as a moral obligation towards the needy. The emotional reason (compassion for the beneficiaries) is the least strong one, but is nevertheless cited by as many as 42 per cent of the Dutch. Finally, only very small minorities of between 8 per cent and 14 per cent explicitly disagree (strongly) with the moral obligation and emotional reasons, and only 5-6 per cent has no answer.

Combining the answers in the motivation scale shows that, apart from it being a legal obligation, actually only 13 per cent of the Dutch perceive no reason at all to contribute to social security. (In this group, people below the age of 25 are over-represented, while older people, welfare beneficiaries and the most highly educated group are somewhat under-represented). Moreover, as little as 20 per cent of the Dutch only perceive self-interest as an additional reason (the younger more so than the older respondents), while two-thirds perceive the moral obligation and/or emotional reasons as more important than self-interest. Clearly, the Dutch social security system has a strong legitimacy base among the population as a whole. Its strongest foundation lies in perceptions of self-interest, but it is firmly sustained by considerations of moral obligation and feelings of mutual identification and emotional ties.

Table 3.1: Benefit receipt (% of population 16-65 years)

	Unemployment benefit WW	Disability benefit WAO	Sickness benefit ZW	Social assistance ABW.	at least one of these
1. respondent at this moment (excl. 65+)	3	5	2	3	12
2. other household member at this moment	6	9	3	?	16
3. near acquaintance at this moment	38	46	29	36	71
4. respondent in past	23	8	39	9	55
5. perceived high future chance by respondent (excl. 65+)	40	45	59	34	59
6. respondent now, in past or high chance in future					79
7. idem + other household member or near acquaintance					92

These results can be understood if one recognises that most of the Dutch are personally involved in, and dependent upon, the social security system. Normally, such involvement is expressed in statistics showing how many people are receiving the various benefits at any one moment in time. From this perspective a minority of about 15 per cent of the Dutch are involved and dependent in terms of being actual recipients of insurance schemes (except pensions) or assistance programmes. However, this offers too static and individualistic a picture of personal involvement. It is too static because people may have been receiving benefits in the past or might expect to be dependent upon them in the (near) future. It is also too individualistic since people will sense personal involvement too if a family member, relative or close friend is dependent upon benefits. Table 3.1 shows how the picture of personal involvement in social security changes from a more 'dynamic' and 'socialised' perspective.

Indeed, Table 3.1 confirms that only a minority of the Dutch (12 per cent) were receiving benefit at the moment the survey was conducted. However, a dynamic view on personal involvement in social security shows that no less than 79 per cent of the Dutch have either received a benefit, are receiving it now, or perceive a (very) large chance of receiving benefits in future. If the picture is further 'socialised' it even shows that 92 per cent of the Dutch are directly involved in the receiving side of the system.

Nevertheless, there are differences in the reasons which apply to various individuals. The following sections describe the differences between social groups and analyse and discuss the factors which directly and indirectly influence reasons for paying for welfare.

Differences between groups

Table 3.2 shows that social groups do not differ very much in their reasons for supporting welfare schemes. Only in a few cases did the percentages on agreeing or disagreeing deviate more than 10 per cent from the overall ones. This coincides with findings in Denmark and Sweden, two other countries with comprehensive welfare systems (Ploug 1996, Aguilar and Gustafsson 1988). In all the categories, the order between the three reasons is the same as in the overall case. In each category, most of the respondents agree with the self-interest, less with the moral obligation, and least with the emotional reason. There is clearly a general motivational base for welfare support in the Netherlands.

Males tend to be somewhat more motivated than females on the grounds of self-interest and moral obligation, but the difference is not significant. There is no sex difference regarding the emotional reason. These results refute the expectations formulated earlier: no greater interest in welfare among women, nor any stronger adherence on their part to values of caring and mutual responsibility are reflected in our data. However, only bi-variate relations are involved here and the result might be specific for the Dutch situation, with its low full-time labour participation. The multi-variate analysis will provide greater insight into the influence of sex and the other personal characteristics.

Table 3.2: Reasons to pay for welfare by personal characteristics [in cells: % (strongly) agree] [N=1403]

	Perceived self-interest	Moral obligation	Emotional reasons
Overall	82	64 – 8	42 - 14
Sex			
- male	84	65	42
- female	80	63	42
Age	*	*	*
- =< 29	75	54	26
- 30-49	84	60	39
- 50-64	84	71	52
- >= 65	88	81	65
Educational level		*	*
- low	80	62	42
- medium	82	61	36
- high	86	75	50
Income level			
- low	83	66	50
- medium	81	61	38
- high	82	66	40
Welfare use	*		*
- no	82	63	40
- yes	89	69	53

* = significant differences: Chi-square tests, p < .000

Agreement with the three reasons increases with age, indicating that social security has a higher legitimacy among older than younger people. Self-interest is regarded as less important by the youngest age group, though the difference is rather small with the other groups. Age differences are greater as regards the moral obligation and emotional reasons, especially in the latter case. The overall pattern confirms the expectations based on the greater personal interest on the part of older people in welfare arrangements and provisions and on young people's more individualistic value pattern. However, the lower agreement level of the youngest cohort is not proportionally mirrored in their greater disagreement with the three reasons. Instead, many of the younger people said that they neither agreed nor disagreed. This implies that they might have clearer opinions on the subject as they grow older, so that the difference between the younger and older categories is an age effect, not a generational difference. As to educational level, it shows that the respondents with the highest educational level are the most motivated. Although all the categories perceive a similar degree of self-interest, the better educated ones agree more on moral obligation and emotional reasons, thus supporting the hypothesis of their higher 'moral consciousness'. The greater 'post-materialism' presumed to exist among the better educated does not manifest itself in our data. With regard to emotional reasons, there seems to be a non-linear relation: the more poorly educated respondents, who might be closer to beneficiaries or have more personal experience with benefit dependency, agree more with emotional reasons than people with a middle level education, but still less than the better educated ones. Quite surprisingly, the income level does not differentiate as expected. Dutch people with higher incomes are motivated by considerations of self-interest to the same degree as people with lower incomes. The comprehensive nature of the Dutch welfare state might play a role here. However, the income effect might be suppressed by the educational level. No specific hypotheses were formulated regarding the relation between income and moral obligation and emotional reasons. There are no significant differences, although there is an indication of a U-shaped relation: the respondents with medium incomes agree least with these two kinds of reasons. With regard to welfare use, as expected the data show that the welfare beneficiaries agree more with the self-interest and emotional reasons than the others. They also seem to be motivated more by moral obligation, but this difference is not significant. All in all, the differences between the welfare beneficiaries and the others are not very large, which might indicate that the Dutch welfare state is indeed 'close' to many people, including those who do not receive benefits themselves.

Influencing factors

To gain greater insight into the factors influencing people's reasons for paying for welfare schemes, multivariate LISREL analyses were carried out. The results are presented in Table 3.3. The total model shows a reasonable fit (GFI > 0.95 and RMSEA < .08: cf. Browne and Cudeck 1993).

As regards the effects of the set of opinions, perceptions and attitudes, the results show that a general solidarity attitude has the strongest direct effect on motivation (ß=.24). This means people who generally take the interests of others more into consideration, find pleasure in doing something for others, and do not believe that everybody should take care of themselves are more strongly motivated to pay for social security. Furthermore, a relatively strong influence is exerted by people's perception of the social effects of social security (ß=.14), their perception of dependency control (ß=-.13) and the attitude towards income solidarity (ß=.17). In other words, as expected, people who more strongly believe that social security prevents societal unrest, large-scale poverty and misery and promotes a fair distribution of life chances are more motivated. The same applies to people who do not tend to blame welfare recipients and believe that beneficiaries have little control over their own situation, as well as to people who favour redistribution more and think more positively about the principle that the higher income groups should pay more for social security. Other direct effects are smaller but significant. As expected, people with more general trust in others are more motivated, as are people with a stronger leftist political orientation. This confirms many previous findings on welfare support. Surprisingly, people's beliefs about characteristics of the social security system as such do not influence their motivation to contribute to it. There is no relation between their motivation and how people evaluate the system at large, and whether they perceive the benefits as adequate or not. There is not even any relation with the perceived degree of abuse of the system, nor are there any influences of people's perceptions of the individual, moral and economic effects of social security. The fact that religiousness, measured as church attendance, has no influence is most probably due to an overruling effect of age and educational level, since in the Netherlands, where secularisation is nearly as high as in Denmark and Sweden (Dobbelaere 1995), it is mainly older people and people with a lower educational level who attend church.

As to personal characteristics, most of the bi-variately observed relations are confirmed. Older people are more strongly motivated to contribute to welfare schemes, especially on moral and emotional grounds, than younger people (ß=.21). People with a higher educational level are more strongly motivated (ß=.09), as are welfare recipients(ß=.06), and as in the bi-variate case there is no direct effect of income level.[5] As to gender, the multi-variate analysis shows a significant effect (ß=-.08) in contrast to the bi-variate analysis, but the direction is the same: men are more strongly motivated to pay for welfare than women.

The total effect of personal characteristics on motivation for welfare support is different from their direct effect. This is because most of them, with the sole exception of welfare use, also have an indirect effect via various perceptions, beliefs and attitudes. In the case of gender, the total effect (ß=-.02) is smaller than its direct effect (ß=-.08). The reason is that although men are more in favour of income solidarity and have a stronger left-wing political orientation - factors increasing their motivation to pay for welfare - they also generally have less of a sense of solidarity, less trust in others, a more negative perception of the social effects of social security, and they believe more strongly that social risks are under people's own control - factors reducing their motivation. The net total effect of these opposing factors is that gender has a significant but rather small overall effect on welfare motivation. The relatively large direct effect of age (ß=.21) is reinforced (to ß=.30) by the fact that older people believe less that beneficiaries have personal control over their situation, they endorse income solidarity more strongly and have more general solidarity than younger people. As regards the educational level, the reinforcement is even stronger: the total effect (ß=.18) is twice the direct effect (ß=.09). People with a higher educational level are more motivated to pay for welfare schemes as such, perceive the social effects of social security more positively, endorse income solidarity more strongly, and have greater trust in others and a stronger sense of solidarity. The total effect is somewhat diminished by the fact that better educated people believe more strongly that welfare recipients have personal control over their situation. As regards income, there is no direct effect on the reasons for welfare support, but there are indirect effects. People with higher incomes are

---

5 The bi-variate analysis suggested that there should be a U-shaped relation between income level and reason to contribute to welfare. Consequently, the square of the income variable was put into the LISREL analysis. However, this variable did not have a direct or indirect effect.

only somewhat less motivated than those with lower ones (ß=-.02) because they believe more strongly that benefit dependency is under the control of the beneficiaries and have a more right-wing political preference. Lastly, welfare recipients do not differ from other people as regards the opinions and perceptions in our analysis. Clearly, there is no large cultural gap between the two categories in the Netherlands.

Conclusions

Many people have several simultaneous reasons for being willing to pay for welfare schemes. No fewer than two-thirds of our respondents said they were motivated by various combinations of perceived self-interest, moral obligation and emotional ties with the beneficiaries. This implies that earlier prognoses of negative trends in welfare support based solely on assumptions of self-interest or norm-regulated behaviour and attitudes are bound to be wrong. It is not only on the basis of self-interest or values that people are willing to support welfare and social security (as suggested by Pettersen 1995), in many cases there is even a combination with a third type of reason, emotional ties and identification with the plight of beneficiaries. More specifically, our data showed that virtually all the Dutch feel they have a personal interest in social security, and nearly two-thirds feel they have a moral obligation to contribute to welfare and a bit less than half sympathise with the plight of beneficiaries.

Clearly, the legitimacy of the Dutch welfare system seems to rest chiefly on the issue of self-interest. Its comprehensive nature seems to have generated its own legitimacy as a beneficial institution for everyone. Although there are no directly comparable data, the situation can be assumed to be similar in other broad welfare states such as Scandinavia, Germany and France. In countries with a more selective or residual welfare system like the United States, Canada, the Central and Eastern European welfare states and perhaps the United Kingdom, one would expect fewer people to be motivated to support welfare schemes on the basis of perceived self-interest. Since our data show a positive correlation between the various reasons, it can be assumed that in these countries the number of people who agree with the moral obligation and emotional reasons might also be smaller than in the Netherlands. In residual systems, the people who usually do not need or receive benefits are generally less 'close', socially as well as culturally, to people who do. From this perspective one could say that a broad welfare state generates its own legitimacy and a residual welfare state inhibits it. Due to popular support levels, it might be as difficult to cut down on a broad welfare state as it is to broaden a residual one.

In addition to the fact that so many Dutch people perceive the welfare state as beneficial to them, the moral and emotional basis for its legitimacy appears to be substantial as well. In our view, the fact that still more people are motivated by considerations of self-interest does not imply that 'the value base' of welfare legitimacy is generally any less important than 'the interest base'. Current welfare states only might have become broad and encompassing once sufficient levels of 'sameness' (Offe 1988) and 'a culture of solidarity' (Hinrichs 1996) were established. In residual welfare states the emotional and moral obligations derived from 'sameness' and 'solidarity culture' might be relatively more important than in other types of welfare states in underpinning any degree of welfare redistribution to the needy (cf. Goodin 1988). Moreover, in a retrenching welfare state, substantial levels of moral and social motivation might effectively cushion the drop in overall legitimacy, which is bound to occur if retrenchment policies limit the welfare revenues for the upper and middle classes.

Generally, our data show that whether people are more or less strongly motivated to contribute to welfare schemes depends more on individual factors - like solidarity, trust in others, political ideology, general attitude towards welfare redistribution and concern for societal cohesion and order - than on their perception of the fair workings of the welfare system as such - regarding perceived abuse, preferred benefit levels, and the effects of social security on individuals and the economy. These findings suggest the existence of a 'solidarity-oriented' personality type, possibly as opposed to the 'calculating citizen' that figures predominantly in the Dutch social debate. Further research is called for to explore this suggestion.

Finally, with regard to the total influence of structural variables, the reason for supporting welfare schemes appeared to be stronger among men, older people, welfare users and the respondents with the highest educational level. Surprisingly, income level had no direct effect on their motivation. It is only because people with a higher income blame the beneficiaries more for their dependent situation than the other income groups and because they have a more right-wing political orientation, that on the whole people with higher incomes tend to be a bit less motivated to pay for social security. It was also surprising that welfare recipients do not differ much in their motivation from other respondents. Both findings confirm that virtually the entire Dutch population perceives to be benefiting form welfare schemes.

Table 3.3: Direct, indirect and total effects on reasons for welfare support (LISREL analysis, max. likelihood, standardised coefficients of effects significant at p < 0.05; N=1407)

	Direct effects on reasons	Effects of personal characteristics on...						Total effect on reasons
		SE	*PC*	*IS*	*TO*	*SA*	*PP*	
Sex *male-female*	-0.08	0.09	-0.06	-0.07	0.06	0.27	0.13	-0.02
Age *young-old*	0.21		-0.16	0.11		0.15		0.30
Educational level *low-high*	0.09	0.26	0.10	0.23	0.08	0.09		0.18
Income level *low-high*			0.10				0.06	-0.02
Welfare use *no-yes*	0.06							0.06
Social effect *SE* *neg-pos*	0.14							
Perception of control *PC* *low-high*	-0.13							
Attitude income solidarity *IS* *neg-pos*	0.17							
Trust in others *TO* *low-high*	0.06							
Solidarity attitude *SA* *low-high*	0.24							
Political preference *PP* *left-right*	-0.06							
Rsquare (%)	24	6	8	6	1	10	2	

Chi-square = 304.59, df=40, p=0.0; RMSEA = .07; GFI = 0.97; critical N = 295

Appendix　　　*Explanatory variables*

PERSONAL CHARACTERISTICS
SEX male - female
AGE young to old
EDUCATIONAL LEVEL low - medium - high
INCOME LEVEL gross annual household income, low - medium - high
WELFARE USE not on benefit (excluding old age pension), on benefit

OPINIONS, PERCEPTIONS and ATTITUDES

INDIVIDUAL EFFECTS OF SOCIAL SECURITY (Lickert scale, alpha=.64, m=2.2, sd=.55, negative to positive). Whether the respondent believes that because of social security (a) many people's lives are more pleasant and free (b) the Dutch population at large is happier (c) everybody gets a chance to make something of their life.

MORAL EFFECTS OF SOCIAL SECURITY (Lickert scale, alpha=.67, m=2.0, sd=.54, negative to positive). Whether the respondent believes that because of social security (a) people become lazy (b) people's sense of self-responsibility decreases (c) people become egotistical and calculating (d) people get divorced too easily (e) people no longer want to take care of each other.

SOCIAL EFFECTS OF SOCIAL SECURITY (Lickert scale, alpha=.67, m=2.2, sd=.55, range=1-3, negative to positive). Whether the respondent believes that because of social security (a) societal unrest is prevented (b) large-scale poverty and misery are prevented (c) there is a more just distribution of opportunities.

ECONOMIC EFFECTS OF SOCIAL SECURITY (Lickert scale, alpha=.65, m=2.0, sd=.55, negative to positive). Whether the respondent believes that because of social security (a) Holland can compete less successfully with other countries (b) labour costs are too high (c) unemployment increases.

PREFERRED LEVEL OF BENEFITS (Lickert scale, alpha=.71, m=3.0, sd=.54). Opinion on whether benefit levels should be decreased or increased (unemployment insurance, unemployment assistance).

CONTROL (Lickert scale, alpha=.63, m=2.1, sd=.77, not at all to absolutely). Degree to which the respondent believes that benefit dependency due to unemployment, disability, sickness and being on social assistance is under the control of beneficiaries (degree to which they are to be blamed for it).

EVALUATION OF SYSTEM (Lickert scale, alpha=.82, m=2.9, sd=.77, negative to positive). Feelings about the system of social security: positive vs negative, badly administered vs well administered, unjust vs just, content vs discontent.

ATTITUDE TOWARDS INCOME SOLIDARITY The degree to which the respondent feels it is right that people with higher incomes pay higher social security premiums (very much to not at all).

PERCEPTION OF BENEFIT ADEQUACY (Lickert scale, alpha=.78, m=3.4, sd=.59, easy to difficult) Perception of the adequacy of benefit levels in enabling people to make ends meet (unemployment insurance, unemployment assistance, disability insurance).

ABUSE OF SYSTEM (Lickert scale, alpha=.79, m=3.7, sd=.57, low to high) Perception of degree of abuse of social protection (employees stay home sick too easily, many disabled people could work if they wanted to, the unemployed are too passive about looking for jobs, beneficiaries work off the books).

TRUST IN OTHERS (Lickert scale, alpha=.65, m=2.8, sd=.51, no to yes) Perception of the social orientation of other people, i.e. whether other people (a) usually promote their self-interest (b) take the interests of others into account (c) are only driven by the pursuit of money and personal profit (d) are always inclined to help.

SOLIDARITY (Lickert scale,alpha=.72, m=2.3, sd=.49, strong to weak). Whether one generally acts in one's own interest or in the interest of others, measured by reactions to statements (a) solidarity is nonsense, everybody has to take care of himself (b) in life you have to follow your own plans and not be bothered by others (c) mostly I put my own interests above those of others (d) I enjoy doing other people a favour (e) if I do something for someone else, I want something in return (f) I never think of the interests of other people (g) I easily get interested on behalf of other people.

RELIGIOUSNESS frequency of church attendance.

POLITICAL PREFERENCE (which party would the respondent vote for if there were elections next week) left to right (Green Left, Socialist Party, Social Democrats, Christian Democrats, progressive liberals, conservative liberals, religious right, extreme right).

Chapter 4

Non-Discriminating Social Policy?
Policy scenarios for meeting needs without categorisation

Helen Bolderson and Deborah Mabbett

Introduction

Categorisation is one of the basic techniques or practices of social policy. We have argued elsewhere that 'social policy allocates, distributes and delivers benefits and services to households and individuals on the basis of need which people are deemed to have by virtue of belonging to a category' (Bolderson and Mabbett 1991:15). If we think optimistically of social policy as developing progressively towards a wider and deeper sense of social obligation, we might expect that the development of categories for identifying needs would advance with improvements in social knowledge and the development of social research. It is one reflection of problems facing social policy that categories which might be thought to have long established their usefulness and legitimacy have become highly contested.

Jochen Clasen (ed.), *What Future for Social Security?*, 53-68
©2001 Kluwer Law International. Printed in the Netherlands.

This contest is particularly striking in the area of disability, where the definition of the category is challenged from several directions. We have suggested elsewhere that disability scores poorly on most indicators of a 'successful' category. The indicators we proposed were 'the ease with which categories or cases are identified, the viability of the exclusions which must be made in the process, legitimacy (whether members of the category are seen to deserve their membership) and the perceived "fit" between need and membership' (Bolderson and Mabbett 1991:15). We argued that disability scored high on legitimacy, but low on ease of identification.

Arguably, the rise in numbers of people classified as disabled even jeopardises the legitimacy of the category. Rising numbers on the 'rolls' and increasing expenditure on invalidity/incapacity benefits may be attributed to failures, sometimes thought to be deliberate, on the part of individuals to seek and obtain work. A related but less 'blaming' view is that the growth in claims on these benefits reflects an insufficient supply of jobs, especially for older people who have been in receipt of benefit for some time; and/or discrimination in recruitment and retention of disabled workers (Berthoud 1995). Depending on the welfare map of the country and the state of the labour market, unemployed people may be re-categorised as incapacitated at times of rising unemployment. Early retirees may be so categorised in the absence of flexible age pensions. The categories 'disability', 'unemployment', and 'early retirement' may not be easily distinguishable and yet the benefits for each may differ considerably in value and accessibility, making category membership highly salient.

While concern is expressed in many countries about large and rising numbers of invalidity/ incapacity benefit recipients (see Lonsdale 1993; Bolderson and Mabbett 1997; UK, 1998, paras 21-35), other, possibly more fundamental, questions about the disability category have been raised from the viewpoint of those who are categorised. Priestley argues that the 'broad categories of welfare entitlement have remained fairly static in the development of British social policy during the age of modernity' (Priestley 2000:435) and that they rest on idealised constructions of normalcy which devalue the lives of children, elderly and disabled people. Disability rights activists have criticised traditional policy-orientated definitions of disability which stress individuals' in-abilities and in-capacities (e.g. inability to work or care for oneself as a result of loss of function) and are seen to locate the 'problem' of disability in the individuals concerned. Critics of this 'individualisation' of disability have argued for a 'social' model, which sees activity limitation as caused by barriers in society (e.g. exclusions from employment, inaccessibility of buildings and transport). 'Individualistic' or 'medical' models are seen to create dependency, pity, conformity to normality, to be in the interests of professionals rather than disabled people, and to lead to oppression (see, for example, UPIAS 1976; Finkelstein 1981,1991; Oliver 1983; Oliver and Barnes 1990; Abberley 1993; French 1994; Drake 1996; Barnes, Mercer and Shakespeare 1999).

The social model has antecedents in the epistemology of social constructivist theories where meanings are imputed, and reflect the perspectives of those who are imputing them, generally for purposes of control (hence the link with oppression, see Albrecht and Levy 1981). There are also echoes of the older debates about the relative importance of individual pathology and social structure in the causation of social problems. Applied to the current debate about the relationship between 'poverty' and 'social exclusion', the social model implies that disability should be understood as a problem of exclusion. Using Room's (1994) terminology, it should be addressed by 'relational' policies to change social structures, not 'distributional' policies which merely ameliorate the outcomes of disability.

In recent years the social model has become influential, leading, for example, to a revision of the international classification of disability (World Health Organisation 2000) and to new policy directions in Europe (Commission 1996, 1999; see also Bolderson and Hvinden 1999). The Commission has developed priorities in disability policy geared to: a rights-based' or 'civil rights' approach rather than a traditional service-based approach; 'awareness' or 'visibility' of disability/people with disabilities; 'mainstreaming' (rather than 'segregated' provisions); and 'equal opportunities'. On the basis of Section 13 of the Amsterdam Treaty on combating discrimination, a Council Directive, outlawing discrimination in employment and occupation on grounds which include disability, has now been adopted (Official Journal 2000).

In some ways, the social model is in harmony with governmental concerns about the rising cost of disability benefits. Policy-makers and disability rights activists seem to agree that the disability category is deficient. The promotion of equal access and counteracting of discrimination could, arguably, reduce the need for special benefits to support the living standards of people with disabilities, although anti-discrimination policies in themselves will still need to be directed at a class or category of identifiable people (Bickenbach et al 1999). However, in other ways, current directions of policy conflict with the social model. Governments have responded to rising benefit costs by drawing the boundaries between categories more tightly and by defining disability in strict medical and functional terms, thus creating clear frontiers but artificial groupings. Narrow, medical, rather than socially constructed, definitions may provide less punitive and more generous benefits because they erase doubts about contamination with other forms of less acceptable disadvantage. However, they emphasise exclusion (Diller 1996).

It is not at all clear how best to implement the values of the social model. They sit uncomfortably with Member States' social policy traditions of meeting need, or providing restitution or rehabilitation, or, indeed, with member States' various modes of welfare governance. For example, a Danish commentator has contrasted the confrontational anti-discrimination and rights-based stance with the Danish emphasis on participatory and 'negotiative' government (Bengtsson 2001). The United Kingdom (UK), Ireland and Sweden have introduced legislation which outlaws discrimination against disabled people at work, but it seems that the social model has not displaced the traditional ways of defining disability for benefit purposes.

Implications

In this section, we identify three scenarios, which, in different ways, reflect the concerns of policy-makers, and social model advocates. We see policy-makers as concerned with the insecurity/instability of the disability category-boundary, while the social model ideally requires that people are not categorised and boundaries are not drawn. In calling for universal access to all activities in society, the social model implies a shift in emphasis from the *distribution* of benefits and services to the *relations* of rights and citizenship.

Our three scenarios are:

1. The abolition of separate 'incapacity' benefits: all people who are unemployed or unable to work will be eligible for the same unemployment benefit or job-seekers allowance.

2. The replacement of disability benefits based on loss of function and inability to perform tasks with payments made as compensation for loss or damage arising vicariously from social structures and barriers.

3. The abolition of the category disability and promotion of universal access to all services and activities in society.

The abolition of incapacity benefit

This is the least radical scenario; arguably, policy-makers are coming close to adopting it now. The history of long-term sickness benefit, invalidity pension and incapacity benefit in the UK illustrates the instability of the boundary between incapacity and unemployment. In writing his blueprint for social security, Beveridge (1942) did not think that indefinite statutory sickness benefit, which he recommended, should differ in level or in duration from unemployment benefit (see Bolderson 1991:149). Both were intended to provide subsistence at times of interrupted or lost earnings. In so far as disabled people had additional needs, they were to be met by supplementary, voluntary insurance. The retention of a separate category by Beveridge was largely historical.

This position was not maintained in the post-war social security arrangements. Beveridge's recommendation for indefinite unemployment benefit was rejected but indefinite sickness benefit became policy (with difficulty; see Bolderson 1991:152-157). This created a 'preference' for long-term sick people over the long-term unemployed. The advantages for a claimant of achieving a disability-related categorisation became even greater with the introduction of Invalidity Benefit (IVB) in 1971, which provided a long-term benefit, at a higher rate than short-term sickness benefit, for people who remained sick or disabled beyond six months.

The immediate reason for introducing IVB was that indefinite flat-rate sickness benefit became non-viable after 1966 when earnings-related benefits were introduced for short-term benefits. Their introduction meant that once again there would be a reduction in benefit for people with long-term sickness, after six months, as in the pre-war days. In the social policy context of the 1960s, this anomaly was unacceptable.

The change to a more generous long-term sickness benefit in the form of IVB, with its permeable frontier, did not develop as a result of any enunciated principle, but because the changes in adjacent benefits had inadvertently created inequities in the way in which people with long-term disabilities were treated relative to the short-term sick. Admittedly, welfare values, which stressed the costs of long-term incapacity, played a part, but, as in the case of many social policies, the change also constituted a pragmatic move.

IVB consisted, to begin with, of a standard flat-rate sickness benefit (later to become more generous with the addition of an earnings-related component) plus a small allowance. The latter varied according to the claimant's age at onset of incapacity to work, on the grounds that the longer the incapacity lasted the more pressing the need for income and the less the opportunity to save. This meant that a new notion of 'need' was introduced into the insurance scheme. Moreover:

> 'The emphasis on satisfying needs rather than providing earnings replacement was taken further by complementary measures which favoured the recipients of invalidity benefit relative to sickness benefit claimants. There was no reduction for contribution deficiencies, higher increases were paid for dependent children, and there was an easier test of dependence for a working wife. The trend was reinforced when, in 1979, an earnings-related component was added to the invalidity pensions.' (Ogus and Wikeley 1995:152).

Thus a new territory - invalidity - was mapped out where the grass was greener than on the side of unemployment benefit, which remained of limited duration, provided less generous benefits, and by 1982 had, in any case, reverted to being flat-rate. The frontiers guarding this new territory were not hard and fast. To be eligible for IVB a person had to be incapable of remunerative work 'by reason of some specific disease and bodily or mental disablement'. However, the work was such as he/she could 'reasonably be expected to do' (UK 1975) which was simply a recognition of the way that the term had traditionally been interpreted (Corrigan 1985).

A Social Security Commissioner (a second tier independent appeal lawyer) gave an unreported decision in 1948 that the availability of work could be taken into account, but this decision was reversed in 1951. Later, being 'incapable of remunerative work' was formulated as meaning that the incapacity was for work and not in obtaining work (see Ogus 1995:177 referring to R (S) 2/82 11(2)). However, in deciding whether it was 'reasonable' for a person to be expected to work, regard was to be had not only to medical factors but also to the personal capacities of the individual including his/her 'age, education, experience, state of health and other personal factors' (R (S) 11/51).

These individual and situational factors were thus similar to those which might affect any person's employment or unemployment situation. This 'contextual overlap' between unemployment and incapacity made it difficult to draw the line between eligibility for the two benefits, one of which was now substantially more generous than the other. This fed into suspicions that long-term unemployed people might try to get classified as incapacitated.

Since 1995, as Wikeley (2000) has shown, the territory has been redefined, and the preferential treatment of the disabled has become diluted. Invalidity Benefit was replaced by Incapacity Benefit (IB), which has a less generous benefit structure. In particular, the assessment of incapacity was changed to harden the distinction from unemployment. The 'All Work Test' was introduced, which 'focussed purely on specified physical and mental health (in) capabilities...taking no account of [the claimant's] age, work experience, or training' (Wikeley 2000:370). A whole range of factors which determined a person's employment opportunities were written out of the assessment, thus making 'incapacity' objective, measurable - and artificial.

Further changes were made in 1999 in the Welfare Reform and Pensions Act. IB was retained but its contribution requirements were increased, with the effect that it no longer became possible to move straight from unemployment on to IB (Burchardt 1999:12). The narrow 'All Work Test' under another name - the 'personal capability assessment' - was also retained but at the same time personal and contextual factors were re-introduced in schemes employing 'personal advisers' designed to assess a person's capabilities for work in an attempt to place him/her into employment. Thus, paradoxically, a person who is entitled to IB, and who is by definition categorised as 'incapable of work' (fully, since there is no partial incapacity benefit) is nevertheless assumed to be capable of work.

It is arguable that the UK Government is moving towards Scenario 1 by bringing IB and Job Seeker's Allowance (JSA) into line and, ultimately, creating a single benefit for the not-employed where benefit levels and administrative procedures are the same for all claimants. For example, contribution conditions for IB and JSA have been aligned, the means-testing of pensions when paid in addition to the benefits are partly aligned, and the delivery of IB and JSA (as well as benefits for lone parents) will be undertaken by a single, new Agency which straddles Department of Social Security (DSS) and Department for Education and Employment (DfEE) responsibilities.

The abolition of IB might, in principle, appeal to proponents of the 'social model' who are critical of benefits which stress in-abilities and which rely on medical assessments of functional shortcomings. However, the merging of IB and JSA would arguably replace one form of exclusion (arising from categorisation as disabled) with another (membership of a larger, but nonetheless stigmatised, group of benefit recipients). This adverse outcome will necessarily prevail as long as the benefit system as a whole is exclusionary in its operation. Furthermore, a merger would create downward pressure on benefit levels (because JSA is lower than IB), although it could be argued that including a manifestly deserving group among the recipients of the not-employed benefit would generate pressure for benefits to rise from the current JSA level.

While the needs-basis of disability benefits is not always clear, there is a problem with creating a single benefit when some of those with disabilities face higher living costs as a result of their disability. To surmount this problem, the government could retain Disability Living Allowance (DLA), which provides non-contributory, non-means-tested benefits to offset some of the costs of attendance and transport. The different rationales for DLA and IB are reflected in the fact that only 36 per cent of all IB recipients (which includes beneficiaries of short term IB) were also in receipt of DLA (UK 1999a).

The retention of DLA would deviate from the 'ideal' version of scenario 1 because it would involve the continuation of a disability assessment. The assessment for DLA is based on a person's inabilities to perform in the areas of caring for him/herself or walking. This method eschews precise clinical measurement, but, in taking in wider factors, such as the manner of walking or whether or not it is achieved with severe discomfort (see Wikeley 2000:380) it also suffers from the problems of an unstable category. Moreover, the focus on an individual's failure in performance does not fit easily with the social model. While DLA does not have the *same* problems of assessment as IB, it still requires the identification of a disabled group. It is therefore not consistent with an entirely non-discriminatory approach.

Payments made in compensation for damage vicariously caused by society

An alternative structure for statutory disability benefits exists in the UK in the form of compensatory payments for loss of amenity, an idea that emerged out of the development of war pensions. War pensions came about in the First World War because there were injured service people who were no longer, as previously, drawn from the poorest and least articulate sectors of society. The latter, if 'invalided out' had been left largely to the mercy of a somewhat arbitrary service pension and the old Poor Law which was locally administered, mean and punitive. When campaigns were mounted for the recruitment of soldiers, it was felt that something better would have to be put in place to encourage people to join up.

In 1915 a pension was provided for those who had been 'invalided out', returned to civilian life, and become incapacitated from work as a result of their war injury. If they subsequently became employed, the pension was reduced on a sliding scale, and extinguished if, or when, the wage equalled it. However, by 1917, this arrangement was suspected of causing work disincentives: it was thought that it might not be worthwhile for pensioners to seek work if earning a wage involved loss of benefit. As a result, it was replaced by the pension which has remained in force ever since: a War Pension which is payable regardless of whether a person is earning or not.

The 1917 War Pensions were the product of war-time imperatives, and a need for labour which led to concern about disincentives to work. However, in 1919, the scheme was scrutinised by a Select Committee (UK 1920a) and at this stage a 'principle' was enunciated. The principle was established in Committee by the Minister of Pensions who said that the 1917 scheme was justified because 'the minimum wage applies to eight hours a day whereas a man's disability applies to 24 hours a day. It is a loss of amenity as well as a loss of wage' (UK 1920b). This formulation meant that the level of benefit should be related to the loss suffered, and not to income maintenance or meeting minimum income needs. In war pensions, this concept of the 'loss of amenity' which had been inflicted on a person was reflected in the structure of the main pension, which was paid regardless of whether a person was working or could 'perform' in specific areas of living.

The 1917 principle is still retained in war pensions and in the statutory Industrial Injuries Scheme, parts of which are being run down. It is, however, unpopular both with governments and with most disabled people's lobbies. One problem is with the concept of causation. In the existing statutory compensatory schemes, eligibility is related to the cause of the injury or disease. This is a big step away from the confrontational tort based idea that 'fault' has to be established and the perpetrator identified and held responsible. Nevertheless, 'cause' as a determinant of eligibility limits the scope of the benefit, and scores particularly badly on two of the indicators of success for a social policy category with which we introduced this paper, namely, viability of exclusions and 'fit' between membership and need. Exclusion based on failure to satisfy the causality criterion means that people with similar needs and circumstances are treated dissimilarly. Gal (2000) is critical of this arrangement because it employs a form of social justice which is about 'just deserts', and does not serve equity, which is preferable. However, it might be argued that 'just deserts' has the advantage of establishing a claim on the collectivity, thus securing a right to redress from damage.

Furthermore, the idea of 'cause' can be extended. The concept of socially rendered 'disservices' is useful here (Titmuss 1968). The notion of socially rendered disservices establishes a nexus between societal causes and individual damage. Arrangements which 'compensate' in the sense used for war pensions or industrial injuries, can also take on board the social inclusion objectives of the social model. The nexus enables us to turn from the idea of disability as solely an 'attributed' characteristic adhering to the individual and requiring resources to be distributed directly to the damaged individual, to the idea of disability as an 'acquired' situation. It is 'acquired' in the sense that a disabled person is in this situation as a result of socially created factors and impediments. The policy response in this case concentrates on the relationship between a person and a group of people who are disabled and society, and on increasing participation and empowerment, rather than amelioration.

What would be the implications of extending the concept of cause in this way? One implication is that social arrangements, which worsened the consequences of a disability, would imply that higher compensation should be paid. Ideally, there would be some feedback in the decision system so that high compensation led to reconsideration of social arrangements - a sort of 'cost-benefit' analysis in which the cost of changing social arrangements would be weighed against the benefit of reduced compensation payments.

The idea of feedback is important in addressing the second major criticism of the compensation model, that it is individualising in its approach. The availability of compensation may suppress issues about how social arrangements are affecting the recipients. We can see this in the heavy reliance on cash benefits in the creation of the UK's war pensions. Only weak training and employment arrangements were put in place for injured ex-servicemen, in contrast to other European countries, which, at the time, had less generous cash benefits.

The feedback mechanism is what might transform an individually-oriented, distributional measure (compensation) into a social, relational measure (changes in social arrangements). Feedback does occur. There is evidence that commercial organisations examine their exposure to compensation liabilities and change working practices or the conduct of their business accordingly (Worrall and Butler 1988; Moore and Viscusi 1990). Equally, feedback may be suppressed because the organisation which could take action to change arrangements does not have to bear the costs of the harm it inflicts, which instead fall on government or on the harmed individuals themselves.

This suggests that one problem with government-financed compensation is that it constitutes an implicit subsidy to those who profit from current social arrangements. Governmental efforts to introduce feedback (for example, to achieve social security savings by reducing discrimination against those with disabilities) are stymied by resistance from those who bear the costs of social reform (the beneficiaries of discriminatory practices). Where government itself is a discriminatory actor, the problem is partly one of fragmentation: costs arising in the social security budget may not be linked to benefits from better practices in other parts of the public sector.

We see here a dilemma in the compensation principle. Statutory compensation may be preferred to private compensation (obtained by legal action using principles of tort) because it escapes from narrow concepts of fault. Statutory schemes make it possible to redistribute collective resources in the direction of those harmed, often indirectly, and maybe unwittingly, by a range of processes and events which may benefit others in society. However, this recognition of the complexity of social processes also reduces the prospect of feedback, making compensation a passive policy.

For all its potential, the compensation approach remains 'individuated'. If social disadvantages really were to be priced accurately for compensation purposes, the process could be highly intrusive on the person seeking compensation. Ideally, the government would recognise the social disadvantages imposed on those with disabilities without involving them in rigorous assessment of their personal circumstances.

Universal access to all services and activities in society: abolition of the category 'Disability'

In this third scenario we imagine that there is no such term as disability - in its modern sense. The governing principle for policy is to remove the social and physical barriers which limit opportunities to participate in society for those with illnesses and impairments. We use the term 'equal access' for short. The paradigmatic example of the equal access approach is that of access to public buildings. Wheelchair users have a 'negative' right to enter a public building, but, in the absence of ramps or lifts, they do not have equality of access. The principle of equality of access dictates that buildings should be designed so that all have access to them. If this is done, it is not necessary to select and identify those with disabilities for special treatment. Once designers and builders make the effort of imagining a range of abilities among users, the design features become a public good, useful for those in wheelchairs but also for those with buggies. Because the use of access-promoting design features does not usually need to be rationed, it is not necessary to classify some users as 'disabled' in distinction to the able-bodied others.

The claim for equal access is explicitly relational. It addresses the structures which generate the distribution of welfare, rather than just ameliorating or compensating for their effects. However, the right to equal access therefore has to be 'mediated' before it becomes 'actual' (Carey 1999) and, in doing this, it is not always possible to avoid specifying beneficiaries. Equal access in some areas therefore has clear (re)distributional consequences despite the use of 'relational' language.

One way of looking at the example of access to a public building is that there is non-rivalry in consumption of ramps (once built). In many areas of public sector provision (health, education, social services) there is rivalry in the consumption of goods and services. This means that any claim by one person for more resources (which equal access requires) must mean that others get fewer resources. Wasserman (1998) discusses the application of the principle of equality of access in education. In cases where a child needs a lot of resources to participate in classroom activities, equality of access turns into a right which may trump the claims of other children on educational resources. By contrast with the example of building design, there is clear rivalry between potential users of educational resources.

The other feature of the ramp is non-identification, whereby it is not necessary to class users as 'disabled'. Again, this feature only inheres in particular types of goods and services. In the education example, the child is selected and identified as a special case, generating all sorts of boundary problems between disability and social deprivation or other causes of low attainment, and highlighting the paradox that it is necessary to identify the child as disabled before 'non-discrimination' measures can be taken on his or her behalf.

Two concepts therefore seem to be important to applying equality of access: non-rivalry and anonymity. In the ideal case of public buildings, both features prevail. In many traditional areas of social policy (education, health and personal social service provision) neither prevails.

This suggests that the scope for applying the principle of equal access is limited. Not many goods and services are both non-rival and anonymous in allocation. Generally, services provided by the welfare state are rival, and identity is central to allocation. We can note the contrast with market allocations, which are generally anonymous, even though rivalry is fundamental. The levying of a price eliminates the requirement for identification and classification of consumers and mediation about the 'deservingness' of their claims.

There may be some scope for enhancing equality of access in the market sphere. Some commodities provided via the market, by commercial organisations, have public good components. Notably, design is a public good to the extent that it is non-rival in consumption, as a design can be repeatedly re-used. The regulation of design through patenting and the establishment of industry standards are areas of considerable public policy importance. Patenting restricts the dissemination of designs in order to provide rewards to inventors; standard-setting, by contrast, enhances dissemination. Carey (1999) argues for the adoption of standard-setting policies which ensure the incorporation of design features which enhance equality of access. Carey's focus is on features which allow people with certain impairments to use the product as effectively as the unimpaired, and which cost less to incorporate in the standard specifications of a unit than to add on to a unit already built. This standardisation would imply that inventions which enhance access would not be patented, so incentives for their development would have to be addressed in some other way.

One obstacle to improved standard-setting is its low political salience and dominance by technical experts, to the detriment of user participation. Many areas of design are subject to industry self-regulation, although the creation of the Single European Market has seen the European Commission become involved in mediating between the national industry associations which have traditionally set standards. Competition between companies within the industry may prevent them agreeing on the best standard. The companies selling to the most price-sensitive part of the standard market may oppose any enhancement of standards, as may those which sell the feature as an add-on.

One attraction of access-promoting standard-setting is that it is efficient, because it promotes the dissemination of design, which is non-rival in consumption. However, we would argue that this is not its only attraction, and it therefore should not be the only criterion for judging whether to incorporate the feature. There are (at least) two other attractions:

(a) Because the design is put in place for *imagined*, not identified, beneficiaries, the decision on standards is made behind a veil of ignorance as to who will actually benefit. Much of the theory of distributional justice is constructed around the thought experiment of a veil of ignorance, but in reality people often know whether they are going to be beneficiaries of a policy or not, so the social contracts which might be made behind the veil cannot be sustained in practice. Devices to maintain the veil are valuable.

(b) The benefits of incorporating accessibility features in a standard design will accrue to those who need the features. We can assume that they will be some subset of those with impairments, but it is not necessary for another party (e.g. a state agency) to identify and select them. Instead, they select themselves in their use of the product. It is not necessary to create a category of beneficiaries for the benefits of the feature to accrue to those who need it. Nor does identity have to be static: a person who uses one feature will not necessarily use another.

Both of these advantages are aspects of *anonymity*. They utilise the capacity of markets in commodities to allow consumers anonymity. This suggests a further question: would it be desirable to extend the scope of market-based anonymity to transactions which are not currently anonymous?

One area where the principle of anonymity could be extended is in the provision of insurance. If insurers are not able to gather information from proposers, they must treat all equally, generating a pooled outcome and charging everyone the same premium. The gains from imposing anonymity would be considerable. Levels and costs of insurance could be achieved that resemble the ideal that might be derived from behind a veil of ignorance - in effect, again, because the veil is maintained. Privacy is maintained; information which may lead an insurer to classify a person as high risk is denied.

However, it is unlikely that an industry association in a competitive market would be able to maintain a policy of privacy, because the benefits of cheating are too great. The Association of British Insurers has half-heartedly adopted a privacy policy on genetic testing, but it is unlikely to be able to maintain it once testing is refined to become a more effective instrument for discrimination than the information already available to insurers. Countries with less competitive insurance industries have adopted stronger policies, but all will be undermined when people with favourable genetic attributes become able to seek bargains through cross-border purchasing. While firms in an industry may sometimes be able to repress competition, they cannot withstand efforts by the unimpaired to select themselves out. This is part of the more general problem of allocating rival goods and services: only when there is no rivalry do the unimpaired have no incentive to re-create discrimination to eliminate cross-subsidies. Similarly, the unimpaired may undermine accessibility standards by seeking out cheaper products which incorporate lower standards. Only if accessibility standards can be incorporated cheaply will their maintenance be viable in a competitive market.

We can see that the possibility of regulating markets to improve the terms on which those with impairments participate has several interesting features. Clearly, if our concern is with the de-construction of social barriers, we should look at the structure of markets, which are one of the primary domains of social interaction. Equally, it is in the nature of markets that it is difficult to identify 'culprits'. Instead we have 'forces': competitive pressures, profit-maximisation, free-riding by self-interested consumers and so forth. Market structures can have a discriminatory impact, and policies to combat that impact do exist, but they may involve the suppression of market forces.

Conclusion

In this paper, we have tried to imagine the consequences of avoiding classifying people as disabled. In the first scenario, those with disabilities would find themselves treated in the same way as any people of working age who could not support themselves through employment. We argued that it would not benefit those currently classified as disabled to have equality of treatment with the unemployed. After all, one interpretation of the history of the term 'dis-ability' shows that it was coined in Britain to 'excuse' or exclude, those who were ill and unable to work, from the rigours of the workhouse test under the nineteenth century Poor Law (Stone 1984). Disability led to the relatively favourable treatment for the 'dis-abled'.

On the other hand, amalgamating the categories could be part of a policy to reduce exclusion among all the affected groups. That there is a boundary problem between unemployment and disability is undeniable. One issue for disability rights campaigners is whether it is possible to justify preference for disabled people with the argument that impairments deny equality of opportunity while deficits in talents and skill do not (see e.g. the discussion of Daniels in Wassermann 1998:154). Daniels argues that there is a qualitative difference between impairment, which involves a loss of 'normal' functioning, and poor skills possessed by people who have, at least, in his view, started from the same baseline. However, this becomes a difficult argument as soon as the social model approach is introduced, because the social model does not give centrality to loss of function. Instead it highlights social barriers which hinder social inclusion. From this viewpoint, a 'skill deficit', caused by lack of educational facilities in a deprived area, might qualify for the same priority as the 'capacity deficit' of an impaired person, unless a further argument for 'impairment preference' is found.

In the second scenario, we envisaged determining cash *compensation* for the disadvantage imposed by society on a person, rather than trying to measure the needs of that person. The principle of compensation would certainly generate a different structure of entitlements than the needs-basis in scenario one. In practice, however, it is hard to see how individualisation could be avoided.

The strengths of the compensation model are that the 'twenty-four hour' notion of loss of amenity makes it possible for compensation for the loss to be paid regardless of earnings or income from benefits or elsewhere and also provides a rationale for making preferential benefits available to impaired people. The concept of 'loss' itself presents difficulties since it is not clear whether the loss is that which has actually been foregone by a particular individual as a result of the impairment, or a loss which is imputed by making comparisons between him/her and a 'normal' person. In either case the concept of loss tends to make the circumstances of the individual more central than that of society, contra to the objectives of the proponents of the social model.

The third scenario abandoned the disability category altogether and replaced it (subject to the existence of basic, universal survival benefits) with social arrangements which combated and minimised the barriers to access faced by those with impairments. Some of these arrangements would be used only by specific groups e.g. people with sensory impairments, but they would be universally available; others would be used by a wide range of people including the aged and young mothers. These social arrangements would not be category-bound.

Trends in demography, the structure of society and social relationships may further this approach. The relevance of demography lies in the proportion of the UK population over the age of 60/65 (18 per cent) and, in particular, over 75 (7 per cent) (UK 1999b Table 1.5) many of whom are likely to experience disabilities. One view is that this may increase the disability-awareness amongst those of working age since they will be looking forward to it in the future. This is seen as a step towards the realisation that there may not be a hard and fast line between those termed 'disabled' and others. Making transport, shops, buildings, communications etc accessible is therefore a general problem. Examples are the access difficulties experience by buggy-pushers (often women) in shops and on the underground (6 per cent of the population are aged 1- 4); the handling of heavy equipment such as lawn mowers or wheel jacks and braces by the less strong; or the use of fiddly gadgets by mildly arthritic or left-handed people.

The problem with this scenario was how far it could be taken. Clearly it can be applied with considerable effect to the design of public spaces and infrastructure. We suggested, following Carey (1999), that there is also considerable scope to apply the principle of equal access to the provision of commodities in the market, where there are large areas of anonymised interaction. More could be done in some low-visibility areas of public policy to make such policies genuinely public and universal.

However, it is inappropriate to apply concepts of non-identification and non-selection to transactions which are personal and personalised, such as the provision of care or classroom education. To avoid selection, one would have to anonymise the delivery of the service, which would conflict with its very nature and purpose. In effect, we do not think that social policy can be replaced by public policy. It is not possible to eliminate the discriminatory function of social policy and still meet people's diverse needs and/or achieve a just distribution of resources. We note that, paradoxically, 'anti-discrimination' policy can also be discriminatory, in so far as it is used to make claims for additional resources for those who can establish that they are members of a minority which is discriminated against.

If discrimination is inevitable, one task is to make it as unobtrusive and unstigmatising as possible. Here we find another paradox. In social policy, categories are seen to be successful if boundaries can be drawn readily and consistently by administrators. In disability provision, the medical model has been attractive to social policy-makers because it appears to provide some of the necessary 'objectification' for consistent administration. Arguably, it also promotes the legitimacy of the category by defending the impaired person against the charge of malingering. But the medical model of disability is strongly rejected by disability rights campaigners, as it ignores the social construction of disability.

Is there an acceptable approach to identification (for the purposes of positive discrimination) which is not medical? Arguably, the alternatives are more personal. A personal advisor or social worker may be able to take a more complete view of the interaction between impairment and environment, but this would point towards a more discretionary mode of administration in the benefit system than now prevails.

We have argued that universalistic public policies are attractively anonymous, but they cannot recognise and respond to all individual circumstances, even if they were formulated in a more pluralistic, less majoritarian way. We have suggested that eliminating the category of disability within the benefit system might reduce the resources allocated to those with impairments. Endeavouring to compensate for social barriers could increase the resources allocated, but might involve more intrusive enquiries to establish the losses arising from the social consequences of impairment.

We have not found an ideal solution. We suggest that there may not be one. The debate over disability is marked by a deep-rooted ambivalence in our attitudes to identity and anonymity. We ask, on the one hand, to be recognised and validated as individuals, yet, on the other, we value our privacy and are drawn towards policies which are consistent with anonymity. It is not possible to devise an approach which reconciles these irreconcilable ideals. The process of categorisation in social policy must be a process of balancing, negotiation and compromise between them.

Chapter 5

Equality, Employment, and State Social Policies: a gendered perspective

Ann Shola Orloff

Introduction

Gender relations, including cultural and ideological preferences about the inevitability, naturalness and rightness of gender difference, have shaped systems of social provision since their origins in the late nineteenth and early twentieth centuries, through periods of expansion and consolidation in the 1940s through 1960s, and into the present period of restructuring of social provision across the world. In the decades since World War II, some features of gender relations have undergone significant transformations in the direction of equality – notably, in the political sphere, the extension of suffrage, the elimination of patriarchal elements in family law and the ending of *de jure* discrimination in most countries, and, in the sphere of work and labour, the increasing employment of women. However, there remain important gender differences, most significantly in the gender division of labor, in which women do the majority of caregiving and domestic work. These patterns are linked with continuing problems of

Jochen Clasen (ed.), *What Future for Social Security?*, 69-86 women's economic vulnerability or inequality and, where not ameliorated by state benefits, the disproportionate poverty of single mothers and elderly widows. This also means that most women workers face problems of reconciling employment and family life; but to the extent that employment and social security systems remain geared to a model of worker with no caring responsibilities, any employee – man or woman – who wants to be involved in caregiving will face difficulties.

Social changes in gender relations have stimulated, and been stimulated by, political changes in the direction of greater gender equality. As women's equality projects gained power within old and new political organizations in the 1960s and 1970s, a range of reforms across many countries attempted to move toward greater gender equality. Many states abolished de jure discrimination and made the provisions of welfare state programs formally gender-neutral. Currently, countries in the developed world are committed to the standard of 'equal treatment' for men and women (Brocas, Cailloux and Oget 1990). Discrimination based on sex is outlawed. What this means is that when men and women are 'equally situated,' they must be treated the same. This is certainly an advance over earlier systems of regulation and provision, which permitted outright discrimination, as when men received higher relief benefits than women, were paid more for doing the same job, or when women were simply excluded from certain categories of occupation and social protection.

The equal treatment standard is alone insufficient to bring about gender equality, for it is confined to the sphere of paid work. Thus, it does not address a key source of men's and women's 'unequal situations', a continuing gender division in the provision of caring labor (Hobson 1999; Ostner and Lewis 1995). Thus, we see – and these cases are more numerous than those where women and men are indeed 'equally situated' – men working more paid hours, women more unpaid; women interrupting careers to care for children or elderly parents, men not doing so; women unable to freely choose jobs, work schedules or careers because of caring responsibilities, while men's choices are more or less unaffected by family status. These arrangements mean that men and women are not in the same situation with respect to their capacities to claim employment-based benefits.

Under the rubric of 'equal treatment' alone, positive action to change arrangements with respect to care are ruled out of bounds because these are considered 'private'. At most, some states have provided services to replace women's caregiving in families in order to allow women to participate in the labor force. Yet even with such services, women continue to bear more of the burden of care, are not equally situated with men, and often suffer in terms of pay and opportunities for advancement. Problems with equal treatment arise not only in policies for working-aged people. How is one to craft equitable pension provision for people who have spent their lives according to different patterns of paid and unpaid work? Is it fair, for example, that those who have spent their lives caring for others, but making no individual contributions to social insurance systems receive lower pensions than those who earned wages and made contributions to pension systems? The links between women's caregiving (and men's absence from caregiving), their economic vulnerability and the family- and gender-related problems facing social provision must be made central in order to overcome gender inequalities.

What standard of evaluation?

Today, explicit discrimination against women in access to valued resources is not politically acceptable. But while few would contest that men and women should be treated 'equally', it is important to underline that there are different meanings and models of gender equality underlying the term across different countries and regions, especially around notions of gender sameness and gender difference. Moreover, analysts of equality have made clear that the concept is multidimensional. How can we assess systems of social provision with respect to their promotion of gender equality, and with enabling new gender and family roles? Social policy analysts have used a number of standards for assessment, which include lessening income inequality, providing income security, or the elimination of poverty, including gender gaps in poverty (what is often popularly referred to as 'the feminisation of poverty'); as well as institutionalising social rights that provide a measure of personal independence.

Ameliorating poverty and preventing it through insuring against socially-recognised risks of income interruption are the most fundamental aspects of state social provision. State social provision protects against the failures of the market – unemployment, work accidents, old age, sickness and disability, and also addresses problems following from 'failures' of the family, particularly the break-up of marriages by death or other circumstances (or their failure to form) – widowhood (i.e., dependence on a wage earner who has died), desertion and single motherhood. This at first reflected the ideology of the male breadwinner family, in that wage earners should be able to support wives and children; the state steps in only when breadwinners are absent. But as many analysts have noted, the old male breadwinner-based order has significantly eroded. There are new risks to be insured against – risks, particularly facing women workers, of income interruption due to maternity and participation in caregiving activities. And the risk of single parenthood may be understood as a more 'normal' event, in which children should be able to gain access to economic support from both parents, both of whom are understood as providers and caregivers. We can then assess how well states do in providing against these different risks, in particular by looking at gender differences in poverty. And the presence or absence of programs to provide for these new situations is also telling.

Social citizenship rights affect the relative balance of power across a range of social relationships, including gender relationships within families and in the workplace, by shaping the terms of participation in these significant social spheres. Do people have real choices about their employment and their personal relationships by virtue of having some politically-guaranteed alternative modes of personal support?

The *capacity to form and maintain an autonomous household* identifies rights relative to family and household formation (Orloff 1993). Having the capacity to form a household without depending on the economic support of anyone else increases one's range of choice and enhances leverage within families or partnerships; it is both about the right to have a family (Saraceno 1994) as well as the capacity to exit from relationships. Speaking of a *capacity* to form an autonomous household does not indicate a preference for separation or a denial of interdependencies. Rather, it indicates a belief that equality and freedom of choice – including a choice to partner – require an absence of coercion, including the kind imposed for years on women to marry because of their own dismal economic prospects (O'Connor, Orloff and Shaver 1999). Thus, this capacity is relevant for all women, married or not, but the conditions facing single parents are good barometers of the extent to which it exists (Hobson 1990, 1994).

There are at least two possible sources for women (or men, for that matter) to gain this capacity (in wage economies): paid work (and necessary services to allow people with caregiving responsibilities to enter paid employment) or cash benefits from the state for staying at home to care. The two routes to economic independence reflect the two main strategies pursued by women's movements in different times and places; distinctive visions of gender equality have guided different women's movements. Gaining access to employment is the predominant strategy today, particularly in the English-speaking countries and in Scandinavia, while 'maternalist' strategies to attain state economic support to full-time mothering were more common in the past and retain some viability in many continental European countries, notably Ireland, Italy and Germany (Ostner and Lewis 1995; Bock and Thane 1991). It is important to note – given how common it is to assume that women's movements have pursued only women's entrance into waged work – that women have pursued the equivalent of a citizen's wage for mothering (a 'mother's allowance'), which also would have given them freedom from dependence on male breadwinners (Pedersen 1993; Lake 1992). Moreover, women have worked to gain access to employment in different ways. Scandinavian and French women have tended to pursue a strategy of supporting the position of women workers who are also principal caregivers; this was also the premise of socialist countries' policies before 1989, but changes in the social policy frameworks of the transition economies have in general meant less public support to employed mothers (Heinen 1999). North American liberal feminists have tended to work to make traditional breadwinner positions in the workforce available to women (Fraser 1994; O'Connor, Orloff and Shaver 1999). Similarly, strategies in the developing world vary cross-nationally and across regions, but have for obvious reasons tended to focus more on questions of basic survival and human rights than has been in the case in the affluent West (Moghadam 1993; Folbre 1994). Thus, while those committed to gender equality differ on the question of the gender division of labor – should women be full-time mothers (at least part of their lives), part-time workers and principal caregivers, or full-time workers as are men (with caregiving publicly provided) – they do tend to agree on the notion of reducing women's economic dependence.

Rights relative to employment are critical in protecting 'individuals, irrespective of gender, from total dependence on the labor market for survival.... [a] protection from forced participation, irrespective of age, health conditions, family status, availability of suitable employment, [that] is obviously of major importance to both men and women' (O'Connor 1993:513; see also Esping-Andersen 1990). But there are other rights necessary for creating gender equality. *Access to paid work* refers to citizens' right to employment – the dominant mode of securing citizenship rights, economic independence and political capacities. Such access is guaranteed on the one hand by outlawing gender discrimination. But in the context of the continuing gender division of caregiving labor, women also need services in order to enter employment, as well as some accommodation for maternity and time for caregiving. Thus, we may consider rights relative to care, especially the *right to have time to care* (e.g. parental leaves, or leaves to care for elderly or disabled relatives) (Knijn and Kremer 1997). But one may also ask if women, like men, are free *not* to care – that is, to pursue their own career and interests (Land and Rose 1985; Lewis 1997a; Orloff 1997). (Note that this applies to caregiving responsibilities not freely assumed; to the extent that childbearing is by choice, one cannot speak of a 'right not to care'). This implies that there must be public alternatives to kin-based caregiving, for all of us need to be cared for at some points in our lives – rights to be cared for refer to public guarantees that services will be provided whether or not we have friends and family willing and available to help (Knijn and Kremer 1997; Fineman 1995).

Social provision and gender (in)equality

Systems of state social provision give insurance against risks of income interruption (unevenly), but at the same time shape social relations, particularly in the developed economies where systems cover almost the entire population. And one sees diverse effects on gender relations, however assessed.

Poverty

After the identification of the 'feminization of poverty' in the U.S. in the late 1970s (Pearce 1978), a number of analysts investigated cross-national variation in policy outcomes (see, e.g., Kamerman 1986; Goldberg and Kremen 1990; McFate, Smeeding, Rainwater 1995). Studies focusing on the poverty of single-mother families consistently find that, among the developed countries, the United States has the highest poverty levels, followed closely by Canada and Australia; according to materials presented by the OECD (1997c), all have rates of poverty among solo mothers above 50 per cent. Britain looks considerably better than its 'daughter' countries in terms of solo mothers' poverty, with rates closer to 20 per cent, while Germany's and the Netherlands' poverty rates for solo-mothers – at about 30 per cent – are higher than might be expected given their reputations for having comprehensive systems of social protection (OECD 1997c, Table 2.4). The Scandinavian countries have kept poverty rates relatively low (6 per cent – 14 per cent) among solo mothers. Single (widowed, never-married or divorced) elderly women also are more likely to be in poverty than are elderly men or couples, reflecting primarily their lower pension benefits and lesser access to occupational pensions and savings – direct results of these older cohorts' patterns of labor force participation (OECD 1997c, Table 2.4).

Analysts link cross-national variations in poverty rates to a key characteristic of social protection schemes – the relatively generosity of benefit levels and levels of overall social spending; particularly among elderly women, raising benefits has been a successful strategy in fighting poverty (e.g., in Canada). Variation in poverty between men and women also reflects to some degree the ways in which paid versus unpaid work is treated in social security systems. In the developing world, and to a somewhat lesser degree the transition economies of eastern Europe, poverty is far more widespread than in the West. But here, too, women appear to bear the brunt of deprivation, certainly when they maintain households on their own, but also, in some areas, within households where resource distribution is skewed by sex (Sen 1990; Dwyer and Bruce 1988; Heinen 1999; Deacon 1999). And universal provisions of services like health care and safety net programs do make a difference in reducing hardship and promoting human development (Moghadam 1993).

State anti-poverty spending is not the only factor in ameliorating poverty, especially among working-aged women. In comparisons of women's poverty across several industrialised countries, Goldberg and Kremen (1990) and McLanahan, Caspar and Sorenson (1995) found that several factors in addition to the level of public benefits – the proportion of families headed by single mothers, the extent of women's labor force participation, and the degree of gender equality in the labor market – affect the level of women's poverty. In Sweden, good labor market conditions and generous benefits minimize single women's poverty; in Japan or Italy, despite very unequal labor market conditions and low benefits, feminization of poverty has not emerged as an area of concern as few mothers are single. A focus on poverty rates alone can be misleading; when marriage rates are high, one sees relatively low poverty rates for women and low gender poverty gaps, but the extent of women's *vulnerability* to poverty is occluded. And while Swedish social policy is recognised in most cross-national studies of poverty for its effectiveness in virtually eliminating poverty among women, analyses concentrating on poverty alone may miss other issues significant for gender relations, such as the high concentration of women in part-time employment and their continuing disproportionate responsibility for housework and care of children and the elderly (Ruggie 1988).

Recent critiques of state social provision focus on various negative dimensions of depending on welfare – indeed, in some places, the U.S. and the UK most notably, have made 'welfare dependency' a pejorative term. In the industrialised countries, some conservative analysts argue for finding ways to bolster the 'traditional' family as a way to undercut such dependence, although this leaves women's economic vulnerability (deliberately) untouched. But even those who do not look with disfavour on welfare provision per se may criticise 'welfare traps' and note the long-term difficulties which attach to being out of the labor force. Thus, they have embraced enhancing women's capacities and incentives to take (even low-wage) employment as the key to preventing poverty while avoiding such economic vulnerability and 'welfare traps' (e.g., Esping-Andersen 1997). It is clear, given gender wage differentials and the extra burden of care that affects single parents, that single mothers will still need some public supports to be able to maintain their families while working (e.g., Spalter-Roth et al. 1995; Hobson and Takahashi 1997). Many of these supports – child care most notably – are also critical for other women to take up paid employment. Thus, from a number of directions, fostering women's employment – if it is well-paid and under good conditions – is emerging as a key anti-poverty strategy which can have significantly increase women's options and resources. This is as true for the developing as the developed world (see, e.g., Moghadam 1993).

There are some parallels to this anti-social provision thinking in other parts of the world. International financial agencies have in the last decade often advocated cutting social expenditures in the developing countries of the South, the 'ailing tigers' of Southeast Asia, and transition economies of Eastern Europe alike (Huber 1996; Standing 1996; Hort and Kuhnle 1999; Deacon 1999). Again, family and employment are to replace state provision in this vision, but in a context of far fewer societal resources. Without denying that restructuring may be needed, the situation for poor women and children, left without any form of social protection, in many of these cases is quite dire, and may well undermine future development efforts that depend on human capital.

Household autonomy and single parenthood

Only some states during some historical periods have given male or female citizens any kind of political guarantee – a social right – to household support. Prior to the initiation of programs that have come to be called the 'welfare state,' states gave little or no support to single mothers, which meant that almost none could escape familial dependency, or, for those without families, institutionalisation or destitution, given the abysmally low wages available to the vast majority of women workers. One could look at the early systems of social provision as political guarantees of male breadwinners' capacities to support households in event of income interruption due to unemployment, disability or illness or retirement; these programs have been expanded and institutionalised over the course of the century. Although these systems are now being subjected to some tightening, most male workers in the industrialised world retain good social protection that allows them to maintain their households, albeit usually not on their own wages alone. These guarantees have not developed beyond rather limited groups of workers, mainly male, in the formal sector in the developing world, however.

In the contemporary period, some states in the industrialised world do offer a guarantee of support to single mothers (i.e., women who have exited marriage) who do not work for pay at least until their children reach school age – the Netherlands, Britain, Ireland, Australia, and Germany (Ostner 1997; Platenga 1998; Knijn 1994; Conroy 1997; O'Connor, Orloff and Shaver 1999). But this is based on the needs of mothers who find themselves without male breadwinners; the economic dependence of married women and the need for mothers to care full-time for their children in these systems is not challenged. And these mothers face substantially greater chances of living in poverty or at a low income than do married mothers or men. Still, benefits for solo parents offer a bottom-line capacity for household independence (critical in cases of domestic violence), which does enhance women's bargaining position in marriage. Yet even in these countries which have been strong supporters of the male breadwinner and female (full-time) caregiver, there have been moves to encourage lone mothers' employment, usually part-time, after children reach school age, as well as to get absent fathers to contribute towards their children's needs (O'Connor, Orloff and Shaver 1999; Knijn 1994). Household independence will be less publicly supported – solo mothers will partially depend on employment and on absent fathers.

The countries of southern Europe, while also upholding a male provider, female caregiver (but also often secondary earner) ideal for marriage and family life, do not offer benefits to lone mothers; support must come from families or work (Bimbi 1997; Saraceno 1994). But since there is little support for mothers' employment generally and employment opportunities for women have not been aggressively pursued by the state, few mothers would find it possible to support themselves on their wages alone – and indeed, there are few lone-mother families in these countries, and in those that do exist, mothers' labor force participation is considerably higher than that of married mothers. Most find no alternative to marriage or staying with their natal families. Women's economic dependency on husbands and other family members is the norm, even though it is often coupled with secondary wage-earning.

The Scandinavian countries and France assist solo mothers to be employed – as they do all mothers – with generous leave policies and public services (Hobson and Takahashi 1997; Siim 1997; Gornick et al. 1997). They also offer some special supplements for single mothers. In these countries, women and men gain personal independence through employment, but in the context of a rather extensive public system of social supports which has been updated to apply to women's special needs with regard to caregiving. There were some parallels between these cases and the policies pursued by the socialist countries of eastern and central Europe; solo and other mothers were given special supports to facilitate the combination of employment and caregiving (although without the Scandinavians' commitment to enhance men's participation in caregiving). But restructuring of social policies in the wake of the transition from socialism has ended such supports, and solo mothers find themselves with only means-tested and inadequate public assistance, while married mothers find themselves more dependent on husbands (Heinen 1999; Haney 1997).

Canada and the U.S. have withdrawn the political guarantee – i.e., entitlement – to social assistance that once existed for single non-employed parents (O'Connor, Orloff and Shaver 1999). Yet, because of rising real wages among women and policies directed at opening workplace opportunities to women, many women do earn enough to support themselves and their children, gaining the capacity to support a household as most U.S. and Canadian men do, through the market. Needed services are supplied by the market - meaning that there is a fair amount of unevenness in the quality and cost of services. Thus, in North America, it is the market that guarantees personal autonomy for married and single men and women alike – there are no political guarantees of services, employment or income. Some recent initiatives at bolstering the income of low-wage workers in North America through tax credits have made even low-wage employment a relatively more attractive option for single mothers (Orloff 2001). Canada has done more than the U.S., however, in directing benefits also to non-employed households, including those of elderly women, and has thereby reduced the poverty rates of these groups, and prevented the deep poverty among children that is such a troubling aspect of U.S. society (O'Connor, Orloff and Shaver 1999; Myles and Pierson 1997).

Employment and care

Research has focused especially on the issue of whether or not women's – actually, mothers' – paid work is accepted and supported, and, if it is, how caregiving is organised to allow women's employment. This reflects both gender ideologies and practices about women's work and the character of the institutional 'division of labour' among states, markets, families and other organisations in the provision of care and income. Much attention has focused on the extent to which services and welfare broadly speaking are to be publicly or privately provided. Successful privatisation depends upon strong family and kin networks available and able to provide support to people in need – elderly needing physical care, employed mothers and fathers needing care for their children, and so on – or upon a level of economic affluence in which people can afford to purchase services or insurance on the market. These conditions, however, are far from universally applicable across the countries where privatisation has been promoted as a solution to problems of social provision.

Contemporary comparative analyses show that women's paid work is far more accepted and promoted in Scandinavia and France than has been the case for women in other parts of Europe and Australasia (e.g., Hernes 1987; Lewis 1992; Hobson 1994; Ruggie 1984; Leira 1992; Jenson 1986). In Ireland, Italy, the Netherlands, Spain, Germany, Switzerland and Austria, social provision has been shaped by social Catholicism and Christian Democratic parties, with their valorisation of gender difference, an ideal of full-time mothering rather than wage work for women, and family 'solidarity' and unity – implying women's economic dependency, but not (explicitly) gendered inequality of resources (Jackson 1993; Knijn 1994; Bussemaker and van Kersbergen 1994; Cousins 1995; Schmidt 1993; Ostner 1993, 1997; Saraceno 1994; Duncan and Edwards 1997).

Yet feminists, too, have been influenced by these notions of gender difference and the valorisation of mothering (Ostner and Lewis 1995). In the UK, Australia, and New Zealand, the male breadwinner – (full–time) female caregiver model was championed by strong trade union movements, led by men, who were able to establish provision supporting men's position as breadwinners and women's as caregivers, including relatively generous allowances to single mothers to allow them to stay home (Cass 1994; Castles 1994; Lewis 1992; Pedersen 1993). The North American countries were initially similar to, albeit less generous than, these countries, and institutionalised a system based on male breadwinner–female caregiver. But recent changes have undermined support for full-time female caregiving, and indeed for caregiving activities of all kinds, while employment is valorised for all (Orloff 2001). The formerly socialist countries of eastern and central Europe have eliminated supports that facilitated the combination of caregiving and employment for mothers (Haney 1997; Heinen 1999). Yet unlike the North American countries, these states are not moving to open opportunities to women in the workplace; beyond a very small stratum of entrepreneurs, most women are suffering declines in various aspects of their work lives, including social provision; thus, these cutbacks are reducing women's access to employment (Heinen 1999). In East Asia and Latin America, women's reliance on family support networks to enter employment is vulnerable to disruptions in those networks.

These distinctive approaches to women's employment are reflected in a number of policy areas (on child care, see Gustaffson 1994). Public services (the European approach), providing partial substitution of women's care of children and the elderly in the family or in family networks, or state subsidies (the American approach) allowing the purchase of services on the market, are key. Provision for elder care has not been as extensively researched as child care, but is clearly central in resolving the care 'crisis' (Knijn and Kremer 1997). (On child care as part of a package of public provisions supporting mothers' employment, see Gornick, Meyers and Ross 1997). While almost all European countries provide care for children from age 3 to 6 as part of their educational mission, care for under-3-years-olds, essential for mothers' employment, is much less developed outside of Scandinavia. Care for school-aged children is de facto provided by elementary schools, but there is less provision for after-school hours, and school days in certain countries, for instance Germany, are irregular. Again, Scandinavia provides services most comprehensively.

Income security programs also play an important role in allowing women to take up employment on more equitable terms. Maternity leave and benefits to replace lost income are well-established parts of the systems of social provision in almost all countries. However, outside the developed world, coverage is quite restricted; even in some industrialised countries, coverage is limited by the exclusion of certain categories of workers or by stiff eligibility requirements (Moghadam 1993:11). And across the world, especially where women workers are not well-organised, there are problems of gender discrimination around women's need to utilise maternity leave provisions. The European Union mandates a leave of at least fourteen weeks; Canada provides a similar leave within the unemployment insurance system while Australia offers leave through the mechanism of arbitrated labor agreements, which reach many but not all women (O'Connor, Orloff and Shaver 1999). The U.S. offers no paid maternity leave; some women can take time off under parental and care leave provisions. Parental leave, more recently developed, is also a way to allow workers to maintain their connection to employment while attending to caregiving. The European Union mandates an individual leave of at least three months for all workers, men and women, but it need not be paid. The U.S. has an unpaid care leave of three months, open to men and women, but restricted to the workers of large employers. Canada and Australia also have short leaves, some paid, available to men and women. Unpaid leaves are unlikely to be of much help to the low-paid. Yet parental leave is a right used mostly by women, as very few men avail themselves of their rights to take parental leave. Several countries – Sweden, Norway, the Netherlands, Austria, France and Greece – have attempted to encourage men to take parental leave by lengthening the total family leave if men take part. Yet still only a small minority of men take them up (e.g., on Sweden, see Haas 1992).

Leave provisions are varied, and their effects are not always easy to discern (for good descriptions, see OECD 1995; Gornick et al. 1997; and Gauthier 1996). Eligibility conditions restrict the coverage of leave in most countries to those with six to twelve months previous continuous service with the same employer; this may serve as a further incentive for women to work (OECD 1995:179). In countries where leave provisions are generous but other employment supports are not well-developed (e.g., Germany, Italy), leave may reinforce the traditional division of labor and women's non-employment. In states with better-developed employment supports, such as the Nordic countries and France, taking leave to give birth and care for very young children is important for most women, but the fact that mostly women take leave may affect their employment opportunities – employers may prefer men for certain sorts of jobs. Such employer preferences may help to reinforce men's reluctance to become involved in care activities. Taking leaves may be preferable to dropping out of the workforce entirely, but may also be associated with the confirmation of mothers as families' secondary earners.

In the Nordic countries, childrearing and paid work have been made easier to harmonise through social policy initiatives, but costs are high and the state has emerged as 'employer of first resort' for many women, contributing to occupational and sectoral sex segregation and concerns about levels of taxation and countries' capacities to compete internationally (or, more pragmatically, their capacity to meet fiscal goals for regional unification efforts). The systems without care services force women to choose between employment and bearing and child rearing, which may also be responsible for depressing fertility – most notable in the countries, like Italy and Spain, where services are least developed (see, e.g., Saraceno 1994; Ostner 1993; Bussemaker and van Kersbergen 1994). Care may be of high quality, but women's employment options are constrained. The formerly-socialist countries have cut services, moving away from a policy orientation that had been somewhat similar to the Nordic one of supporting women in combining paid work and caregiving. But unlike the southern European scenario, the quality of care currently suffers from depressed living standards and health services; in the future, it is possible that the situation for caregiving will improve, but women's options will remain limited without some social supports for employment. In the United States, Canada and Australia, a liberal orientation in favor of private provision prevails, and there is very little publicly-provided child care. As a result, the capacities and resources for reconciling childrearing and employment are quite uneven. However, because of government-encouraged private provision of care services, tax credits to employed parents and some state provision of services (especially on behalf of low-income women), services have been developed and women have entered the workforce, some rather successfully (O'Connor, Orloff and Shaver 1999). Yet care is of variable quality, and income inequalities contribute to inequalities in access to good quality care. Although Britain has shared a tradition of social policy liberalism with her 'daughter' countries, care services are less developed there, with the result that women's employment is, as in the continental situation, constrained. However, overall levels of labor market regulation are much lower, and a large part-time labor market offering precarious employment mainly to women has emerged.

Gender and regime types

Do these different dimensions of policy relative to gender equality hold together in any way? In other words, can we identify gendered social policy regimes, or make use of existing regime typologies, such as Esping-Andersen's (1990, 1999)? There are certain significant similarities with respect to gender among the countries within the regime clusters identified by Esping-Andersen. But there appear also to be significant gendered differences within regimes, reflecting especially differences in the assumptions about the gender division of labor institutionalised in policy – differences which may be better captured by Lewis's (1992, 1997a) regime formulation. Finally, there are also likenesses between countries from different regimes in terms of outcomes, even if the institutional modalities for achieving these outcomes are distinctive.

The social-democratic regimes are notable for their extensive service provision; this has been critical in supporting women's, especially mothers', employment. This has also been significant for undermining 'familism', that is, in mitigating women's dependency on family and marriage (as well as men's dependence on wives for servicing). But within the social-democratic cluster, Norway differs from Denmark and Sweden in terms of 'models of motherhood', according to Leira (1992); this is reflected in less extensive service provision and somewhat lower participation rates by Norwegian mothers with very young children. In other words, the gender division of labor differs among the social-democratic regimes.

The social-democratic countries are not the only ones which have developed arrangements supporting women's employment and their economic independence. France and Belgium, among the conservative-corporatist cluster, feature extensive public child care services, leaves and so on, and mothers' employment rates are higher than in other continental European countries, where service provision is most notable by its absence. The U.S. and Canada, liberal regimes, also display relatively high rates of mothers' employment and women's economic independence, but without extensive public services. How is this possible? Low wages make child care affordable for many families, aided by tax subsidies; targeted public services enable others to work. Liberalism favors private provision; but 'private' can mean market or family. The North American countries have supported market provision in various ways, which has facilitated women's employment. Note that while outcomes – relatively high levels of women's employment – are similar, the policies by which they are achieved differ, especially between the liberal North American countries and the social-democratic Scandinavian ones.

The conservative-continental countries are notable for the 'familism' of their welfare regimes, which has meant that caregiving burdens are borne by families – especially women, creating difficulties in reconciling employment and care, lower participation rates and lower fertility rates than elsewhere. Yet French and Belgian patterns of women's employment differ from the patterns in Germany, Spain, Italy, the Netherlands and Austria. Again, we can recognise a somewhat different gender division of labour – what Lewis (1992) has called a 'modified male breadwinner regime,' in contrast to the 'strong male breadwinner' model institutionalised in, for example, Germany. We have already seen that France and Belgium partly escape from some of the problems associated with 'familism' by pursuing a service-provision strategy similar to the Scandinavian one. However, judging from historical analyses of the origins of France's family policy (e.g., Pedersen 1993; Jenson 1986), the sources of this set of provisions is distinctive from that obtaining in Scandinavia. It was not social-democratic forces that led to the initiation (in the pre-WW2 period) of the set of policies which French mothers today use to reconcile work and care, but pro-natalists and state and Church elites who wanted to support reproduction compromising with employers who wanted to employ women workers.

But 'familism' is not limited to continental Europe. Liberal Britain and Australia (and maybe to a more limited degree, social-democratic Norway) also display some features of familism in their systems. However, these countries are not so constrained by strong labour regulation and social security costs, and have therefore seen somewhat higher participation rates for women, and less severe consequences for fertility than in the most familist systems; in addition, stronger systems of support for women's autonomous households is reflected in higher proportions of single-mother households than in the conservative regimes.

The liberal regimes are notable for their residual systems of social provision. Given women's disproportionate economic vulnerability due to caregiving responsibilities, this means that when women find themselves outside employment or marriage, they are left exposed to poverty. All five of the liberal regimes feature very high levels of poverty among woman-maintained households (i.e., single elderly women or single mothers with children). But there are some interesting differences within this group on this score: Britain has done better at protecting single mothers (although the last years under the Conservatives were eroding this), while Canada's recent initiatives in old-age protection have brought poverty levels among older women down dramatically (to 'European' levels). Meanwhile, Germany, with more extensive social protection in other respects, also leaves single mothers exposed to high poverty levels; this has come to be the case in the Netherlands as well (poverty rates among single mothers rose from the mid-1980s to the mid-1990s – before and after policy reforms). And even in the Scandinavian countries, older women are more likely to be poor than other groups.

Finally, we can examine women's independence or autonomy as an outcome. In all the countries which support women's employment (by whatever means), women's economic independence (a lack of 'familism') is a by-product. And this is related to high proportions of single-parent families and non-marital births, characteristic of both the social-democratic regimes and the North American countries. But women's economic independence can also be supported through state benefits, as in Britain, Australia and the Netherlands, where there are also relatively high proportions of solo-mother families. Again, a significant outcome – autonomy, or 'defamilisation' to use Lister's (1997) term, – may be supported by different policy means. It is only where *both* employment-supporting policies and individual rights to social assistance are lacking – in Southern Europe – that we see relatively low rates of divorce and non-marital births.

This pattern of outcomes suggests that there are some significant gender consequences of overall regime architecture (levels of spending and institutional arrangements with respect to the provision of income and care services). To take only some of the most significant: the emphasis on state provision of services in social-democratic regimes supports mothers' employment and reconciliation between employment and care. The antipathy to state provision of income or services – and preference for the market (and secondarily the family) leaves women in the liberal regimes vulnerable to poverty, and reliant on the market for services to support employment (and with no guarantee that the market will provide them). The family-oriented character of the conservative-corporatist regimes constrains women's employment, or forces a trade-off between care/childbearing and employment. But within clusters, while the institutional architecture does condition their expression, gender relations, gender ideologies and policies differ. To take but one striking example: women's employment is politically emphasised in both Sweden and the U.S. In Sweden, this is facilitated through state provision of services and public employment opportunities for women. In the U.S., the market is the key arena - not only because low wages produce affordable child care for many and robust employer demand for workers (especially in the service sector) brings women into the labor force, but through *political* interventions which encourage private provision of services (e.g., tax credits for child care) and private employment of women (e.g., equal-opportunity regulation of employment, affirmative action).

Those outcomes which tend to vary by regimes can be explained with reference to the well-known factors associated with the development of the different regimes (political constellations, patterns of state-building, etc.). But there remains the task of explaining patterns – within and across regimes – of policy differences relevant for gender relations, that is, nationally (or even regionally) specific patterns around (1) women's and men's employment, caregiving and the overall organisation of care – significant aspects of the gender division of labour, and (2) women's capacities to support autonomous households (as compared to men's), and their relative vulnerability to poverty – significant aspects of gendered power. This will require the investigation of gender politics across these countries: the organisation and strength of women's movements (and movements antagonistic to feminism); women's legislative representation and their position within state administrations; women's position within trade unions and the overall situation of labor; the character and representation of men's gendered interests (in unions, legislatures, etc.); and gender ideologies. Of course, gender politics occurs within the context of distinctive policy regimes and their associated political constellations, and is influenced as well by employers' demand for women's and men's labor, labor market characteristics, exposure to global economic pressures, the racial and ethnic makeup of client populations and national populations, and demographic patterns.

Creating gender equality

It is clear even from this brief review of evidence that substantial gender inequalities still exist today – some because of, others despite, systems of income security.

In the developing world, the biggest challenge is regularising women's employment, allowing them access to still-limited social security. Investment in women's physical well-being, and in their educational and employment opportunities have been shown to be significant in enhancing women's relative situation, but also in enhancing the conditions of children. Basic programs to support women and men experiencing some of the less desirable side-effects of economic development and to support investment in human capital can be quite important components of overall development. For example, basic pensions for the elderly will give people greater freedom to reduce family size; this is especially beneficial to women, but is also critical to overall development goals. And even modest family allowances for mothers are effective in getting resources to children and in promoting women's power within families and society. In the newly-industrialising countries, women have greater representation in the formal labor force, but still face serious challenges in reconciling employment and caregiving; the development of services will be essential for continued progress.

In the industrialised countries, equal treatment initiatives have removed most of the most obvious biases from social security systems. For further progress toward gender equality to be made, issues to do with the gender division of labor must be faced. In the short term, we need some protection for women whose caregiving has left them economically vulnerable; for elderly women, enhanced pension benefits are an effective solution to poverty. But for working-aged women, those in favour of increasing gender equality must deal with the issues of how men and women can combine caregiving and paid work. One might think that the general policy thrust toward mobilisation of women's labor should make their goals easier to accomplish given that many governments want more women employed. Yet participation in and of itself is not sufficient to advance women's interests; the quality of jobs in terms of pay, hours, conditions, locations, and how compatible jobs are with caregiving are critical. Many are concerned about whether women's equality projects can flourish under the new conditions of globalisation given pressures by many employers and allied political forces for maximum 'flexibility' from workers and the decline of traditionally well-paid, secure and unionised jobs in the manufacturing sector (O'Connor, Orloff and Shaver 1999; Jenson et al. 1988). But surely 'flexibility' can be imagined from the perspective of employees, men and women, who would like greater control over when and how long they work, and also want social protection. Thus, there must be political will mustered to see that this reconciliation is not be at the expense of the quality of care or of women's employment opportunities. In other contexts, persistently high unemployment rates may cause some policymakers to assume encouraging women's entry to the labor force would be counterproductive. Yet it is arguable that the effects of women's employment in generating demand for services, and hence service employment, would actually help to reduce unemployment (Esping-Andersen 1996, 1997).

Depending on each country's starting point, different strategies may be pursued to combat women's poverty and economic deprivation while ensuring caregiving activities are supported. Where women's employment and employment opportunities are well-established, as in North America, it is caregiving that needs attention: supporting parental leaves more generously and assisting more extensively in the provision of services. In addition, there is a need for financially supporting low-wage workers so that they can in fact provide necessities, including high-quality care, for their families. If all are expected to be (paid) workers, it must be understood that workers have caregiving obligations which should be supported. In Scandinavia and France, where workers who are caregivers have excellent supports but employers discriminate on the basis of caregiving responsibilities, it is women's opportunities in employment – rather than simply their participation in the labour force – that must be targeted, while assuring that services and leaves are not cut back. Here, where men are 'just' workers, despite the rhetoric encouraging them to take up care, but women are care-providers, it is women's roles as workers that must be emphasised while continuing to make clear that men should be carers as well. In the many European systems where women's care work in the family is supported but their paid work is not, the systems of service provision and leave protection which allow women's employment must be built up even as employment opportunities are opened up. In all systems, these initiatives must target men as well as women.

The ultimate solution to the problems of reconciliation of employment and care, women's economic dependency and the care crisis in all systems is a 'universal caregiver' model: to induce 'men to become more like what most women are now – that is, people who do primary care work' (Fraser 1994:611); this would dismantle 'the gendered opposition between breadwinning and caregiving,' and 'integrate activities that are currently separated from one another, eliminate their gender coding.' This would necessitate changing workplaces to accommodate caregiving, and would call upon income security systems to insure that people can take time to care and have access to care services. Encouraging *men's* caregiving is essential, as is encouraging women's integration into paid employment while allowing their continued caregiving.

Chapter 6

Europeanisation and Decentralisation of Welfare 'Safety Nets'

Luis Moreno

Introduction

The process of Europeanisation implies a certain confluence of resources and outputs among the diverse national systems of social security and welfare. This is due to both structural constraints, such as external social dumping and relocation of industries, and institutional inputs, such as sentences by European Court of Justice. This chapter reflects on two ongoing processes which appear to be antagonistic: the adjustment of national systems of social protection to operate within a rather similar European framework on the one hand, and the decentralisation of 'safety net' policies at a meso-level, which is aimed at strengthening territorial subsidiarity and democratic accountability, on the other.

In the first section key concepts and premises are discussed in order to reflect on epistemological considerations around which subsequent analyses of Europe's unity and

Jochen Clasen (ed.), *What Future for Social Security?*, 87-100
©2001 Kluwer Law International. Printed in the Netherlands.

diversity are discussed. The subsequent section concentrates on the so-called 'European social model'. This model refers to most of the EU countries and contrasts with national systems in which an increasing individualisation of welfare is noticeable (such as in the USA). However, the model can also be regarded as the bearer of various historical cultures and national organisations. Notwithstanding a confluence of public expenditure levels and organisational arrangements among EU countries, cross-national differences are briefly examined with regard to the four European welfare regimes.

Mesogovernments, and the increasing role of sub-state governments in the provision of community-centred policies, are the focus of the third section. Demands for stronger decentralisation and a greater regional say in areas of policy-making closer to citizens' perceptions, such as the 'weaving of safety nets', have often been based on aspects of culture or identity. But other reasons such as policy innovation and a more effective management which is facilitated by the devolution of powers have also been put forward. In Southern Europe, for instance, de-concentration and decentralisation of social services have had a much larger impact than privatisation. A brief examination of the case of Spain's devolution of welfare powers to the regions illustrates such claims.

The rationale implicit in the European principle of subsidiarity favours the participation of sub-state layers of government in accordance with democratic accountability. This chapter concludes that in order to build up a macro community of trust in the 'Old Continent' more attention should be paid to the increasing role of medium-size layers of government.

Concepts and premises

Safety nets

'Safety nets' aim at providing citizens and families with basic means which both guarantee the satisfaction of minimum vital needs and facilitate civic integration. 'Safety nets' are bottom-lines of welfare provision and as such institutionalised expressions which vary in degree and form. The complex task for social scientists is to determine the constituent materials by which 'nets' are interwoven. Public programmes of social assistance provided on a means-tested basis are basic constituent elements. In many cases these programmes are not a direct responsibility for social security, although they may be linked to contributory social services and subsidies.

Public policies and associated interventions combined to provide 'safety nets' are often fragmented. Benefits and services are generally targeted on different collectives with no correlation between them (Eardley et al. 1996). Other intervening factors, such as intra-familial transfers, community help, or altruistic help provided by NGOs (Non-Governmental Organizations) and 'third sector' associations, also play a crucial role.

Excessive attention paid to centrally-run governmental output in the area of welfare provision has tended to neglect the impact of those latter factors, which are difficult to measure and assess in quantitative terms. Studies on welfare development have often neglected the importance of the interrelation between state, civil society, family and the individual in establishing 'safety nets', as well as in providing social cohesion and political legitimacy. Despite the fact that the subject of study has many facets, welfare state research has often concentrated on analysing national social spending rather than institutions and organisational relations (Esping-Andersen 1993).

Furthermore, often disregarded by social policy researchers (Alber 1995), sub-national tiers of government have been important institutional actors of policy innovation in the area of welfare 'safety nets'. The concept of welfare 'residualism' is usually correlated to the decline of the centralising 'command-and-control' planning model. However, a growth of institutional 'stateness', or state penetration of the welfare sphere (Flora 1986/87), has also been noticeable in decentralised countries. Obviously, the concept of 'stateness' includes the degree of autonomy of state officials in decision-making and implementation of public polices at all layers of government (central, regional and local). In line with traditional Jacobin tenets, there still persists a misinterpretation as a result of equating central government with state institutions.

Europeanisation

At the beginning of the 21st Century, the unfolding of structures of governance at a supranational European level is taking place by means of formalising interactions between the fifteen members of the European Union. These interactions affect mainly actors and policy networks which traditionally have been confined to operating in nation-state arenas. However, an emerging new layer of supra-national government and an all-round multi-tier concurrence are processes well under way.

Europeanisation can be referred to as a process of economic, political and social convergence in the 'Old Continent'. It relates to all three economic, political and social domains, and comprises of countries which share a somewhat common historical development and which embrace values of democracy and human rights of an egalitarian nature. However, the concept is far from being precise or clear-cut. It is multi-semantic and subject to various degrees of understandings and interpretations. Europeanisation is not a static concept, but rather a dynamic idea which found expression in the gradual development of common institutions in Europe (e.g. the Agreement of Schengen, the European Court of Justice, the Euro currency).

Europeanisation does not necessarily imply the constitution of the United States of Europe along the lines of neo-functionalist prescriptions. This school of thought has generally adopted the view that universal progress requires a kind of integration, which is made equal to cultural assimilation according to a notion and analogy of a 'melting-pot'. An alternative view of non-homogenising integration puts the emphasis on the historical, psychological, and social premises of a plural Europe. Pluralists envisage European rules to be achieved and successfully accommodated by taking into account both history and cultural diversity within the mosaic of peoples in the 'Old Continent'. Neo-functionalists have criticised such an approach as being 'Euro-pessimistic', as it is not centralised and vertically hierarchical.

Decentralisation

Decentralisation is a premise inherent in the process of European convergence. The principle of subsidiarity was enshrined in the Treaty of European Union of 1992, known as the Treaty of Maastricht. It provides for decisions to be taken supranationally only if local, regional or national levels cannot perform the same task more adequately. In other words, the preferred locus for decision-making is close to the citizen, and as local as possible. State political elites, reluctant to advance the process of European institutionalisation, interpreted subsidiarity as a principle which would safeguard the preservation of traditional national sovereignty and, consequently, the powers to intervene centrally, placing the bottom-line of subsidiarity at the level of the nation-state.

As a result of the EU's summit held in Nice in December 2000, an agreement was reached to set up a new intergovernmental conference which would conclude with a new European Treaty in 2004. Countries with a decentralised or federal structure of government are keen on clarifying the divisions of powers and responsibilities in the future multi-tier European Union. Workable schemes should be adopted so that German *Länder*, Italian *Regioni*, Spanish *Comunidades Autónomas*, or the British devolved administrations, could secure their own inputs at European level, as well as to implement and manage EU decisions at their own level of competence. Regional governments have shown resistance to encroachment from Brussels on sub-state political action. They expect the forthcoming intergovernmental conference to reverse a trend to further re-centralisation, not only at a European-wide but also at national level.

European subsidiarity favours the participation of sub-state layers of government in the running of public affairs. At the same time, it encourages intergovernmental co-operation on the assumption that national states will be less 'sovereign' than they have been up until now. To meet these challenges, the process of democratic institutionalisation of the European Union needs to acknowledge, first of all, the diverse processes of state formation and nation-building within the constituent member-states. On displaying his 'macro-model of European political development', Stein Rokkan has already pointed out that the accommodation of cleavage structures forged in centuries of history appeared to be a pre-requisite to any political attempt to dismantle internal boundaries in a supra-national Europe (Flora et al. 1999).

The development of a European supra-national welfare state and social policy is regarded as unlikely in the foreseeable future. On consolidating welfare 'safety nets', national and local cultures will continue to play a crucial role in peoples' expectations, perceptions and values. This area of social policy-making is highly shaped by local cultures and life styles, and is less likely to be dealt with in a homogenous and centralised manner from a supra-national entity.

Unity and diversity in EU social protection

After World War II, West European systems of social protection were based upon the assumption of full employment and on the complementary role developed by the family, and, in particular, on women's unpaid work within households (Lewis 1993). This scenario has dramatically changed during the last decades. On the one hand, processes of economic globalisation and industrial transformations have had wide-ranging effects on national labour markets. On the other, there have been deep structural modifications due to population ageing, an increasing participation of women in the formal labour market, and changes within households as main producers and distributors of welfare and well-being. In addition, fiscal crises and the erosion of the ideological consensus regarding social policies have also conditioned the re-casting of welfare states in Europe.

There is a widely held belief that the 'European social model' is something which provides unity and identity to most of the EU countries in contrast to systems where an increasing individualisation of welfare is noticeable (such as in the USA). However, viewed from below, such a 'European social model' appears much more diverse as a kaleidoscope of sediments and peculiarities (Ferrera 1996b). Indeed, systems of social protection within the European Union are far from being identical and uniform. Any future scenario for a unified EU involvement in the area of policies regarding social protection must take into account the present situation of national differentials and regime peculiarities. A brief review of the diverse welfare arrangements and institutional configurations within the European Union should be clarifying in this respect. To accomplish this I refer to the 'regime approach', which has established itself as a useful methodological tool for analysing the diversity of welfare in the European Union (Esping-Andersen 1990, 1999).

According to this approach, welfare systems are characterised by a particular constellation of economic political and social arrangements. Undoubtedly, the 'regime approach' has proved to be very persuasive in linking together a wide range of elements which are considered to influence welfare outcomes. However, by establishing patterns of fixed interaction an assumption of continuity tends to prevail over that of change. As a consequence, it is implicitly assumed that a particular welfare state will tend to sustain interests and arrangements identified within the three main categories. These are briefly described as follows (see also Table 6.1).

Table 6.1: Features of European Welfare Regimes

	ANGLO-SAXON	CONTINENTAL	NORDIC	MEDITERRANEAN
IDEOLOGY	Citizenship	Neo-corporatism	Egalitarianism	Social justice
GOALS	Individual choice	Income maintenance	Network public services	Resource optimisation
FINANCING	Taxes	Payroll contributions	Taxes	Mixed
BENEFITS	Flat rate (low intensity)	Cash (high intensity)	Flat rate (high intensity)	Cash (low intensity)
SERVICES	Residual public	Social partners	Comprehensive public	Family support
PROVISION	Public/quasi markets	NGOs	Public / Centrally fixed	Mixed / decentralised
LABOUR MARKET	De-regulation	Insiders/outsiders	High public employment	Large informal economy
GENDER	Female polarisation	Part-time feminisation	Occupational specific	Ambivalent familialism
POVERTY	Dependency culture	Insertion culture	Statist culture	Assistance culture

(a) *The corporatist Continental* regime is characterised by a concerted action between employers and trade unions, and financed by contributions made by them. Welfare policies by state institutions uphold this arrangement, which is organised through social insurance. There is a sharp distinction between labour market 'insiders' and 'outsiders'.

(b) *The liberal Anglo-Saxon* type is patterned by its commitment to universality, financed by taxes and incorporating residual means-tested services and flat-rate benefits. It has pursued a shift toward market principles, involving deregulation of the labour market, wage flexibility and containment in social expenditure.

(c) *The social-democratic Nordic* type is premised on the harmonisation of egalitarian ideas with growth and full employment, and the minimisation of family dependence. It is financed by taxes, characterised by the principle of universality, and favouring the public provision of services rather than cash transfers.

This three-fold categorisation of welfare regimes has spawned further taxonomies, including the identification of a fourth South-European or Mediterranean category (Ferrera 1996a; Rhodes 1996; Moreno 2000). The discussion revolves around the contention whether the Mediterranean type of welfare belong to the 'continental' model of social insurance and are merely lagging behind (Katrougalos 1996) or whether it is a distinct 'Latin rim' type which is characterised by a rudimentary level of social provision and institutional development (Leibfried 1992; Gough 1996). In broad terms, similar social-demographic trends, macro-economic constraints and pattern of public policy can be observed in all four South European countries (Giner 1986, Morlino 1998; Castles 1998).

Beyond the discussion of both parsimony and reduction of variance in the classification of welfare regimes (see Table 6.1), a confluence in the level of public expenditure and in organisational arrangements among EU countries is noticeable. Europeanisation and the adaptation of the European labour markets to global competition have undoubtedly induced such a convergence. The idea of 'encompassing' welfare arrangements, whereby universal coverage and basic security form the base upon which income related benefits are to be erected, was recently proposed for the Nordic countries (Korpi and Palme, 1998). This approach is in line with the Bismarckian contributory principle of social insurance and aims at providing income-related benefits to all gainfully employed individuals. It is a criterion already introduced in some Scandinavian welfare programmes (Eitrheim and Kuhnle 1999).

If a reduction in the level of protection which welfare benefits provide, in addition to a hardening of access and eligibility criteria is observable in Central and Northern Europe, the trend in Southern Europe has run somewhat in the opposite direction. Based on a Continental-style contributory system of social security, recent reforms implemented in Mediterranean countries have pointed towards generalisation –and even universalisation - of benefits and services (e.g. education, health, non-contributory pensions). In the case of Britain, welfare reforms have put an emphasis on workfare in trying to avoid universal 'dependent' welfare. Such a course of action has implicitly adopted the philosophy of the 'contributory principle', although a transfer of responsibilities from the public to the profit-making private sector is the underlying trend.

Among the various factors affecting this observable trend towards 'unity' in social policy provision developed by European member states, macro-structural constraints such as external social dumping, industrial relocation and financial globalisation are to be accounted for. But the European institutional inputs are also crucially important, particularly those related to European law and European Court of Justice's jurisprudence. Let us refer to one example which appears to underline this very clearly.

The impact of European law on social security is growing in importance and has potentially far-reaching consequences. Article 2 of the EC Treaty provided the EC legislator with the competence to harmonise provisions of the national systems of social security in order to secure the freedom of movement of workers. In recent times, social policy matters have been brought to the forefront of EU interests. The Social Charter regarding the right of workers, as well as the agreement on social policy of the Maastricht Treaty and its inclusion in the Amsterdam Treaty as a separate chapter on social policy, are significant steps in the direction of developing a 'Social Europe'.

Jurisprudence of the European Court of Justice can be regarded as a decisive institutional input shaping the future of social security in the European Union. The decision of 1998 on the Kohll and the Decker cases constituted a turning point in the juridical concept of the relation between EU law and national health insurance laws.[1] The Court ruled that, in the absence of harmonisation at the EU level, each member state could determine the conditions concerning the right and duties of those insured within a social security scheme, as well as the conditions for entitlement to benefits. Nevertheless, and this was the crucial aspect of the Court's decision, national member states should comply with European law when exercising their powers to organise their social security systems (Kötter 1999).

It remains to be seen whether the Kohll and Decker rulings by the Court of Justice will have a 'visible' impact on an area of 'exclusive' national competence.[2] The weight of the

---

1 Mr. Kohll, a Luxembourg citizen, had requested authorisation for dental treatment for his daughter in Germany (Trier). Mr. Decker, also a Luxembourg citizen, had solicited the reimbursement of spectacles with corrective lenses he had purchased in Belgium. In both cases, national social security administrations rejected the claims. Kohll and Decker appealed subsequently to the European Court of Justice.

2 On the allegation that the financial implications of this ruling could undermine the balance of the national systems of social security, the Court held the view that the reimbursement of costs at a flat-rate level, or in accordance with the tariff of that established in the country of origin, would have no effect on the financial equilibrium of the national social security system.

institutional inputs produced by the Court's jurisprudence will have the highest levels of legitimacy in the process of building a 'Social Europe'. Until now, decisions and rulings by the Court have enjoyed an uncontested degree of legitimacy *vis-à-vis* national interests defended by the governments of the member states. At the root of such attitudes lies the acceptance not only that political life in Europe depends on the rule of law, but the conviction that human rights and values of an egalitarian nature are embraced by EU countries without exception.

Mesogovernments and 'safety nets'

Recent social and economic transformations have brought about a higher degree of uncertainty for wide social collectives which were previously covered by social protection schemes and now face increasing vulnerability. In this context, 'safety nets' have become focal points of attention. There is a growing European concern expressed in EU programmes aimed at combating poverty and social exclusion. The EU Commission 'Strategic Objectives' for the period 2000-2005 envisage a reform of social protection based on solidarity that can remain fair, caring and inclusive in a climate of '...cautious pubic spending' (Commission 2000). According to these views, the new European governance is not considered to have the 'exclusive' responsibility of European Union institutions. Neither are national governments or national parliaments regarded as the sole actors of European governance. Instead, local authorities and the regions are recognised as decisive and emerging actors.

Indeed, both processes of bottom-up Europeanisation and top-down decentralisation have facilitated a considerable extension of some form of European *cosmopolitan localism*, and provided an increasingly important role for sub-state governments in the provision of community-centred policies (Moreno 1999). This is reflected in societal interests which are aimed at developing a sense of local community and at participating simultaneously in the global context. In this respect, the role played by medium-size polities is acquiring relevance in most aspects of contemporary life. In Europe, the renewal of community life at the meso-level derives mainly from the combination of two main factors: a growing rejection of centralisation at the national level coupled with a strengthening of supranational politics, and a reinforcement of local identities and societal cultures with a territorial underpinning.[3]

---

3 European community life should be seen as distinct from that prescribed in North America for local communities (Etzioni, 1993). In the case of the USA, many of the communitarian experiences may be regarded as reactions to specific social cleavages and pressing social fractures (the criminalisation of social life), as means of socialisation in response to urban constriction (suburban isolationism), or as alternative lifestyles to dominant values (possessive individualism). Thus, North-American communitarianism can be seen mainly as socially defensive.

In policy making, mesogovernments are no longer dependent on the state building programmes of rationalisation carried out during the 19th and 20th century. Regionally-based entrepreneurs, social leaders and members of the *intelligentsia* have adopted many of the initiatives and roles which were once reserved for 'enlightened' elites, who in the past held the reins of power at the centre of their nation states. Positions of influence are now more evenly distributed at central, meso-level and in local institutions. The co-option of regional elites to the central institutions of government is no longer the exclusive route available to 'successful' political careers.

A re-assertion of sub-state identities is acquiring major relevance within the supranational framework provided by Europeanisation. Manifestations of such developments in Western Europe are not confined to electoral deviations within national contexts (e.g. CiU-Catalonia, CSU-Bavaria, Lega-Northern Italy, SNP-Scotland). Social movements and industrialists of the 'new economy' have found a more flexible context for action at the regional level. The central state apparatus is often clumsy and inefficient in dealing with bottom-up initiatives. Medium-size nation states (Denmark or Finland), stateless nations (Catalonia or Scotland), regions (Brussels or Veneto) and metropolitan areas (London or Berlin) are well equipped for carrying out innovative policies in a more integrated Europe. To be underlined here is particularly the quest of medium-size communities to run their own affairs and to develop their potentials outside the *dirigiste* control of central state institutions.

Demands for decentralisation and a greater regional say in areas of policy-making closer to citizens' perceptions, as is the case of social policy and welfare development, are based not only on cultural or identity considerations. There is also a case for the better management of welfare programmes associated to the weaving of 'safety nets'. Deconcentration and decentralisation of social services have had a much larger impact than privatisation in Southern European. Programmes of 'minimum income guaranteed' constitute important components in the process of weaving such 'safety nets'. The case of their implementation in Spain offers a good illustration of the growing role of mesogovernments in this respect.

The case of Spain's decentralisation

In 1988, the Basque Government announced the implementation of a regional *Plan de Lucha contra la Pobreza* ('Programme against Poverty'). This innovative policy sparked off a regional mimesis, or 'demonstration effect', on the part of the other 16 Spanish *Comunidades Autónomas*. By the end of the 1990s, all Spanish mesogovernments had implemented regional programmes of minimum income, which combine means-tested cash benefits with policies of social insertion (primarily employment promotion and vocation training schemes).

In parallel, Spanish mesogovernments also passed legislation in their regional parliaments to develop integrated networks of social services based upon the constitutional principle which entitles them to request 'devolved powers'. According to the criteria for the implementation of the new regional networks of social policy and welfare services, local governments are to carry out the bulk of service provision, but the powers of legislation, planning, and co-ordination with the private and altruistic sectors would rest upon regional executives and legislatures.

The Spanish regional laws considered the networks of social services as integrated public systems with unrestricted access to all citizens. Traditional public policy was 'updated' in order to avoid stigmatisation of the beneficiaries. The aim shared by the mesogovernments was one of modernisation of the social services by means of taking into account the needs expressed by users in a more efficient manner, as well as their complaints and 'feedback'. With the purpose of rationalising and adapting the provision of new social services, the idea of the 'welfare mix' was also embraced enthusiastically. The combination of efforts with private and altruistic organisations has proved to be very effective in the implementation of programmes to combat poverty and in the gradual weaving of 'safety nets'. Non-profit and voluntary organisations, in particular, were incorporated in the general provision of social services, and many of them were subsidised by the regional public systems of social services (Moreno and Arriba 1999).

Social policy-making by the Spanish mesogovernments followed EU recommendations, some of which were put into practice by neighbouring France. First implemented in December 1988, the French RMI (*Revenu Minimum d'Insertion*) aimed to establish a linkage between benefit receipt and the objective of insertion of beneficiaries into their communities of residence. Deconcentration of the management of the programme at the regional and local level was implemented. This policy was geared towards adapting the general objective of social insertion to the characteristics and structural constraints of the particular local communities concerned.

In France, as in the case of the Spanish mesogovernments, 'minimum income guaranteed' programmes have been conceptualised as public instruments to 'fill in the gaps' of contributory social security systems. Let us remember that with the growth of unemployment in the 1980s and 1990s, increasing numbers of 'new poor' who had formerly occupied gainful jobs in 'lame-duck' or non-competitive industries, had to face situations in which contributory unemployment benefits ran out. The new social assistance benefits were granted to them not so much due to their status as former employees confronting permanent unemployment, but as citizens entitled to minimum income for purposes of social integration.

In financial terms, the expansion of social assistance programmes has meant an increasing economic burden for local authorities and regions, which runs somewhat contrary to general aspirations of cost containment at national level. In many European countries, central treasuries finance regional budgets via transfers from general taxation by means of 'block grants'. The key aspect to be considered in this respect is whether the final destination of such funds is 'earmarked' or non-categorical. Once again, the case of Spain illustrates potentials for policy innovation and cost reduction when policies of welfare 'safety nets' are a regional responsibility within a general framework of non-discrimination. Spanish mesogovernments have the final budgetary say in the running of *ab novo* programmes, which have been the product of their own political initiative. This usually implies the setting of budgetary priorities within the aggregate of policies and services which are to be complied with statutorily. Certainly, the Basque Country and Navarre with a system of fiscal quasi-independence have been able to fund their programmes of minimum income more generously.[4] Nevertheless, the setting of political priorities in policy funding appears to be the most compelling explanatory element. Mesogovernments have found new arenas for political legitimisation with the autonomous implementation of welfare programmes.

It remains to be seen whether these welfare programmes will continue to be a priority for the Spanish mesogovernments. Up until now the expansion of regional public expenditure has allowed the financing of new 'safety net' policies. The following table shows the territorial re-allocation of public spending in the last twenty years, with an impressive expansion of regional expenditure.

Table 6.2: Territorial distribution of public expenditure in Spain (per cent)

	1981	1984	1987	1990	1992	1997	2000*
Central	87.3	75.6	72.6	66.2	63.0	59.5	54
Regional	3.0	12.2	14.6	20.5	23.2	26.9	33
Local	9.7	12.1	12.8	13.3	13.8	13.6	13

*Government's estimates

Source: Spanish Ministry of Public Administrations (MAP, 1997).

However, the potential role played by European mesogovernments in the redefinition of the 'safety net' implies scenarios of uncertainty. If it is true that they are well placed at an intermediate level to integrate social services and social assistance policies into a common network, the latent risk of exacerbating inter-regional inequalities in welfare provision has to be acknowledged.

---

4 Spanish mesogovernments collect main taxes such as income tax, corporation tax, VAT and (since 1997) 'special taxes' (petrol, tobacco and spirits). Basque and Navarran institutions collect practically all taxes. Subsequently, they transfer a previously agreed quota to the Spanish central treasury. These transfers represent a form of compensation for Spanish general expenditure, and cover the costs of running state administrative bodies which are located in the Basque Country and Navarre.

In explaining the differences in policy outcomes, the variable financial manoeuvrability of the mesogovernments involved is a main explanatory factor to be accounted for. The degree of financial autonomy for the design and implementation of welfare policies highly conditions the capacity of policy innovation. As I have commented on in the case of Spain, the fact that the Basque Government had sufficient resources has been a key factor in the development of the 'minimum income guaranteed' programme since 1989, which provoked a 'domino effect' in the rest of the Spanish regions. The latter did not have the same financial manoeuvrability as the Basque Country. However, not wanting to be left behind they were able to finance their programmes, although some of these have not been as 'generous' as in the Basque and Navarran ones.

This issue can be linked to the discussion of 'welfare tourism', which was initially analysed in the USA. The main argument here revolves around the contention that the poor and excluded would change their residence in order to obtain more generous welfare benefits. This, in turn, would initiate a 'vicious circle' by penalising financially those states and communities which make extra budgetary efforts in favour of more comprehensive and generous welfare programmes. However the argument does not seem to have the same degree of plausibility in Europe, since the level of geographical mobility is much lower than in the USA, and where social bonds, kin and networks of friends have a much greater influence in people's attachment to their territorial contexts. Besides, cultural factors are also crucial aspects which deter 'welfare tourism'. These include not only linguistic barriers and differences in customs and habits, but also the more accessible path towards social integration. In fact, territorial identities at regional and local level can provide better means for insertion for the excluded.

Further arguments supporting local and regional involvement in the 'weaving' of welfare 'safety nets' concern the maximisation of available information for policy-makers, and a better 'tailoring' of insertion programmes in accordance with the needs of local labour markets. Critical commentators draw attention to the fact than an excessive autonomy for the richer regions would be detrimental to the poorer ones. This in turn could widen the gap between more developed and less developed regions, and to fuelling of cross-regional grievances. All things considered, a better access of civil society to political decision-making at the meso-level can be regarded as the means for fortifying accountability in a global order that put at risk the democratic quality of post-industrial societies.

Conclusion: subsidiarity and accountability

The provision of social policies according to the principle of decentralisation opens up new opportunities for policy innovation at the regional level. Mesogovernments, and medium-size states, are no longer dependent on state-centred welfare programmes or supra-national EU intervention provided in a top-down manner.

The implementation of regional systems of social protection and welfare 'safety nets' is in line with the assumption that a more efficient welfare provision is plausible by means of a more effective development of community care services. It appears more suitable for purposes of monitoring means-tested programmes, and for maximising economies of scale. Besides, it provides institutional means for facilitating democratic accountability at both meso and local levels.

Subsidiarity favours the participation of sub-state layers of government in the running of public policies, among which social provision appears to be an obvious priority. At the same time, it encourages intergovernmental co-operation on the assumption that the role of the national states would be less hierarchical than it has been up until now.[5] Territorial identities, as sources of legitimacy, are intertwined in a manner which expresses the degrees of citizens' attachments to the various institutional levels: municipalities, regions, nations, states, and European Union.

Democratic accountability and full involvement of citizens were given priority by Prodi's Commission in a fully-fledged statement at the beginning of the millennium (Commission 2000). However, the ways and means by which the two guiding principles of subsidiarity and accountability are to be put into practice are understood to be on the basis of the delegation and decentralisation of day-to-day executive tasks in any future form of European governance. The difficulties of implementing transnational policies from Brussels, particularly in the area of social policy and welfare development, were implicitly acknowledged in such a statement. Further to this, the agreement taken at the 2000 Nice summit, in order to work out a EU treaty in 2004 based upon a new intergovernmental balance of powers, seems to give support to the quest for more extensive decentralisation.

Efforts of Europeanisation to build up a macro community of trust which would dismantle internal boundaries need to be reoriented towards transferring more responsibilities to intermediate layers of government. Europeanisation would thus develop into a meaningful system by incorporating existing cultural systems and collective identities at both national and sub-national levels. These interact in a differential and contingent manner and should be integrated - rather than assimilated - into a process of convergence. In this way, Europeanisation would avoid being seen as an exogenous process which is superimposed on the internal interaction of communities with long-standing culture and history.

---

5 This would also take full advantage of a period of peace and relatively stable economic growth characterised by the absence of wars between once powerful nation-states. The ever-latent possibility of rivalries between nation-states is nevertheless potentially explosive (Chomsky 1994).

PART II

REFORMS

II. A

REFORMS IN THEORETICAL PERSPECTIVE

Chapter 7

Beyond Retrenchment:
four problems in current welfare state research and one suggestion how to overcome them[1]

Bruno Palier

Introduction

'Welfare states in transition' (Esping-Andersen 1996a), 'Recasting European welfare states' (Ferrera and Rhodes 2000b), 'Welfare state futures' (Leibfried 2000), 'Survival of the European Welfare State' (Kuhnle 2000a) and 'The new politics of the welfare state' (Pierson 2001a) - all of these are among the most important recent publications on the welfare state. Collectively, they indicate that the focus of the academic agenda has moved beyond the crisis of the welfare state and towards an analysis of actual social

1 Earlier versions of this chapter have been presented in the University of Stirling, the University of Tokyo, the Max Planck Intitute in Cologne and to some fellows at Harvard University, Center for European Studies. I wish to thank all the commentators from those venues, and particularly Olli Kangas, Mari Miura, Fritz Scharpf, Peter Hall and Rosemary Taylor for their very useful comments.

Jochen Clasen (ed.), *What Future for Social Security?*, 105-120
©2001 Kluwer Law International. Printed in the Netherlands.

policy changes which have occurred during the last 20 or 25 years. Probably under Anglo-Saxon influence (Reagan and Thatcher pursued explicit anti-welfare agendas) first analyses of these changes have been phrased in terms of retrenchment (after the 'golden age' of growth). They sought to discover how deep and to what extent governments had reduced social expenditure since the late 1970s. After a couple of decades of debates on the crisis of the welfare state, and countless welfare reforms adopted throughout the industrialised world, many commentators agree on the fact that the welfare state is much more solid and robust than what had been assumed and argued in the 1970s. To date, most welfare state analyses have concluded that in the last 25 years there has either been stability, little retrenchment or 'path dependent' changes. Even if expenditure on certain programmes has been partially cut back, recent reforms do not change the nature of post-war welfare states.

The idea of only limited changes is particularly linked to continental 'conservative corporatist' welfare states. More precisely, it has often been argued that these welfare states have hardly changed at all and the changes which were introduced were counterproductive ('adjusting badly', as Manow and Seils 2000, put it). Among the 'frozen' continental European welfare state landscape (Esping-Andersen, 1996c), the French social welfare system in particular has often been regarded as one of the most 'immovable objects' (Pierson 1998:558, note 8). In France, social expenditure continued to increase rapidly throughout the 1980s, but no fundamental reform seems to have been introduced in health services or in old age pension systems. Attempts to introduce reforms have been fiercely opposed by strikes and demonstrations, especially in 1995 (Levy 2000).

However, this gloomy picture must be modified. I have argued that during the last 25 years, French governments have implemented three different kinds of policies aimed at coping with welfare state problems (Palier 2000). During the late 1970s and the 1980s, they have responded to social security deficits by mainly raising up the level of social contributions; policies which only changed the level of the available instruments. In the early 1990s a second type of change appeared with sectorial reforms, such as new medical agreements in health care, a new benefit in unemployment insurance and new modes of calculating retirement pensions. Such policies introduced new instruments but remained within the traditional (historical and institutional) logic of the French welfare system. However, since these two kinds of changes appeared to be insufficient and since the French welfare system itself appeared to exacerbate economic and social problems (unemployment, social exclusion), governments have also decided to act indirectly by tackling the institutional causes of these problems. The French welfare state was felt to be resistant to change to such a degree that governments decided to introduce structural reforms so that the French welfare state would become less of a 'immovable object' (Pierson 1998). These structural reforms, such as new means-tested re-insertion policies (RMI), new financing mechanisms (CSG) and a new role for the state, introduced both new instruments and a new logic of welfare, i.e. structural change which will transform the very nature of the system (Palier 2000).

The thesis of 'eurosclerosis' or the 'path dependent continuity' argument, commonly found in recent welfare state literature, seem to neglect the latter kind of reforms, even though they may lead to profound welfare state changes. The structural reforms adopted by French governments in the early 1990s imply the abandonment of some elements of the French (Bismarckian) tradition and a progressive transformation based on the development of means tested benefits, the growing importance of tax finance and the empowerment of state representatives within the system at the expense of the social partners. Resistance to change may now be progressively overcome, leading to new patterns of social protection in France (Palier 2001). However, it remains true that, until recently, change has been difficult to implement in France, as in other Bismarckian social insurance welfare systems. There should be a specific comparative analysis of why these countries are more difficult to change than others. As far as France is concerned, Giuliano Bonoli and I have shown that some of the peculiarities of the French social policy-making system help to explain why major retrenchment has not occurred. In particular, these are: a highly popular but particularly fragmented social insurance system which is largely financed by social contributions; numerous divided trade unions, which are particularly eager on keeping their position in the system because of their weakness in industrial relations; and a central state which is relatively weak in this field and thus obliged to negotiate with the other social protection actors (Bonoli and Palier 1998, 2000).

There might therefore have to be a twofold agenda in comparative welfare state research. On the one hand, we should be able to identify more changes than are usually recognised. On the other, we should be able to understand why continental welfare states are more resistant to change, or at least change differently, than other welfare states. For this, I suggest that we need to draw on and combine public policy analysis and the role of welfare institutions in order to develop and arrive at a more adequate framework of analysis.

With reference to my previous work (Bonoli and Palier 1998, 2000; Palier, 2000, 2001) and in line with that of others (for instance Visser and Hemerijck, 1997), I would argue that current research on welfare state changes should go beyond the notion of retrenchment so as to be able to embrace the different kinds of developments which have occurred. Recent European welfare state changes should be analysed by differentiating between both different time periods and different types of changes introduced by governments. Some reforms may prove to enforce continuity, some others may prove to introduce a new logic in the welfare system. In contrast to the general notion of retrenchment, reforms do not always imply less welfare state. Inspired by general public policy analysis, in this chapter a specific analytic framework is proposed which emphasises the role of welfare institutions, and distinguishes three types of changes. This framework has been influenced by some dissatisfaction with current research on welfare state changes and in particular with four aspects: the notion of retrenchment, the concept of path dependency, institutionalist approaches of reform and the analysis of change. Taking each of these four issues at a time, I will conclude with putting forward a proposal for an analytic framework to study recent (and future) social policy changes.

Beyond retrenchment

Retrenchment seems to have become one of the most common terms employed to describe recent welfare state developments. The notion lends itself to a stage or functionalist model of analysis of the history of welfare states: emergence (late 19th Century until 1945) is followed by growth (the golden age, mainly until the 1970s), to limits (or even crisis, the 1980s), and then retrenchment (since the late 1980s). The notion of retrenchment harbours the same problems as those of development, modernisation or growth of welfare states. All of these have been criticised for assuming a uniformity of the processes of welfare state development. If all changes which have occurred since the 1980s can be termed retrenchment this would imply shrinking welfare states. Therefore, in this framework, the main question is often to measure how much retrenchment has been applied, with large or small cuts as the dependent variable and a focus on spending. A great deal of academic discussion during the 1990s was aimed at demonstrating that even if expenditure levels were similar, different welfare states spent money differently, under different principles, for different purposes and with different institutions (Esping-Andersen 1990).

These debates should be kept in mind when focusing on recent changes and it should be taken for granted that different welfare states are changing differently. Even if this is increasingly recognised in social policy research (Esping-Andersen 1996a; Scharpf and Schmidt 2000; Pierson 2001a), there is still a need for a systematic cross-national differentiation of processes of retrenchment, as there has been differentiation between welfare states during their 'golden age' (Esping-Andersen 1990).

It might perhaps even be that retrenchment is not a useful term since some changes in some social protection systems might not be bringing about less generous benefits. As the trente glorieuses could not be analysed merely in terms of more welfare state, current developments are more complex than simply representing less welfare state. Firstly, data show that most of the OECD countries have increased their social spending over the last two decades. In the early 1990s Pierson (1994) argued that, if anything, overall welfare spending had gone up during the years he had studied and concluded that retrenchment efforts had failed. I would propose another point of view. In recognition of new problems which welfare states were confronting, some governments were, or were at least proposing to, spend more rather than less. This, at least, applies to many Bismarckian countries in the late 1970s and during the 1980s (Palier 2000; Manow and Seils 2000).[2]

Secondly, for governments the question may not be a quantitative (of more or less spending) but a structural one: how can welfare states be transformed in order to promote new principles and to develop new institutions which are more adapted to the

---

2 'The 1980's were not a time of simple retrenchment. Under conditions where neither federal nor state government was obliged to pay the welfare bill, the door was open for increased benefits or expanded entitlements' (Manow and Seils 2000: 279).

current situation? In this case, the measurement of change should not be quantitative (in terms of expenditure, benefit levels, scope of coverage, etc.) but should provide an assessment of the degree of innovation introduced by changes. Typical questions would be whether reforms introduced new institutions or a new logic or led to the involvement of new actors? However, recent analyses usually focus more on continuity than on change.

Path dependency and continuity

Comparing Reagan and Thatcher's reform ambitions with actual outcomes Pierson (1994) emphasised the stability of (American and British) welfare arrangements. He explained this resistance to change by the force of past commitments, the political weight of welfare constituencies and the inertia of institutional arrangements which all engender a phenomenon of path dependency. Thus, 'any attempt to understand the politics of welfare state retrenchment must start from a recognition that social policy remains the most resilient component of the post-war order' (Pierson, 1994:5). Broadening the scope to other developed countries in order to analyse 'national adaptation in global economies', Gøsta Esping-Andersen (1996b) came to a similar conclusion, depicting a general 'frozen landscape' and emphasising the rigidity of continental welfare state arrangements. He concluded that 'the cards are very much stacked in favour of the welfare state status quo' (ibid.:267). While the conclusion was that, once again, no dramatic changes could be (fore)seen, analyses of developments within different welfare regimes allowed the deconstruction of the general notion of retrenchment into different processes which are linked to specific institutions within each welfare system.

Nevertheless, among others, John Myles and Gill Quadagno (1997) demonstrated subsequently that things were not that fixed. Some changes could be identified, specifically in pension reforms. To put their argument in a caricatured nutshell, retrenchment means targeting for universal benefits, reinforcing selectivity and adding conditions to already targeted benefits, and tightening the links between contribution and benefits (and going from defined benefit to defined contribution) (Myles and Quadagno, 1997:247-272). Pierson and Myles have recently argued that these changes were always path dependent, demonstrating more continuity than radical changes. While pension reforms often reduce the level of benefits, all are framed by past commitments and specific institutional arrangements. They operate differently and each perpetuates (and sometimes even reinforces) the historical logic in which the pension system has developed (Myles and Pierson 2001).

Recently, several studies have broadened the scope of comparison beyond pension reforms, pointing out that there are different processes of welfare state adaptation (Scharpf and Schmidt 2000; Pierson 2001a). Through their empirical evidence, these comparative analyses of changes seem to confirm the notion of 'three worlds of welfare capitalism' (Esping-Andersen, 1990). In the context of the historical and institutional constraints it seems that there re three paths for welfare state changes. Scharpf and

Schmidt (2000) convincingly show that the three worlds do not have the same kind of vulnerabilities in the face of the new global and European environment. Examining the implementation of several policies, Pierson proposes that in each world a specific type of reform is predominantly pursued: commodification in the liberal welfare states, cutbacks in the Nordic countries and re-calibration of the Continental systems (Pierson 2001b).

Very convincingly these analyses provide us with a much better understanding of what is going on than others which simply focus on curtailments. They demonstrate that there are (broadly three) different ways of reforming welfare states and that differences between the welfare regimes explain difference in reforms implemented. However, they still frame their approach in terms of retrenchment or adaptation, as if there has been, within a single country, only one single trend of reform over the last 25 years. Clearly, as Visser and Hemerijck (1997) claimed for the Netherlands, there is a need to differentiate between different kinds of reforms within the same country (or welfare regime). Governments have not always implemented the same recipes. They did not display the same behaviour in the late 1970s as during the 1980s or during the 1990s. There is a need for an analytical framework for studying reforms which allows a differentiation between countries, but, in accordance with the type or period of reform, also within countries.

Usually, recent comparative studies have concluded that reforms had a limited impact on the structure of the different welfare states, not threatening but preserving the very nature of each system. In fact, reforms are seen as merely reinforcing the logic of each welfare system. Due to the different processes of marketisation of their social policies liberal welfare states have become even more residual and liberal. The social democratic welfare states, thanks to an egalitarian distribution of cuts (around 10 per cent across all benefits) and a rediscovery of the workline, have returned to their traditional road to welfare (Kuhnle 2000b). Also most of the continental welfare states have remained the same, not only because reforms have reinforced their characteristics but also because of an apparent inability to implement any susbtantial reform (giving rise to terms such as 'eurosclerosis or 'frozen fordism'). In short, it seems that fundamental structures of welfare states have remained to a large extent unaltered. The (neo-institutionalist) path dependence approach often leads to the conclusions of prevailing continuity.

The role of welfare institutions : from independent to dependent variables

In order to explain the kind of continuity revealed by recent research, the impact of institutions is regularly referred to. The emphasis has mainly been put on the variables of general political systems, including constitutional rules, party systems, veto points or players and state structures (unitary versus federal, single actor versus multiple actor systems, strong versus weak, etc.). However, the role of welfare state institutions themselves is rarely analysed in any systematic fashion. It might be argued that welfare institutions play a major role in shaping the problems which welfare states face, but they also partly determine the kind of resources which different actors can mobilise, and shape the kind of solutions adopted to face the problems. By welfare institutions, I refer here to institutionalised rules of social policy legacy.

Explaining continuity: the role of welfare institutions

During the last ten years, research has been emphasising the importance of institutions in understanding the differences in timing in the development of the welfare states, as well as differences in the content of social policies. In order to account for these differences, it is necessary to refer to the general political institution of each country (Bonoli 2001) as well as to the political orientation of governments (Levy 1999; Ross 2000, Huber and Stephens, 2001). With Giuliano Bonoli, I have previously argued that there is a need for more attention to be paid to the institutional dimension of the social protection system itself in order to understand differences in timing and in the content of recent reforms (Bonoli and Palier 2000).

Drawing on Ferrera (1996c:59) in a previous contribution we identified four institutional variables which are helpful in describing social protection systems (Bonoli and Palier, 1998). Accordingly, a welfare state scheme may be characterised by four institutional variables:

Mode of access to benefits; for example citizenship, need, work, the payment of contributions, or a private contract.

Benefit structure; benefits can be service-based or in cash. Cash benefits may be means-tested, flat-rate, earnings-related, or contribution-related.

Financing mechanisms; this can range from general taxation, to employment-related contributions or premiums.

Actors who manage the system; these are those who take part in the management of the system and might include state administration (central and local), social partners (representatives of employers and employees) and the private sector.

These welfare institutions shape the politics of the reform. Institutional factors structure debates, political preferences and policy choices. They affect the positions of the various actors and groups involved. They frame the kind of interests and resources which actors can mobilise in favour or against welfare reforms. In part they also determine who is and who is not participating in the political game which leads to reforms. Depending on how these different variables are set different patterns of support and opposition can be encountered. In general, one may expect these variables to influence the politics of social programmes in the following ways:

Mode of access; as it delimits the beneficiaries and thus the likely supporters of a scheme this factor is crucial for shaping the politics of a given social programme. The mode of access also relates to the objectives of a programme, i.e. income maintenance, poverty alleviation or equality. As a result, support for a scheme might come from groups with an ideological orientation congenial to one of these objectives. Generally, left-wing parties have tended towards equality, Christian-Democrats have supported income maintenance and liberal parties have been keener to alleviate poverty (Esping-Andersen 1990:53)

Benefit structure; to some extent this variable is related to the previous one, as typically earnings-related benefits are granted on a contributory basis while universal transfers are flat-rate. The nature and the generosity of benefits is also determining the kind of support they will receive. Targeted or (low) flat-rate benefit are less likely to be supported by middle and upper classes than earnings-related benefits. Moreover, the higher someone's income, the less flat-rate benefits will contribute to his or her living-standard. Politically, a flat-rate benefit structure - combined with a low level - might be related to lack of programme support from the middle and upper classes. As earnings inequality increases in many industrial countries, it will become ever more difficult to set a flat-rate benefit which is at the same time affordable and significant for a majority of the population. Targeted benefits are supported mainly for philanthropical reasons or fear, rather than based on material interest, and are thus more readily subjected to criticism. The political support of the benefits is the reverse image of their financial cost. As a consequence, it is more feasible to reduce flat-rate or means tested benefits than earnings-related ones.

Financing mechanisms; while related to the two previous factors, this variable has some significance in its own right. If the mode of access delineates the beneficiaries of a programme, the financing mechanism determines who is paying for it. The political support for a financing mechanism is likely to be stronger if those who pay for a programme are also those who receive the benefit. The looser the link between benefit and payment, the less legitimate the financing mechanism becomes. As a result, there is a crucial difference between tax- and contribution-financed schemes in their ability to attract public support. Whereas taxation goes to the state, social contributions are perceived as a 'differed wage' which will return to the insured person at times of sickness, unemployment or retirement. Paying health insurance contributions for instance, 'buys' a right to health care which guarantees protection during periods of sickness. From a political point of view contributions are raised much more easily than taxes, especially income taxes.

Actors who manage the system; this dimension determines the accountability and legitimacy of different actors. The more the state controls a system and its generosity, the more the political class is likely to be held responsible for any changes. When benefits are increased, the government is credited; when benefits are reduced it will be blamed (Pierson 1996). When management is shared with trade unions and employers, responsibility tends to be diluted, thus diminishing the state capacity to control the development of the social protection system, and particularly levels of expenditure. This variable also determines the range of actors which are regarded as legitimately participating in welfare reform debates. In a state controlled system the debate is confined to political parties. When the management is handed to the social partners, their participation in the debate is legitimised. In the latter case trade unions are also seen as important actors in social policy-making, and widely regarded as defending the current system against retrenching governments. This institutional setting gives rise to tensions over controlling social security between governments on the one hand - often regardless of political persuasion - and trade unions on the other. Union involvement in the management of social security grants unions a de facto veto power against welfare state reforms (Bonoli and Palier 1996).

From independent to dependent variable

References to welfare state institutions contribute significantly to the understanding of details regarding both mechanisms of path dependency and differences between welfare regime changes. The institutional shape of the existing social policy landscape poses a significant constraint on the degree and the direction of change. For instance, a comparison between the UK and France, countries with extremely different social policy legacies, show two particular institutional effects. Schemes which mainly redistribute horizontally and protect middle classes well are likely to be more resistant against cuts. Their support base is larger and more influential compared with schemes which are targeted on the poor or are so parsimonious as to be insignificant for most of the electorate. The contrast between the overall resistance of French social insurance against cuts and the withering away of its British counterpart is telling. Also, the involvement of the social partners, and particularly of the labour movement in managing the schemes, seems to provide an obstacle for government sponsored retrenchment exercises (Bonoli and Palier 2000).

However, not only social scientists acknowledge the role institutions play in shaping, and sometimes preventing, change. Through learning processes, experts and politicians also recognise this effect - and sometimes therefore decide to change the institutions and thus alter the political game which is blocking reform projects. Two particular institutional features which prevent welfare state are contribution financing and the involvement of social partners in the management of social security (two characteristics of the Bismarckian welfare systems, widely regarded as the most 'frozen' systems). Some recent reforms, mainly in Bismarckian countries, have been aimed at modifying these institutional arrangements (financing and the management of social security). This is certainly the case in France (Palier 2000, 2001), but one could also mention reforms introduced in other Bismarckian countries (for example, the introduction of a 'green tax' in Germany to replace some social contribution funding, or the introduction of private employment services in the Netherlands). These developments are not aimed at benefit levels or access and thus cannot be considered as retrenchment (nor as improvement of the generosity of the benefits). Yet they may prove to be extremely important reforms since they could introduce changes in the very nature of national welfare state systems as well as in their politics. Thus, what is needed is a framework of analysis which helps to distinguish, identify and assess these kinds of changes.

Differentiating between social policy changes

Welfare state analyses which focus on the evolution of social policy, or processes of adaptation tend to forget the kind of reforms referred to above. Emphasising the inertia of institutions, they tend to ignore the structural impact which public policies can have. While integrating phenomena of path dependency in welfare state analysis is essential, this should not prevent us examining the impact of such reforms on social policy. In other words, recent developments within the social protection systems are not only due to their own evolutionary dynamic, but also to the implementation of public policies. Incorporating public policy aspects of change into the study of the ways in which social protection systems adapt requires using the tools of public policy analysis, and particularly of Peter Hall's approach to change[3]

Social policy as public policy

Peter Hall (1993:278) proposes that we 'can think of policymaking as a process that usually involves three central variables: the overarching goals that guide policy in a particular field, the techniques or policy instruments used to attain those goals, and the precise settings of these instruments…'. According to this approach, it is possible to recast our understanding of welfare regimes in terms of public policies. The instruments of social policy are mainly the four institutional variables mentioned above (the mode of access, the benefit structure, financing mechanisms and management arrangements).

The 'overarching goals' can be related to the three different political logics which are associated with three welfare state regimes (Esping-Andersen 1990); the centrality of the market in the allocation of resources and residuality of state intervention in the liberal regime; the centrality of equality, citizenship and 'harmonisation' of the population in the social-democratic welfare regime; and the centrality of work, status and occupational identity in conservative-corporatist social insurance systems.

If the above regimes are interpreted as ideal-types rather than precise descriptions of specific realities, three major combinations of these principles, logics and institutional instruments can be derived from the classic typology. These three combinations can be seen as three different repertoires of social policies which are more or less salient in any one specific social protection system. Table 7.1 (at the end of this chapter) summarises their main characteristics.

While these kinds of categories cannot pretend to describe the reality of any specific social protection system either in its entirety or in detail (because no social protection system would be this consistent, and all combine different logics and instruments to

---

3 An increasing number of scholars are using this framework of analysis for understanding social policy reforms (see for instance Visser and Hemerijck, 1997 or Hinrichs in this volume).

some extent), they are nevertheless useful for the comparative analysis of a specific programme. Each social protection programme is close to one of three goals and presents a specific setting of the four institutional dimensions. Therefore, these categories represent indicators against which changes can be located. By identifying the specific characteristics of a programme (i.e. its goal and the specific combination of the four institutional variables) before and after a reform, objective criteria for assessing changes will have been established. For example, did the reform only lower benefit levels, or did it introduce new modes of access or new rules of calculation - or did the reform set new goals? In other words, it is possible to assess whether a reform did change one or several of the institutional dimensions, and whether it implied a change in the goals.

Instrumental, parametric, or paradigmatic changes: three orders of policy changes

Elaborating his framework for analysing macro-economic policy changes, Peter Hall (1993) distinguished three different types of changes.

> 'We can identify three distinct kinds of changes in policy... First, [a change of] the levels (or settings) of the basic instruments. We can call the process whereby instrument settings are changed in the light of experience and new knowledge, while the overall goals and instruments of policy remain the same, a process of first order change in policy... When the instruments of policy as well as their settings are altered in response to past experience even though the overall goals of policy remain the same, [changes] might be said to reflect a process of second order change... Simultaneous changes in all three components of policy: the instrument settings, the instruments themselves, and the hierarchy of goals behind policy... occur rarely, but when they do occur as a result of reflection on past experience, we can describe them as instances of third order change' (Hall 1993:278-279).

This approach helps to differentiate between impacts a reform will have, depending on whether or not it changes the instruments and the overall logic. It provides a grid for assessing the type of change beyond a pure quantitative approach (more or less retrenchment) and a means for judging the degree of innovation introduced by a specific reform. A first order change will not imply profound changes as far as a historical path is concerned. It just implies a change in the instrument settings (such as raising the level of social contributions or lowering benefit levels) without implying a change in the general principles and logic. This type of change might be called instrumental change. Second order changes, often referred to as 'parametric changes' in the pension literature, involve the introduction of new instruments (i.e. the introduction of new calculation rules or new entitlement rules). These types of change appear to be path dependent, as Myles and others have shown for pensions. They may lead to substantial changes once they have been in place and developed over time.[4] However, more directly, some reforms may involve a change both of the instruments and of the goals (such as changes in the financing mechanisms or in the organisation of the management of the system), and thus represent what Hall has termed 'paradigmatic changes'.

Policy learning: the role of ideas

In addition to identifying different types of change, the aim is also to explain under which condition and how changes occur. Peter Hall's approach is based on processes of policy learning. First order changes can be understood as the first response which governments may adopt when faced with a difficulty which at this stage is not perceived as a new problem. By only changing the settings of the usual instruments, 'old recipes' are resorted to, repeating what governments are used to doing. Hall points out that as a response to the first oil shock in the early 1970s British governments applied 'traditional' Keynesian policies with the aim of boosting demand. Similarly, I have shown that the French government after the mid 1970s merely did what they had done before, i.e. raising social contribution rates in order to finance the growth of social expenditure, rather than reducing social expenditure (Palier, 2000).

However, when something is progressively perceived as a new context, old recipes produce unintended effects or 'anomalies'. Advised by different kinds of experts (among them, at times, social policy comparativists) governments become convinced that they need to abandon the previous, and now perceived to be the wrong, ways of doing things, and innovate. Two different paths seem available: the introduction of an innovation which is aimed at preserving the given logic of a system (for example, the so-called 'consolidation' reforms implemented in Germany at the end of the 1980s and during the early 1990s, or the French sectoral reforms (see Palier 2000:122-126), or a more substantial change of some of the rules of the game, as well as its goals.

An important process here is a change in peoples' perception of problems and solutions. I have shown that an explanation of the implementation of structural changes in France requires one to take account of different intellectual processes. First the idea occurred that former recipes were not adequate any longer (such as Keynesian use of social spending). Second, existing social and economic difficulties had been re-interpreted. In the new explanation which emerged in the late 1980s, the position of the social insurance system shifted from that of victim to being the cause of the problem.[5] Third, a

---

4 Myles and Quadagno (1997) illustrate this. Within pension systems, a transition from a defined benefit to a defined contribution scheme implies a change in the mode of pension benefit from deferred wages to savings, for instance.

5 The social insurance system became accused of partly causing some economic, social and political problems through three broad mechanisms: the weight of social contributions preventing job creation; the contributory nature of most social benefits reinforcing social exclusion and the

large majority of the actors concerned about social protection problems agreed with the new measures bringing about structural changes. However, the precise analysis of the different positions which actors adopted towards the new measures shows that the reasons which made them agree with those measures were very different, and sometimes even contradictory. Indeed, an important element for the acceptance of a new measure seems to be its capacity to aggregate different – and even contradictory - interests, based on different, and sometimes contrasting, interpretations. Structural changes are achieved through ambiguous measures rather than via a clear ideological orientation. Finally, such changes have been introduced gradually but progressively. Fairly marginal at first, they will play a major role within the core of the social protection system to come (Palier 2001).

Conclusion

Analysing all recent reforms of the social protection systems as forms of retrenchment, as has often been the case, represents a linear reductionist, developmental and purely quantitative view of what is going on. Instead, it is imperative to differentiate between different reform modalities or paths with the help of qualitative analysis. When differentiating between several (usually three) paths of reform, conclusions are often reached that processes are path dependent, but also that outcomes are marked by continuity: after 10 to 20 years of reform, that different welfare states have apparently remained all but untouched in terms of their own logic and main features. The, often seen as inevitable, link between path dependency and continuity needs to be questioned (see also the following chapter by Goul Andersen in this volume). Continuities are usually explained by references to the impact of institutions. However, while institutions shape the particular context in which problems, interests and solutions are framed, apart from the role played by political institutions, those of the welfare state created by social policy legacies (both as independent and dependent variables) need to be acknowledged more. Emphasising continuity rarely takes account of public policies which can have an important impact on welfare state structures. Finally, there is a need for a better differentiation between types of reforms: some are reinforcing the pattern of a particular system, others are introducing structural change. In order to identify the different kinds of reforms, one has to assess whether the latter merely imply a change in the settings of given instruments, a change of instruments, or a change in both the instruments and in the goals.

With these analytical tools, we will be able to identify more adequately social policy changes which occurred in the recent past and will continue to occur. The analytical framework put forward here confirms that Continental welfare states are more difficult to reform than others. Reference to the impact of welfare states institutions help to understand why this is the case. For example, contributory benefits enjoy a particularly

---

joint-management of the system by social partners engendering irresponsibility and a management crisis of the system.

high level of legitimacy and are therefore difficult to cut back radically. Transfers are 'paid' by social contributions, workers assume that they have 'bought' social rights, and benefits are usually generous. In this sense their loss would be more significant than the reduction of a benefit which is already at a low level. Finally, insurance-based transfers are well defended by organised interest, and in particular by trade unions of different branches corresponding to the different professional schemes.

However, this framework of analysis also helps to realise that structural, paradigmatic changes have occurred, and particularly in Bismarckian countries. In order to cope with structural problems (regarding benefit financing, entitlements and capacities to change), these countries have created new benefit programmes according to new logics (means-tested benefits, private funded schemes in pension and health systems), they have developed new modes of financing, partly replacing social contributions, and are implementing new management arrangements (privatisation of some administrative tasks, empowerment of the state at the expense of the social partners). These changes are the result of a process of policy learning. They have been (or will be) implemented very gradually. Probably because of their marginal scope and because of the fact that they do not directly affect the level of expenditure, few analyses have concentrated on these changes. However, the increasingly visible impacts of these structural reforms indicate a need for a change in the analytical framework. Social science should not be more resistant to change their paradigms than, arguably, welfare states themselves!

Table 7.1: Three repertoires of social policy

Three Different Logics			
According to Titmuss According to Esping-Andersen	Industrial-achievement Conservative-corporatist	Residual Liberal	Institutional-redistributive Social-democratic
Geographic situation Historical reference	Continental Bismarck	Anglo-Saxon Beveridge	Scandinavian Beveridge
Aims	Workers' income maintenance	poverty and unemployment alleviation	Equality, income for all, egalitarian redistribution
Functioning Principle	Contributivity	Selectivity	Universality
Technique	Social insurance	Targeting	Redistribution
Four different types of instruments			
Mode of access	Status, Work	Need, Poverty	Citizenship, Residence
Benefit structure	Proportional (contribution related, earnings-related)	Means-tested	Flat-rate
Financing mechanisms	Employment-related contribution	Taxation	Taxation
Management, control, decision	social partners	Central State	State, Local government

Chapter 8

Change without Challenge?
Welfare states, social construction of challenge and dynamics of path dependency

Jørgen Goul Andersen

Introduction

Current explanations of welfare state change and stability may be summarised in three very broad categories (which are not mutually exclusive): (1) *interest* explanations which have in particular stressed class mobilization (Esping-Andersen and Korpi 1984, 1986) and class alliances (Esping-Andersen 1990); (2) *economic* explanations which stress the economic crisis or challenges to the welfare state (e.g. Lindbeck 1994; Pierson 1998); and (3) *institutional* explanations which stress path dependency and the legacy of past decisions.[1] Very broadly, one could say that interest explanations have mainly been put forward to

---

1 This is close to the well-known distinction between political, functional and institutional explanations of change (van Kersbergen 1995: 6-30; Goul Andersen 1998). However, functional theories not only include economic theories but also theories about integrative or cohesive functions of the welfare state, while economic explanations are not by definition functionalist.

explain the historical expansion of the welfare state; economic explanations mainly serve to explain retrenchment and restructuring; and institutional theory is used to explain the inertia of the welfare state.

Around the Millennium, welfare state theory has tended to give particular emphasis to economic challenges. This is not very surprising: the welfare states of Europe faced much economic hardship during the 1990s, and according to many economic analyses, future challenges will be even greater, due to ageing populations and problems of competitiveness of European welfare states in a globalised economy. Whereas a key question about the future of the welfare state a couple of decades ago was how it could improve equality, the key question now rather is whether it is robust enough to meet the economic challenges of the future.

Along with economic challenges, current research has focussed much on resistance to change (institutional as well as attitudinal), and on how such resistance can be overcome by a number of techniques of retrenchment (Pierson 1994). Although current research increasingly acknowledges welfare states' 'declining resistance to change' (van Kersbergen 2000), institutional perspectives and in particular the notion of path dependency have mainly been put forward to account for the relative inertia of welfare states.[2]

The point of departure for this chapter is that something must be missing. The current mix of approaches, in particular the emphasis on economic challenges, seems to have difficulties in explaining why some of the welfare states which have undergone the most far-reaching changes are those where economic challenges appear to have been rather modest. Briefly, current research often seems to over-emphasise economic challenges and under-emphasise the importance of *agency*, that is, the interests, and in particular the formation of ideas, perceptions, and preferences among decision-makers (Scharpf 2000). Next, current research often seems to equate institutionalism and path dependency with a notion of inertia that is not necessarily implied by this approach. Below, I shall argue for a more *constructivist* approach to the 'challenges' facing contemporary welfare states, for more emphasis on agency, and for a more dynamic approach to path dependencies. This approach also questions the widespread premise that welfare retrenchment should be explained in quite different terms than welfare expansion (Pierson 1994).

Our empirical illustrations below are mainly drawn from Denmark. Although in some respects atypical (there are few 'veto points' if a majority coalition can be established in Parliament)[3], this case provides some very good illustrations of the problems involved in

---

2 Some applications of path dependency are becoming more dynamic. For example, Palier (2000) links the concept of path dependency to Hall's (1993) distinction between changes of the first, second and third order, i.e. change of levels, change of instruments and overall change of perceptions, logics and goals (in short: paradigms). He suggests reserving the label 'path dependency' for changes at the second order which may at times be quite far-reaching.

3 Obstacles for change undoubtedly remain stronger in Bismarckian welfare states, especially if they are federal countries, than in Denmark with a strong government control over the welfare state and weak minority (coalition) governments building on ad hoc coalitions in Parliament (see Bonoli and

an approach based on the two components of 'challenges' and 'institutional inertia'. In the 1980s when the Danish welfare state faced severe 'challenges' or even a structural crisis, nothing really happened to the welfare state, at least in qualitative terms. By contrast, during the 1990s when economic prosperity facilitated high growth rates in public consumption, one may almost speak of a 'silent revolution' within the welfare state. It is still unclear whether reforms introduced should be considered a matter of degree or represent a fundamental change in kind. Certainly, many observers, and politicians, would emphasise stability rather than change. But even though changes may be small from a perspective of short-term outcomes, quite a few changes of principles have taken place which may have potentially far-reaching implications. Such ambiguities seem rather widespread across welfare states at present. As the economic situation in Europe is improving, the Danish situation of relatively weak links between challenges and change may become more typical.

Economic challenges or economic philosophies?

Before the first oil crisis, theories about the relationship between the welfare state and the economy were typically functionalist, emphasising the positive, indeed 'necessary' functions for society performed by the welfare state.[4] The model of a welfare state adapting to external change applies to economic welfare theory in the 1950s and 1960s as well as to economically oriented Marxist theories in the early 1970s, notably 'capital logic' which 'translated' concepts such as collective goods and externalities into a Marxist language (for an overview, see Jessop 1982). In the mid-1970s, the picture changed. 'The crisis of the welfare state' - be it 'fiscal crisis', 'demand overload', 'ungovernability', 'legitimacy crisis' or even 'bankruptcy' (which in a sense summarised all the above) - became a fixed reference point for scholarly discussion about the welfare state (for an overview, see Birch 1984). In the 1980s such notions about the (*endogenous*) politically and economically self-destructive forces of the welfare state gradually disappeared. They were replaced by economists' increasing concern for the negative impact of welfare arrangements on market flexibility and efficiency (Sandmo 1991), and by other social scientists turning their interest to the institutional legacies and the institutional variations of welfare states, not least the discussion about welfare state regimes (Flora 1986; Esping-Andersen 1990).

During the 1990s, the notion of crisis reappeared in another language. Many, if not most, discussions about the future of the welfare state came to take their point of departure in the common 'challenges' facing contemporary welfare states. This also includes non-economic factors such as what might be labelled the challenge of 'post-modernity' (individualisation, changing family structures, etc.). But the most important challenges referred to include

Palier 2000).

4 Another branch of functionalist theories (including Marxism) stressed the socially integrative or cohesive functions of the welfare state. The functionalist roots of comparative welfare state research is explicit in Wilensky (1975) which is sometimes considered as the origin of this tradition.

economic impacts of demographic ageing, and of globalisation and competitiveness in a 'new knowledge-driven economy'.[5] This conception of challenges is one of an 'old system in a new world' (Ploug and Kvist 1994:11) or 'institutional maladjustment between a set of old policy solutions ..... and a set of new societal problems' (Ferrera and Rhodes 2000b:260), i.e. the welfare state is faced with new *exogenous* forces from changing demographic and economic surroundings (Figure 8.1). To this perspective which owes much to functionalism, an institutional perspective is usually added. All welfare states are faced by similar challenges, but depending on their institutional set up, they are affected somewhat differently, have different capacities to overcome the challenges, and choose different paths to react (Scharpf and Schmidt 2000).

The question is how appropriate this approach is, at least if it stands alone. It is of course important to draw attention to the relationship between the welfare state and the economy. But depending on how this is done there are particularly two sets of dangers. First, it may too easily import the implicit functionalism that characterises much economic thinking about the welfare state, and it may sometimes involve taking contested or uncertain economic diagnoses too much for granted, such as the consequences of ageing and of globalisation. Second, and most importantly, the approach tends to draw attention away from the changing definitions or the social construction of economic problems, and also from actors who bring about change[6]. Thus the welfare state becomes a 'black box'. What we need is to open this black box by means of some of the tools from policy analysis which help investigate the social construction of 'problems', and the interplay between actors' interests and ideas, 'problems', and institutions (Clasen 2000; Scharpf 2000).

We can illustrate this argument by means of two figures. Figure 8.1 shows what might be labelled 'modern functionalism' which couples functionalism with institutional diversity. Welfare states face external pressures and have to adapt. This often happens reluctantly, and usually in accordance with their institutional history. Welfare state theory can classify such adaptations into major paths. Even though it may be acknowledged that politics plays a role, the focus is clearly on challenges and adaptation (which means that external pressures are reduced). This approach has indeed some advantages and should not simply be abandoned.

---

5 Sometimes 'economic challenges' also refer to anti-inflationary goals of the Economic and Monetary Union which we shall leave aside here.

6 Besides, it may identify the 'wrong' economic problems. Most importantly, it detracts attention from the *endogenous* economic challenge of *controlling public budgets*. A very large public sector, in particular a large public service sector, does not mean 'ungovernability' or 'demand overload' as claimed a couple of decades ago. But it certainly exerts great pressures, and it is an enormous challenge in terms of having to prioritise between demands that always have and always will exceed economic capacities, and, secondly, to ensure 'value for money' as it is a common observation that the association between input in terms of budgets and outcomes/effects is not always very obvious. Health care expenditure is a well-known case in point. With a public economy that comes close to 50 per cent of GDP, these challenges have become really enormous. This is recognised far too little in comparative welfare state research (Goul Andersen and Christiansen 1991).

However, it may also harbour a bias towards accepting too readily prevailing problem definitions, conceptualising politics as rational problem-solving, perceiving the nature of problems as the only source of uniformity across countries, seeing the changes as inevitable, and underestimating the potentials for change or diversity.

This becomes clear when we contrast this model with what could be labelled a simple 'constructivist' model which concentrates more on the political processes involved (Figure 8.2). This involves basically three processes: interpretations/problem definition, dissemination of ideas, and reception of ideas by decision makers.[7] To begin with interpretations, problems do not really become problems before somebody defines them as such. The question then is how such problem definitions emerge, and who has the power to define problems such as the 'ageing population', or 'inflexible labour markets' in the face of 'globalisation'. Of course, these are rarely invented out of nothing; there are real problems 'out there'. But the way in which problems and problem definition correspond, and the relative emphasis put on some problems and not on others, is not always that evident. Neither is there free and equal access to defining society's problems. Therefore, a core research interest should be who defines problems and in which way. What is the role played, for example, by government bureaucracies, or by inter-governmental organisations such as the OECD, which (without any formal competence) skilfully combines economic expertise, networking and backing by political power? Such issues should be addressed more critically than is often done.

The next stage would be the selection and dissemination of ideas. Again, we know relatively little about the 'who' and 'how'. For example, how do ideas flow within governments; or from experts or intergovernmental organisations to national governments? Why are ideas often so symbolically loaded, not only when they are adopted by politicians but also often when recommended by experts. Examples include notions of 'passive versus active' support for unemployed people; the 'burden of support' for the elderly, 'the demographic time bomb' or the 'ageing crisis'. As to the relationship between problems and solutions, in politics it is in a sense perfectly commonplace that 'solutions' (that is, political ideologies) often seek 'problems' to link up with (see also Kingdon 1995). To which extent is this also the case when it comes to welfare state change?

---

7 For clarification, this is not intended to represent a model of the complete decision making process. The latter would have to include processes of policy implementation, which can at times reveal that formal changes are without effect, or that quite fundamental change has taken place without any formal change of rules (see also chapter 13 by Wright in this volume). For instance, most countries tightened conditions for receiving unemployment benefits in the 1990s (Kalish et al. 1998), not least the 'works test'. But what this meant in actual practice has often remained uncertain.

Figure 8.1: A 'functionalist' model of challenges to the welfare state and policy change.

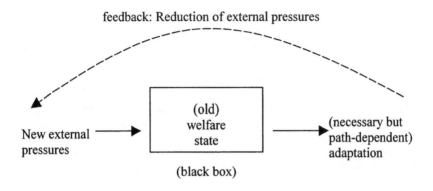

Finally, there is the question about the reception of ideas (problems and solutions) on the part of political decision makers who already have interests and ideas of their own. It may be suggested that political decision makers, apart from being straightforwardly persuaded, are likely to select among the problem definitions those which are compatible with their interests, and between the solutions those which serve their (often tactical) interests.[8] Briefly, there is a case for 'bringing politics back' into analyses of welfare state change (Ross 2000), while recognising that politics is as much about problem solving, ideas and tactical interests, as it is about representation of group interests; and that it is as much about problem definition and agenda setting, as it is about formal decision-making.

It may be argued that this line of reasoning only serves to complicate things, to replace theory for 'storytelling' and to reproduce a chaotic situation rather than aiming to identify and systematically examine broad lines of policy change. This criticism is certainly relevant, and it is not argued here that one type of analysis should be replaced by another. But it must be emphasised that crucial sources of change can only be grasped through analyses of decision-making processes.

---

8 An interesting further question is to what extent political decision makers pay attention to long-term consequences or focus mainly on short-term (e.g., electoral, or distributional) aspects (see also the latter part of Hinrich's chapter in this volume).

Figure 8.2: A 'constructivist' model of changes in welfare policies.

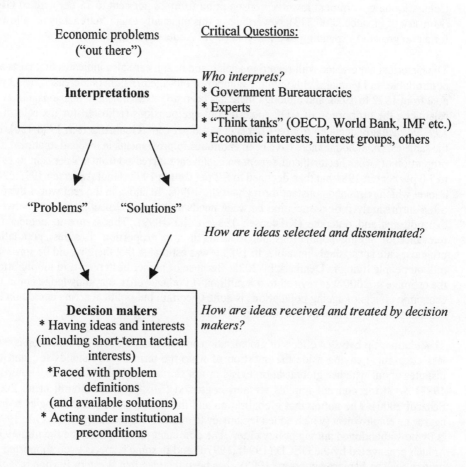

To illustrate the importance of problem definition and to underline why it is not always obvious what constitutes the important 'challenges', two Danish examples will be referred to here: the challenge of ageing and the challenge of globalisation. As to the former, it is of course true that ageing constitutes a challenge. However, focussing too much on 'needs' arising from demographic change may bring the issue out of proportion, while directing attention away from the perhaps more serious challenge of controlling large-scale public budgets. In Denmark, the cost of ageing populations, including elderly care, is typically estimated to amount to 3-6 per cent of GDP over 30-35 years (e.g. Welfare Commission 1995; Ministry of Finance 1996, 1999:104-121; Ministry of Finance 2000:313; but for a contrast see also Economic Council 1998:145). To put this in the context of public budgets, we may note that the additional costs of ageing is roughly equal to half of the Danish public debt interest payments in the mid-1980s, or to the growth in the public economy between 1980 and 1982 (plus 4.6 per cent of GDP) when the economic crisis was exacerbated by a very weak steering of public budgets. To apply yet another comparison, between 1982 and 1990, i.e. the period which comes most closely to qualify as a period of retrenchment in Denmark, the government lowered consumption from 28 per cent to 25 per cent of GDP (Ministry of Finance 2000:313). Nevertheless, this unusually tough 'retrenchment' allowed for a real growth in spending of 5 per cent (Goul Andersen 2000a:71).

The historical experience with regard to ageing and health care also indicates that costs are controllable. In Denmark, although the number of old-age pensioners increased by 33 per cent from 1972 to 1998, and although there has been no retrenchment in pensions, not even relatively, the proportion of GDP spent on old-age pensions (adjusted for tax reform in 1993/94) actually declined from 5.1 per cent to 4.6 per cent (Goul Andersen 1998:130). By the same token, although there have been enormous improvements in medical treatment, the proportion of Gross Factor Income spent on health care increased from 6.3 per cent in 1972 to 7.0 per cent in 1981 but then declined to 6.2 per cent in 1992 (Goul Andersen 1993:228), a level which remained constant throughout the 1990s. In short, in the real world there is often surprisingly little association between needs and public expenditures - or between expenditures and outcome (Kristensen 1987; Lolle 1999). This is not to neglect the relevance of ageing populations but to bring it into proportion. Besides, population prognoses are surprisingly unstable. In 1983 it was estimated that there would be some 4.2 million people living in Denmark by 2025. Because of higher birth rates and immigration, the estimate in 2000 was revised to 5.8 million.[9] In other words, our knowledge about the economic effects of ageing populations is quite uncertain but political actors decide on the basis of their *perception* of this problem.[10]

The relationship between effects of globalisation and discourses about globalisation is even less clear-cut. Leaving aside the question of what the term exactly stands for, and the disputes about whether globalisation exists or not (Krugman 1996; Hirst and Thompson 1997), what the concept implies remains contested (Mishra 1999; Bonoli et al. 2000; Scharpf 2000). The notion that globalisation and the impact of new technologies reduce aggregate employment (which added legitimacy to citizens' wage strategies, see Offe 1996), is by now abandoned among policy elites. The dominant philosophy since the mid 1990s - much propagated by the OECD (1994b,1997d) and in some respects even supported by writers such as Esping-Andersen (1999) - has been the idea that Western Europe is facing a trade-off, or at least a dilemma, between employment and equality. A much used illustration, rich in symbols and with a high capacity for identity-shaping, is the comparison between USA and Europe (OECD 1994b). Until the mid-1970s, the USA had an unemployment rate twice the European average. By contrast, since the 1990s unemployment

---

9 See Statistics Denmark: Befolkningsprognose. *Statistiske efterretninger: befolkning og valg*, 1983:15, 1996:14 and 2000:11.

10 Another problem is hardly debated at all: What will happen when pensioners really start using their pensions savings (which in Denmark amount to well above 100 per cent of the GDP and are estimated to grow at a very high rate)? This could well be a larger 'challenge'.

in the US has been half the European level. At the same time the gap between American and European employment rates continuously increased in favour of the US labour market. Western Europe seemed to suffer from 'Eurosclerosis' due to 'inflexible' labour markets and other disincentives, including distortions due to welfare arrangements (Goul Andersen forthcoming).

However, since the mid-1990s, many European countries have experienced unusually strong labour market improvements, indicating that there are several routes to low unemployment (Goul Andersen forthcoming): The Netherlands, Ireland, the UK, Denmark and Sweden have all experienced a significant fall in unemployment, while Austria, Switzerland, Norway, Luxembourg and Portugal have never really suffered from persistently high levels of unemployment. There are few common denominators to these successes, and their experience often does not conform with what should be expected from dominant problem definitions. To take Denmark as an example, there has been a path-breaking change towards an active labour market policy in the 1990s (Goul Andersen 2000b). Yet, as in other countries, the effects of those policies are weak and can only explain a minor share of the improvement in the labour market (Martin 2000; Ministry of Labour 2000). Surprisingly also, the degree of inequality, at least in terms of disposable incomes, seems to have decreased (Ministry of Finance 2000:67-108). Finally, and contrary to widely held assumptions, the decline of unemployment did not stop at the 'structural level of unemployment', which only a few years ago was estimated to be 11 per cent (Larsen and Stamhus 2000), and the decline was most pronounced among the lower-skilled labour force (Ministry of Finance 2000:109-36).[11]

This accumulation of anomalies indicates that the notion of 'challenges' must be considered with caution, and that the social construction of problems is an important topic for research on its own. It is not that economic ideas are simply wrong. But reasons should be explored how one particular set of interpretations is able to achieve a dominant or even hegemonic position. For research on welfare reform, rather than (merely) considering challenges, we must also examine how decision makers are influenced by ideas about challenges, from where and how such ideas disseminate, and how they interact with the interests of actors. To take Denmark as an illustration, the very idea of structural unemployment and the micro perspective on labour markets entered the political agenda very abruptly in 1988/89 (Government 1989), which was a time when opinion polls indicated that the government was seriously under pressure and in need of propagating a 'new project'. This situation strengthened 'political entrepreneurs' within the cabinet who could supply new ideas, such as the notion of structural unemployment. As these ideas had been available from economic experts for some time, it was just a matter of picking them up.[12] Soon, the underlying

---

11 Some economists have even begun to question whether there is such a thing as structural unemployment. In the Danish case, there are strong arguments against the notion which has guided policies (Ibsen 1992). Still, efforts to avoid bottlenecks on the labour market may have had some effect.

12 Ironically, the government coalition 1988-1990 which was intended to be more centrist than previous bourgeois governments came to pursue (but not to implement) the most radically

philosophy was to a large degree also accepted by trade unions and the Social Democrats, as it was compatible with their interests in adopting more active labour market policies. The social partners did not reach agreements on policies but they reached agreement on problem definitions. Improving qualifications of people with low skills became a 'functional alternative' to lowering minimum wages and unemployment benefits. This was confirmed in the report of one of the major government-appointed commissions on the subject in 1992 (Udredningsudvalget 1992).

Ironically, one of the strongest conflicts over globalisation was fought between two ministries in the Danish government. Regarding globalisation basically as beneficial, the Ministry of Finance argued that negative side effects could be offset by active labour market policies. The Ministry of Industry, on the other hand, focussed on the surplus of low-skilled labour and suggested that there was no alternative to lowering minimum wages by way of subsidising service jobs for private households. An important commission was set up partly in order to increase legitimacy for this policy and, to some extent, it did recommend such policies (Welfare Commission 1995). When unemployment rates declined however, the Ministry of Industry lost the battle. Nevertheless, a 'home service' programme subsidising a number of private household services was maintained.

Institutionalism, path dependency and path dynamics

The increasing academic interest in economic challenges to the welfare state reflects long-standing problems of European welfare states in the 1990s. But it also seems to be influenced by an increasing sense of change that runs somewhat counter to the previously dominant version of institutionalism in welfare state theory, namely the link between institutions and inertia, including the notion of path dependency. Increasingly, it has been recognised that welfare states do change, but this is explained mainly in functionalist terms and due to external pressure. A functionalist perspective suggests that change is needed; an institutionalist perspective suggests that this is likely to take a path dependent course, and increasingly, path dependency has come to mean more than just simple inertia.

The problem with the concept of path dependency is that it can mean different things. Often, it has been used more or less synonymously with simple inertia. A second possible meaning of path dependency is maintenance of basic programmatic structures or preservation of the in-built logic of such structures. When the notion of path dependence is applied in this sense, the criticism against institutionalism for its inability to explain change is not very well grounded. However, there is a third, and even more dynamic meaning which can be attached to path dependency. In this, the path metaphor only implies that policies tend to follow some particular routes with an in-built logic; but this route can at times involve dramatic change, or even a genuine break with the past. At times, such path breaking may be relatively unnoticed, sometimes even by decision makers, until the implications become clear. This

---

bourgeois/neoliberal policies in this period.

dynamic interpretation of path dependency may be criticised as a catch-all explanation. However, it may be highly useful, and it is actually in accordance with the ideas of the founding fathers of 'new institutionalism'.

The most important aspect of this variant of institutionalism is the notion that decisions taken at one point in time strongly affect decisions at a later stage. On the objective side, institutions determine policy effects and, accordingly, which problems are encountered. Also, institutions provide positions of power which determine the strength of particular interests or interest alliances, and serve as gate-keepers or non-decision structures that give preference to some issues or concerns at the expense of others. In a narrow sense, institutions are rules and standard operating procedures.[13] But equally important here is that this variant of institutionalism recognises that decision makers not only 'power', they also 'puzzle' (Heclo 1974), and institutions may strongly affect the perception of problems and even of interests. Actors act in surroundings of uncertainty, and they learn (Simon 1985). Minor changes in institutions may sometimes make the world appear highly different to them. In other words, institutions not only limit or constrain the range of possible choices; they also influence certain ideas, i.e. perceptions of the world, perceptions of problems and solutions, perceptions of interests etc. - and certain paths of action. This does not necessarily mean that people reproduce the same patterns of action however; it can involve sudden and radical change.

In short, institutions should not simply be seen as constraints. It is no accident that the 'founding fathers', when they launched the label 'new institutionalism' (march and Olsen 1984), referred to the idea of 'garbage can' decisions (Cohen, March and Olsen 1972) and went on by adding the idea of 'policy martingales' as an illustration of what they were thinking of. This concept refers to a situation where some small initial change turns out to have self-reinforcing effects which bring about growing deviations from previous policies, but where policies still follow a path which is anything but arbitrary.

Thus, although path dependency is often associated with a notion of inertia, the origin of the new institutionalism does not imply such an interpretation. On the contrary, path dependency can be a highly dynamic concept. In order to avoid misinterpretations, and to distinguish more clearly, we may perhaps introduce the expression of 'path dynamics' as a description of a path which increasingly breaks off some sort of previous 'equilibrium'. Such path dynamics may be intended, but sometimes they are not. Decision makers can be faced with the fact that a decision which initially seemed fairly insubstantial subsequently turned out to bring about major programmatic change caused by 'martingale effects'.

Such a perspective is not unusual in analyses of decision-making processes, but in theorising welfare state change it has so far played a minor role. Borrowing from the language of functionalism (Stinchcombe 1968), one may argue that within European welfare states there used to be a number of stabilising mechanisms ('veto points' as well as others) which

---

13 For the present purpose, it is not necessary to engage in any lengthy discussion about this issue here (see e.g Hall and Taylor 1996).

corrected deviance from an established institutional set-up. By contrast welfare states are currently in a situation where such mechanisms are weakened and the potential for dynamic path-breaking change is stronger.

We can illustrate the two concepts of path dependency in Figure 8.3a and 8.3b. Figure 8.3a represents the classical picture where some deviations from an established path occur from time to time but are corrected. In Denmark, a classical example would be oscillations around the path of universalism, reflecting uncertainty and a deep ambivalence between two basic values of the Danish welfare state, i.e. protection of the poor (universalism originally developed from residualism) and citizenship. When it is discovered that some weak groups receive insufficient support, attention is often directed towards welfare for the better off, and arguments arise in favour of targeting. If such policies are successfully implemented, all the foreseeable problems with targeting (Gilbert 2000:220-24) sooner or later appear on the political agenda, including control problems (transaction costs), inscrutability and unequal treatment, or interaction between means-tested benefits and marginal taxes which produce perverse incentives. As a result, the pendulum swings back towards universalism.

Figure 8.3: (a) Classical model of path dependency and (b) 'policy martingale' model

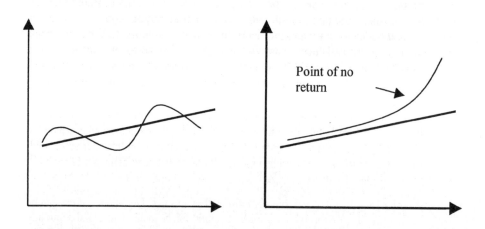

The model of policy martingales is without such correction mechanisms. It refers to a situation of self-reinforcing change or deviations. On a tentative and intuitive basis, one could say that such change may often develop slowly and with a small and insignificant beginning, which is perhaps not even recognised and certainly not regarded as path-breaking change. But at a certain point in time, it reaches a point of no return and develops very fast, with significant path-breaking consequences.

While this is nothing but a metaphor or a model, it is not too difficult to find developments of welfare arrangements which fit this pattern, and it does provide a way of thinking which is useful in welfare state research. More specifically, it helps in reading a situation, alerts to path-breaking potentials of small and incremental changes and, last but not least, represents a source of change which is not necessarily related to either interests or economic necessity.

A similar notion of path dynamics is implied by Esping-Andersen's (1990) prediction that flat-rate universalism in pensions will lead to dual pension systems.[14] The same case also illustrates that at times decision makers think that they maintain a status quo but have in effect produced a path-breaking change. Basically, this happened in Denmark in the 1970s and 1980s. Whereas Sweden and Norway had chosen a path of adding an income-related superannuation scheme to the basic pension in the 1960s, Denmark only added a small, employment-related but otherwise flat-rate superannuation scheme. Due to the subsequent expansion of occupational pensions, a dual pension system had become a reality in the mid-1980s, with one-third of the Danish population relying on a significant supplementary pension whereas the remaining two-thirds had only their basic pensions (Vesterø-Jensen 1985). Paradoxically, the intention of maintaining a particular system led to what could be considered a path-breaking change.[15]

However, the dual pension system was not as unjust as it seemed at first glance: in accordance with the logic of universalism, Denmark had developed what might be called a 'Rolls Royce' version of flat rate universalism in the 1970s and 1980s.[16] In addition to the basic pension and the small second-tier scheme, privileged housing allowances for pensioners, tax privileges, a large number of special arrangements (such as inexpensive public transport and support for heating costs), in addition to individual supplements (provided by municipalities on discretion) ensured very high de facto minimum pensions which amounted to approximately full income replacements for single pensioners from lower income groups. Nonetheless, in the 1990s, one more 'silent revolution' took place in

---

14 The examples of such path dynamics which cannot be subsumed under what is usually referred to as path dependency are innumerable. For instance, with Glennerster (1995:182) Bonoli et al. (2000:31) argue that once a flat rate universal benefit drops below a certain level, it becomes irrelevant and will tend to wither away altogether. By the same token, Palier (2000) identifies incremental changes that might become path-breaking in the financing of the French social security system.

15 Actually, the expansion of occupational pension in Denmark was less extensive than might have been expected in the light of the limitations of public pensions. At the same time, in Sweden, generous public pensions for the new middle classes did not crowd out occupational pensions as much as one could have expected. Protection of class differences and adaptation of expectations have been suggested as possible expectations here (Pedersen 1999).

16 There is an interesting parallel to New Zealand which originally (1898) adopted a purely tax-financed system, partly inspired by the Danish social reform in 1891. However, New Zealand strengthened universal pensions and dropped tax subsidies to all private pensions savings (Overbye 1997).

the same policy field. On demand from the trade unions, and without any formal political decisions or public debates, a funded labour market pension was gradually established in the 1990s as part of collective agreements. Trade unions intended these occupational pensions to act only as a supplement to the universal pension system. Yet a path of gradual substitution is equally imaginable, even though this was probably not envisaged nor intended by the main actors in the field.[17]

While the final outcome of these changes is uncertain, a number of incremental changes would indeed seem to lead towards a path of substitution. From 1990, pension indexation was changed to wage increases after deduction of increased pension contributions. In connection with the 1994 tax reform, a larger share of the basic pension became means tested and in 1998, housing allowances for pensioners became more strongly means tested on income.[18] Finally, even the basic amount has become means-tested against earnings from employment. So far, this represents only a 'retirement test' with small practical effects, i.e. affecting people who have remained in employment, but it could easily be expanded to a fuller means test covering different sources of pension income. What is more, as occupational pensions mature, the implicit notion of pensioners as a weak and deserving group might evaporate. As a consequence, it is conceivable that arguments for abolishing all sorts of special treatment of pensioners will become stronger. Such a change of mentality seems to have in practice already squeezed (discretionary) individual supplements. The consequence is a lowering of the de facto minimum pension which, in turn, might increase demands from trade unions and their members to increase contributions for labour market pensions beyond the current agreed-upon target of 9 per cent (of which employers pay two-thirds) towards, for instance, the 15 per cent which many public employees already enjoy. If this happens, occupational pensions are likely to become the backbone of the pension system, whereas the basic pension may slowly wither away except as a guaranteed minimum (Cox 1997). Because of a lack of regulation and an extremely low degree of risk sharing, this has more far-reaching implications than in other countries where occupational pensions are widespread. Of course, how far things will actually develop, remains to be seen. But the point of no return has been passed long ago, and it is highly conceivable that this 'silent revolution' of incremental adjustments with self-reinforcing elements will add up to what constitutes a 'third order' change (Hall 1993) without any public debate, ideological mobilisation or political conflicts which are usually associated with these types of change.

---

17 From a comparative perspective, there is yet another interesting aspect to this as it was proved possible to build a funds-based system financed by additional contributions alongside continuing payments (via general taxes) to the pay-as-you-go system of basic pensions.

18 The basic pension consists of a basic amount given to everybody (except for a small minority with earnings from active employment) and a pension supplement which is means-tested (against all income) but at present given to a very large majority of pensioners. However, with increasing incomes from private pensions, more and more pensioners will be affected by means testing, and the relationship between basic amount and supplement has been changed from about 4:1 in the 1980s to about 1:1 (by 2001) for single pensioners.

Another classical example, also within the field of pensions, is the first major Danish social reform of 1891 which included an old-age relief. In contrast to Bismarck's contribution-based reform a couple of years earlier, Denmark consciously chose an entirely different path by introducing tax-financed, needs-tested pensions which later paved the way for universal, flat-rate pensions. The reasons for this first choice were agrarian interests, or rather, a misperception of their interests on the part of politicians of the agrarian Liberal Party. The latter believed that such a pension reform would be able to maintain a large agrarian workforce available for the middle-sized farmers (Baldwin 1990:65-76). The Conservative Party had preferred a contribution-based system, and so did the agrarian Liberal Party a couple of decades later. The Social Democrats who subsequently became the main defenders of the system, actually voted against the reform in 1891. But when the Liberal Party changed its mind, it was too late. In many respects, the old-age pension system that had been implemented became the backbone of the universal welfare state in Denmark, and in the first decades of the 20th Century it began to develop according to its own logic of ('creeping') universalism partly because the middle class parties also became preoccupied with the notion of securing a 'fair' share for the social groups which they represented (Baldwin 1990).

Institutions, attitudes and behaviour

Popular support for the welfare state, not least in Scandinavia, has often been seen as a major obstacle to far-reaching change. In principle, however, this is slightly inconsistent with an institutional approach. Institutionalism and the notion of path dependency would rather tend to see attitudes as a dependent variable (Svallfors 2000), and to direct at least as much attention to the actual behaviour of people as to their political attitudes. Even if people may prefer welfare arrangements based on principles of solidarity, they have to make choices and seek solutions for themselves under the existing opportunity structure.

To begin with the example of Danish pensions, the new labour market pensions mentioned above were initially not popular among the rank-and-file of unskilled workers who may have feared a substitution effect (Goul Andersen 1988). However, gradually improving pensions have become a high priority demand in wage negotiations at a time when public debates about the 'pension bomb' has generated widespread distrust in the viability of the public pension system. Private insurance companies and banks have actively sought to exploit and reinforce such distrust, e.g. in advertising campaigns. According to a survey of 'welfare values' in 2000 (Mandag Morgen 2000; Goul Andersen forthcoming), the result is that a majority of the population no longer believes that they can rely on public pensions by the time they reach pension age (52 per cent do not believe that the public old age pension system will continue against merely 35 per cent who think that it will). If this leads to an increase in private pensions savings, the effect could be an even stronger crowding out of public pensions than suggested above.

A similar situation has developed in other areas, such as certain service provisions. For example, medical treatment and elderly care in Denmark is (sometimes wrongly) believed to be of an unacceptably low standard. At present, and ironically with the support of trade unions, insurance against 'critical disease' is mushrooming, not least as part of collective agreements. So far, this insurance typically includes only a cash amount and not medical treatment as such. But even when it comes to medical treatment, there is some uncertainty about the future. Surveys indicate that 58 per cent of the population expects that there will be medical treatment for everybody in the future. But 29 per cent think that this will not be the case and that people will have to insure themselves (Goul Andersen, forthcoming). The question is of course what can be the consequence of such attitudes. Even though there are so far no signs of a weakening of people's support for the welfare state, one possible path could be a strongly increased demand for private welfare.[19]

The argument is that if trust in public welfare deteriorates, it will increase demand for private welfare among those who can afford it, which in turn might trigger a lower support for public welfare as people do not want to pay for welfare twice.[20] There is, it must be underlined, empirical evidence which speaks against such a scenario. Making use of ISSP data in order to examine the implication of welfare regime theory that social variations in support for the welfare state will differ between residual, universal and corporatist welfare models, Svallfors (1996, 2000) found evidence for this theory only as far as aggregate support for the welfare state is concerned. Burchardt and Propper (1999) found that attitudes to public financing of welfare spending was not directly linked to the use of private alternatives. Danish data indicate that a perception of inadequate public services remains positively linked to support for increasing budgets. But it also turned out that during 1998 to 2000, which was a period of persistent criticism of public services, the strength of such associations had declined very significantly. It was also possible to examine the single hypothesised paths in 2000, and although associations were weak, the suggested relationships in Figure 8.4 (see the end of the chapter) were basically confirmed (Goul Andersen forthcoming).

---

19 A further possibility is the introduction of private welfare 'through the back door'. In recent years, companies have started to introduce private health care insurance (mainly in order to avoid waiting lists and to provide a fringe benefit, partly for symbolic reasons). There is a tendency for such arrangements to spread from the top of the occupational hierarchy towards the bottom, partly reinforced by trade unions' instincts to demand for their members the privileges which are given to other groups. In 2000, a few large companies entered into insurance plans for all of their employees. Such a trend could be self-reinforcing, and it is strengthened by the idea of 'social responsibility of firms'. It is no longer unimaginable that it could be considered 'natural' that most companies provide for their employees. Indeed, some insurance companies envisage such a situation, extrapolating from recent trends. Finally, ministers of finance and taxation, always in need of money or in need of getting rid of financial obligations, could grasp the opportunity in a situation of high private coverage and state budget deficits.

20 Bonoli et al. (2000:46) refer to a perceived 'social protection gap' that may be filled by private provision. Increasing resources and increasing expectations might even *as such* trigger an increasing demand for private welfare provision, regardless of the supply of public services.

These data serve only as an illustration. But they do indicate that one should perhaps not put too much emphasis on public attitudes as a constraint to change. Furthermore, it is imaginable that, perhaps not even politically intended, public support may erode once private paths to welfare move beyond a certain level. Once again, path dependency may contain strong and sometimes unintended dynamics.[21]

Conclusion

The messages of this chapter are simple: first, current welfare state research tends to overemphasise the relevance of economic challenges to the welfare state. Second, as indicated by the significant changes during the 1990s in countries such as Denmark or the Netherlands which have not faced acute economic problems, more emphasis should be paid to the social construction of challenges, and more generally, to political agency. Third, welfare states can find quite different solutions to challenges which do not always point in one direction. Fourth, if policies move in one direction across countries, this may stem not only from the nature of 'challenges' encountered but also from the dissemination of ideas. Fifth, path dependency should not be employed only as a static concept; and sixth, at present many dynamic paths away from the welfare state 'as we knew it' are imaginable. To avoid confusion, the concept of path dynamics could serve as an appropriate concept to describe such developments that are path dependent in the sense that they follow a particular logic but at the same time turn out to be path breaking in the sense that they gradually change the programmatic structure. When the point of departure is 'challenges', the question becomes whether it is possible to maintain the welfare state in the face of new challenges. However, this should not be conflated with the question of whether present welfare arrangements are *likely* to survive. At least in the Danish case, it does not seem difficult to answer the first question in an affirmative way. But the answer to the second question is much more uncertain. Finally, there is the question of whether ongoing changes are at all desirable. But that is another story.

---

21 A further case in point is the Danish public child care system that has moved close to full coverage in the second half of the 1990s. Apart from a few progressive reformers, nobody had envisaged such a development. But people's behaviour, including their propensity to move to a municipality where daycare was guaranteed, left municipalities with little choice if they wanted to avoid stagnation. At the same time, public provision of childcare and elderly care has contributed to a level of taxation where the choice of being a housewife (without any sort of transfer income) virtually does not in practice exist anymore.

Figure 8.4: Possible relationships between perceived quality/sufficiency of public welfare support, trust, preference for private alternatives, and welfare support

A. Increased support

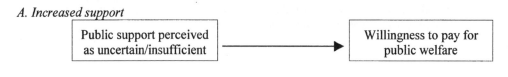

B. Ambiguous situation

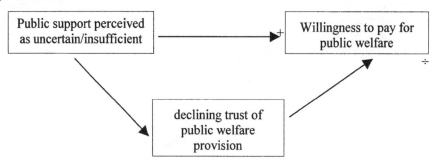

C. Private welfare path/-crowding out

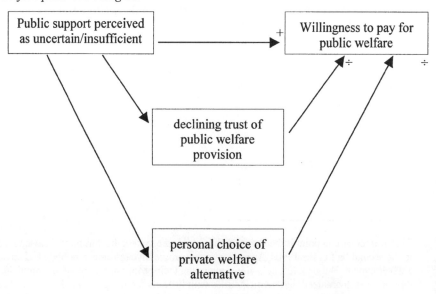

II B

REFORMING PENSION SYSTEMS

Chapter 9

Public Expenditure and Population Ageing: why families of nations are different

Francis G. Castles

Introduction

There is a new spectre haunting Europe, the OECD and, if the World Bank is to be believed, the world as a whole – the spectre of an ageing population! For national economic policy-makers and their international agencies, population ageing has many of the characteristics of a moral panic. The World Bank (1994) talks of 'the old age crisis' and the OECD Secretariat (1996) of 'a critical policy challenge'. Some refer to the aged as a 'selfish generation' (Thomson 1991) and invoke the notion of increasing conflict between younger and older generations over welfare resources. Others note that whatever problems loom in the short to medium-term can only get worse as the fertility rates of many Western nations go into free-fall. National treasuries, irrespective of country-specific demographics, use the supposedly ineluctable consequences of a 'greying' population as a mantra to be invoked against all proposals for enhanced public spending. New commitments are out of the question, when existing commitments to the old (and those who will become old) promise national ruin in a matter of decades. While some scholars and a few agencies of government provide a more measured analysis of national trends, their voices are, almost invariably, drowned by the clamour of those who argue that population ageing means that the modern welfare state can no longer pay its way.

Many of these views have some surface plausibility. The world's population is ageing and that of the OECD countries in particular. It is estimated that between 2000 and 2030 AD, the OECD's elderly population (aged 65 and over) will increase by 61.8 per cent from 13.9 per cent of the population to 22.5 per cent (Bos et al. 1994). At the same time, it is clear that the percentage of the old has direct budget implications. Many of the countries in the world, and all but one of those within the pre-1990 boundaries of the OECD bar Turkey[1], have age pension systems with extensive coverage. All other things being equal, therefore, a more elderly population means proportionately greater income maintenance expenditure as a percentage of GDP.

Nor are these the only implications. A majority of commentators, including the World Bank, argue that ageing has a direct influence on health spending 'since health problems and costly medical technologies are concentrated among the old' (World Bank 1994:3). The OECD concedes the possibility of an alternative scenario that 'the major increase in health costs in later life is actually determined by the lifetime remaining before death occurs' (Roseveare et al. 1996:8), but the former is the argument most commonly encountered in the population ageing literature. Ageing also has other costs. Where governments provide services for the elderly, such as nursing homes and home help, these too must be factored into the financial equation resulting from an ageing population.

Finally, there is the question of how the costs of population ageing will be paid for. International economic agencies and national economic policy-makers are deeply aware of the temptations facing democratic politicians confronted by demands for additional spending from relatively cohesive interest constituencies (for the clearest exposition of this logic, see Brittan 1977). For modern economists, as for their more orthodox forebears, spending without taxing is the primrose path of dalliance, leading on to eternal damnation. If politicians give way to their natural inclination to defer the inevitable fiscal consequences of increased public spending on the elderly by increased borrowing, the cost to the public treasury will ultimately be far greater. This suggests that, in addition to increased spending on pensions, health care and aged services, population ageing is likely to result in a never ending spiral of increasing debt interest payments.

Argued in general terms, these arguments seem persuasive. They appear to gain additional substance from comparative public policy research, which has demonstrated strong linkages between the age structure of the population and the bigger aggregates of welfare spending and public expenditure more generally (see Pampel and Williamson

---

1 Note that not all of the generalisations made here concerning OECD nations apply equally to the newer member states - the Czech Republic, Korea, Mexico and Poland - or to the only relatively underdeveloped older member, Turkey.

1989; Huber, Ragin and Stephens 1993; Castles 1998). Harold Wilensky, a pioneer in this field of research, argued the case most strongly: 'If there is one source of welfare spending that is most powerful – a single proximate cause – it is the proportion of old people in the population' (Wilensky 1975:47). There remain influential scholars who think much the same way. Having devoted a monograph to showing that globalization is not a threat to the achievements of social democratic corporatism, Geoffrey Garrett argues that 'demographic change will increasingly strain the public purse in all countries, including the ranks of social democratic corporatism' (Garrett 1998:152). For commentators already convinced that the welfare burden is already far too great, the disastrous expenditure consequences of further substantial population ageing seem to follow inexorably.

There are, however, grounds for scepticism. Comparative public policy research has made its case for ageing effects on the basis of highly aggregated data for income transfers, total social security spending and total outlays of government. For the most part, such research has not disaggregated spending in the manner required to establish that ageing effects are separately mediated through spending on pensions, health care, age services and debt financing. Moreover, while the policy forecasters' warnings for coming decades are almost invariably couched in universal terms, national expenditure and ageing profiles have varied widely in recent decades. Why should such profiles not vary as much in the future as they have done in the past?

Recent research has concluded that social expenditure levels and social rights of citizenship differ very appreciably in different welfare state regimes (Esping-Andersen 1990) and in different families of nations (see Castles and Mitchell 1993 and Castles 1998). However, there is no reference to possible diversity, when the OECD Secretariat argues forcefully, and without qualification, 'that if pension programmes are not changed, the tax or contribution rate required to finance transfers to the elderly will rise considerably' (OECD 1996a:88). Yet the Secretariat's own estimates show that some nations will be far more affected by this problem than others. For the English-speaking family of nations (Australia, Canada, Ireland, the UK and the USA), the average change in the tax/GDP ratio required to maintain existing levels of pension generosity in the years up to 2030 is around 3.3 per cent of GDP (calculated from OECD 1996a: Table 5.3, 89–90). For the Scandinavian countries (Denmark, Finland, Norway and Sweden), the figure is 5.1 per cent and, for the countries of continental, Western Europe (Austria, Belgium, France, Germany, Italy and the Netherlands), it is 9.7 per cent (ibid).

The exercise which follows is quite unlike those offered by the World Bank or the OECD. Rather than making predictions on the basis of simplified models (Roseveare et al. 1996:6), we examine the evidence of three decades of OECD experience to establish how far and in what ways population ageing has impacted on public expenditure development in the recent past. While the presentation here avoids complex statistical modelling, the findings are derived from an extensive data base which does permit such analysis. Occasionally, we refer to conclusions derived from such modelling. Two concerns are foremost in our discussion. The first is the extent to which the evidence of the past warrants generalisations concerning the catastrophic consequences of population ageing in coming decades. The second – assuming that generalisations give way to more nuanced and varied scenarios for change – is what this evidence tells us about the probable impact of population ageing as a constraint on future public expenditure development in diverse families of nations.

Population ageing: 1965–1995

A likely *a priori* objection to using the experience of the past as a guide to likely future trajectories of development is that the scale of the problems to be encountered in the future is wholly without precedent in the past. Certainly, that would be the view of those who paint the direst picture of the consequences of population ageing. Much of the force of their argument rests on the fact that mankind faces a new and unprecedented problem, rather than an extension of an existing problem with which nations have been grappling with varying success over many years. The data presented in Table 9.1 on the absolute and proportional increase in the aged population in 19 OECD countries over the three decades 1965–1995 allow us to assess the strength of this objection.

We have already noted the projected rise in the OECD's population over the age of 65 from 13.9 per cent in 2000 to 22.5 per cent in 2030, an absolute increase of some 8.6 percentage points. The figures in the final row of Table 9.1 demonstrate that population ageing in the recent past has been of a lesser magnitude than that expected in coming decades. The average change of 4.3 percentage points over the period 1965–1995 is exactly half that projected for the coming three decades. In relative terms, the difference is somewhat less pronounced, with an increase in the proportion of the elderly in OECD countries between 1965–1995 of around 40 per cent compared to a projected increase of just over 60 per cent between 2000–2030. These are significant differences, but hardly of a sufficient magnitude to establish the existence of a problem on an entirely novel scale.

It could be argued that we should be using other measures of the potential impact of population ageing, such as the elderly dependency ratio (i.e. the population 65 and over as a percentage of the working age population), for which the estimated rate of increase over the next 30 years is closer to 80 per cent (calculated from Bos et al. 1994). However, whilst it is certainly true that the capacity of society to bear the cost burden of ageing is best captured by a measure that directly relates spending on the old to the size of the support-base for that spending, this does not make such measures appropriate indicators of the purely demographic aspects of population ageing. The proportion of the population aged 65 and over is only one component of the elderly dependency ratio. Equally important are trends in labour market participation. Increasing participation rates for men and women reduce the aged dependency ratio and declining participation rates increase it. Moreover, because some countries have much lower rates of labour force participation rates than others, their projected dependency ratios are higher. These are not issues of demography and not properly part of the debate on the impacts of ageing.

Table 9.1: Population aged 65 years and over – 1965, 1995 and change over time

Country	1965	1995	Points Change	Percentage Change
Australia	8.5	11.9	3.4	40.0
Austria	13.2	15.1	1.9	14.4
Belgium	12.6	15.9	3.3	26.2
Canada	7.7	12.0	4.3	55.8
Denmark	11.4	15.4	4.0	35.1
Finland	8.0	14.2	6.2	77.5
France	12.1	15.1	3.0	24.8
Germany	12.0	15.8	3.8	31.7
Greece	9.0	16.6	7.6	84.4
Ireland	11.1	11.5	0.4	3.6
Italy	9.8	16.0	6.2	63.3
Japan	6.3	14.5	8.2	130.2
Netherlands	9.6	13.2	3.6	37.5
New Zealand	8.3	11.7	3.4	41.0
Norway	12.0	16.0	4.0	33.3
Sweden	12.7	17.5	4.8	37.8
Switzerland	10.5	15.7	5.2	49.5
UK	12.1	15.7	3.6	29.8
USA	9.5	12.7	3.2	33.7
Mean	**10.3**	**14.6**	**4.3**	**44.7**
Source: OECD, *Labour Force Statistics*, Paris (various years)				

Returning to the data in Table 9.1, it is very important to note how varied the experience of these OECD countries has been. Countries like Ireland, Austria, Belgium and the United Kingdom have aged relatively slowly. On the other hand, there are a number of countries in which the process of population ageing in the recent past has been of much the same order of magnitude that we may expect to be the norm in coming years. These countries include Japan, Greece, Finland and Italy. They also include both Spain and Portugal, which are only excluded from this analysis because of gaps in their public expenditure data. The experience of post-war Japan is worthy of special note in the context of the discussion here. Japan has simultaneously manifested the most pronounced population ageing of any country in the OECD and the lowest level of welfare state spending in the OECD measured as a percentage of GDP. This should serve as a valuable reality check for those inclined to accept the prognostications of the population ageing nostradamuses too uncritically.

The main factors accounting for Japan's weak growth in welfare spending measured as a percentage of GDP are that country's exceptional economic growth rate throughout the post-war period (in fact, the rate of growth of real welfare expenditure was the highest in the OECD) and the persistence of an extended family support system, resting on Confucian values (Goodman and Peng 1996), which partially insulated the state from the impact of an ageing population. Other countries cannot possibly hope to emulate such an experience and, almost certainly, nor can Japan in future years. Our identification of Japan as a key case for the argument here is not because Japan is an exemplar of how to go about avoiding a future old-age crisis, but because it stands as an example of how economic, cultural and other factors can get in the way of an automatic correspondence between the size of the aged population and public expenditure development.

Finally, we wish to note differences between families of nations in patterns of population ageing. In 1965, the countries of continental Western Europe had the oldest population structures (an average of 11.5 per cent of the population aged 65 and over), with Scandinavia not far behind (11.0 per cent), but the English-speaking countries were markedly younger (9.5 per cent). Thirty years later, Scandinavia was marginally older (15.8 per cent) than continental Europe (15.2 per cent), with the divide between these countries and the English-speaking nations (12.6 per cent) increasing still further. Forecasts (Bos 1994) suggest that the English-speaking nations' demographic advantage will continue. Estimates suggest that, in 2030, the population of 65 years and over will be 20.6 per cent in the English-speaking world, 23.2 per cent in Scandinavia and 25.9 per cent in continental Europe. Corresponding estimates for the aged as a percentage of the active population are 33.9 per cent (English-speaking), 39.2 per cent (Scandinavia) and 44.5 (continental Europe). These differences essentially derive from the fertility differentials of earlier generations. The fact that the majority of English-speaking nations have been, throughout the post-war era, countries of overseas migration has been conducive to high fertility and a youthful population. More recently, Scandinavian social policies designed to permit women to combine labour force participation and family formation have promoted fertility rates higher than elsewhere in the OECD (McDonald 1997; Castles 1998; Esping-Andersen 1999). This is reflected in demographic forecasts which show that the extent of population ageing in Scandinavia over the next three decades will be significantly less than in continental Western Europe.

Post-war Pension Programs

Of all the potential ways in which population ageing might impact on the public purse, much the most obvious is through the enhanced costs of pension programs as they expand to cope with an increasingly elderly population. Indeed, in the absence of changes in the coverage and generosity of public pensions, it is axiomatic that as the proportion of the population of pensionable age increases, so too will the burden on the exchequer (OECD 1985).

Table 9.2 provides data on cash transfers to the aged as a percentage of GDP in 19 OECD countries in 1965, 1995 and for change over time. Initial expenditure levels varied extremely widely from a low of 1.2 per cent of GDP in Japan to nearly 11 per cent in Austria, with a mean of just over 5 per cent for the OECD as a whole. By the mid-1990s, the OECD mean level of spending was just over 7 per cent, varying from somewhat over 3 per cent of GDP in Australia and Ireland to more than 10 per cent in Austria, France, Germany and Italy.

Table 9.2: Public expenditure on age pensions as a percentage of GDP – 1965, 1995 and change over time

Country	1965	1995	Points Change
Australia	3.3	3.1	-0.2
Austria	10.8	10.4	-0.4
Belgium	4.5	7.6	3.1
Canada	2.9	4.3	1.4
Denmark	4.9	7.7	2.8
Finland	4.0	7.9	3.9
France	7.6	10.4	2.8
Germany	9.9	10.3	0.4
Greece	4.3	8.5	4.2
Ireland	2.8	3.4	0.6
Italy	7.7	11.0	3.3
Japan	1.2	5.5	4.3
Netherlands	7.7	6.7	-1.0
New	3.9	5.8	1.9
Zealand	4.7	5.8	1.1
Norway	5.1	8.2	3.1
Sweden	3.4	6.7	3.3
Switzerland	4.9	6.5	1.6
UK	4.5	5.4	0.9
USA	**5.2**	**7.1**	**1.9**
Mean Adj. R²	**.30**	**.45**	**.50**

Sources: For 1965, pensions data calculated from OECD (1985). For 1995, old-age cash benefits data from OECD, *Social Expenditure Database 1980–1996*, Paris, 1998 (CD Rom). **Adj. R²** indicates the strength of the relationship between pensions expenditure and the corresponding data on age structure in Table 9.1.

Given the apocalyptic tone of much of the population ageing debate, it should be noted that the average increase in pensions spending of 1.9 per cent of GDP over the period 1965 to 1995 amounted to only 16 per cent of the change in total social spending and to only 11 per cent of the change in total outlays over the same period. Assuming that the ratio of pensions spending change to population ageing (i.e. column 3 of Table 9.2

divided by column 3 of Table 9.1) remains constant, between 2000 and 2030 the average level of OECD pensions spending will go up by 3.8 per cent of GDP.

The final row of Table 9.2 indicates the strength of the relationships between age transfer spending and the age structure of the population. In 1965, some 30 per cent of the variance in spending levels could be accounted for by cross-national differences in the proportion of the elderly. By 1995, that figure had gone up to 45 per cent. Precisely 50 per cent of variance in changing levels of spending could be accounted for by changes in the age structure of the population.

These are strong and statistically significant relationships, but they are a long way from demonstrating the kind of immediate knock-on effects of ageing implied in the population ageing literature. If only 50 per cent of expenditure variance is attributable to ageing, then 50 per cent must be attributable to other factors. In principle, we know what these other factors must be. The axiom that pension expenditure change is a function of ageing, where coverage and generosity are held constant, means that the remaining 50 per cent of the variance in expenditure change must be a function of the joint impact of differences in coverage and generosity.

Historically, the major sources of such differences lie in choices between adopting universal or means-tested, flat-rate benefits and income-related, contributory benefits (see Overbye 1994; Myles and Quadagno 1996). Essentially, income-related benefits are more expensive than flat-rate or means-tested ones and the contributory principle creates a strong sense of entitlement to benefit. This potent combination, stemming from the original Bismarckian, institutional design of the welfare state, underlies the high pensions expenditure levels of the core, continental Western European states throughout the post-war period. It also helps to account for the substantial growth of the age pension systems of Southern Europe over the past two decades. A number of commentators have further noted the tendency for such systems to be abused by governments using them to provide funds for early retirement at times of rapidly increasing unemployment (see von Rhein-Kress 1993; Esping-Andersen 1999).

The welfare states of the English-speaking family of nations are at the opposite extreme from such countries. In 1995, the average level of pensions expenditure in these countries was 4.7 per cent of GDP compared to the overall OECD average of 7.1 per cent. Over the period 1965–1995, average expenditure in the English-speaking countries went up by only 1.0 per cent of GDP compared to the OECD mean of 1.9 per cent. These differences stem from the essentially Beveridgeian design features of most of the English-speaking welfare states, with the majority of benefits provided on a flat-rate basis, either to all citizens or to groupings selected on the basis of need. Along with flat-rates, there is also tendency for replacement levels of benefits to be comparatively low; in several of these nations, typically below 30 per cent of average weekly earnings. Combined with the already established fact that all the English-speaking nations, bar the United Kingdom, have, throughout the post-war period, been blessed with relatively youthful age structures, this lack of generosity has translated into expenditure levels as a percentage of GDP typically only a third to a half of those prevalent in continental Western Europe.

The institutional designs of pensions systems in Scandinavia can be seen as hybrids, with both Beveridgeian and Bismarckian elements. Historically, these countries started out with flat-rate and/or means-tested provision and, in the early post-war decades their pensions systems were characterised by flat-rate, universalism. However, from the 1960s onwards, all, bar Denmark, added contributory and income-related, second-tiers to their pensions structures. This in-between status in terms of institutional design combines with an already noted in-between position in respect of demographic pressures. Consequently, it is not surprising that estimates of the likely burden imposed by population ageing in coming decades suggest that Scandinavia falls somewhere between the English-speaking and the continental, Western European nations in severity of impact.

As we have noted, the lack of generosity and restricted coverage of age pension provision in the English-speaking family of nations follows directly from the institutional design of these nations' social policy systems. Although this makes for enduring contrasts with systems based on Bismarckian and social democratic principles, it is worth noting the recent trend of many European countries to adopt reforms limiting either the generosity or the coverage of existing, age pension provision. Generosity has been reduced by indexing pension benefits to the rate of inflation rather than to the rate of increase of real incomes and by moving away from income maintenance principles to the earlier notion of a benefit in proportion to contributions. Coverage has been reduced by the introduction of partial means-testing or by an increase in the age at which individuals become eligible to receive benefit (for examples, see Ploug and Kvist 1994; Kuhnle 2000).

These reforms are, of course, substantially motivated by an awareness of the dangers posed by high degrees of benefit generosity in the context of an ageing population. Nevertheless, the very fact that they have been enacted suggests that it may be possible to contain the public expenditure impact of age pensions in precisely those countries where the existing problems are greatest. It is also possible that governments may be able to provide for the income needs of the old in a manner that does not make use of the formal structures of public provision. At the same time as a number of countries have been trimming back on the generosity of their schemes, other countries have been redesigning their pension systems to provide greater cover and generosity through government mandated and employer-funded, private provision. In the long-run, anxieties about population ageing may actually lead to a convergence in total spending, as historically generous public systems trim their provision and historically parsimonious ones use mandated schemes to cope with increasing need and growing expectations.

Other welfare state programmes

Apart from aged pensions, the other welfare state programs most likely to be directly influenced by population ageing are health care and service provision for the elderly. Table 9.3 provides data for health care expenditure in 1965 and 1995 and for expenditure change between those dates. Data on services to the elderly is only available from 1980 onwards and not for all countries and Table 9.3 only reports the level of such spending for 1995. Table 9.3 reveals an almost complete lack of correspondence between cross-national variance in population ageing and levels and changes in health care costs. Only in 1965 does the correlation even approach the level of statistical significance. Although this challenges a commonplace argument, it is not really very surprising. OECD research has shown that total health expenditure is almost entirely a function of a nation's level of real GDP per capita (OECD 1993:14–15) and recent research on public funding demonstrates an analogous finding for the early 1990s (Castles 1998:192). It should be emphasised that these conclusions do not necessarily contradict research findings for many nations which suggest that public spending on health will increase with an ageing population. The only point that is being argued here is that trajectories of spending growth in the health area differ very markedly between countries and that cross-national differences in population ageing do not seem to offer much purchase in explaining such differences.

In contrast to health care, there is a modestly significant and positive statistical association between expenditure on services to the elderly and the proportion of the population aged 65 and over. However, this relationship disappears completely when we take into account differences in post-war Left incumbency, which of themselves account for 71 per cent of the variance in aged services. The ideological preference of leftist parties to favour service provision over transfer expenditure is much remarked in the comparative literature (Kohl 1981; Esping-Andersen 1990; Castles 1998) and seems to provide a more satisfactory explanation than an account based on age structure. It is also an explanation which coincides precisely with a perspective framed in terms of families of nations. Here, it is Social Democratic Scandinavia which spends big on services to the aged (an average of 2.9 per cent of GDP), while continental Western Europe (.47 of a per cent) and the English-speaking family of nations (.32 of a per cent) lag way behind.

Table 9.3: Public health care as a percentage of GDP – 1965, 1995 and change over time. Services to the elderly as a percentage of GDP, 1995.

Country	Health Care 1965	1995	1965–1995	Services to the Elderly* 1995
Australia	2.7	5.6	2.9	0.35
Austria	3.3	5.8	2.5	•
Belgium	3.0	6.9	3.9	0.15
Canada	3.1	6.9	3.8	•
Denmark	4.2	6.9	2.7	3.04
Finland	3.2	5.7	2.5	1.69
France	3.5	8.0	4.5	0.77
Germany	3.6	8.1	4.5	0.57
Greece	2.2	4.4	2.2	•
Ireland	3.3	5.2	1.9	0.48
Italy	3.8	5.4	1.6	0.20
Japan	2.7	5.6	2.9	0.27
Netherlands	3.3	6.7	3.4	0.66
New	3.9	5.6	1.7	0.05
Zealand	3.1	6.6	3.5	3.58
Norway	4.4	7.1	2.7	3.37
Sweden	2.3	6.9	4.6	0.05
Switzerland	3.5	5.8	2.3	0.68
UK	1.5	6.5	5.0	0.05
USA	**3.2**	**6.3**	**3.1**	**1.00**
Mean	.09	-.01	.01	.17
Adj. R^2				

Sources: Health expenditure data for 1965 from OECD (1993) and for 1995 from OECD, *OECD Health Data 98: a comparative analysis of 29 countries*, Paris 1998). Age services from OECD, *Social Expenditure Database 1980–1996*, Paris 1998, (CD Rom). *This expenditure item also includes services to the disabled. **Adj. R^2** indicates the strength of the relationships between spending on health care or services for the elderly and the corresponding age structure data from Table 9.1.

Aggregates and sub-aggregates

So far, we have discovered that pensions expenditure is moderately strongly associated with ageing, but that spending on health care and on services for the elderly do not demonstrate unambiguous signs of a connection with the age structure. We have also noted that, for the average OECD nation, change in pensions expenditure over the period 1965–1995 represented only approximately 16 per cent of change in total social spending and around 11 per cent of change in the total outlays of government. This suggests that the kind of age effects we would expect in relation to changes in these big aggregates of public expenditure should be relatively modest. This expectation is based on the assumption that two major sub-aggregates of public spending – total social spending minus pensions and total outlays minus social spending – are themselves unconnected with the changes in the age structure. The data in Table 9.4 serve to test these expectations and assumptions.

The assumption that change in social expenditure minus pensions would be unrelated to age structure change is confirmed by the data in column one of Table 9.4. However, since health expenditures and, to a lesser extent, age services expenditures are significant components of this sub-aggregate, this is really only a reiteration of a previous finding. More surprisingly, despite the adjusted R^2 of .50 for the relationship between age pensions expenditure change and age structure change, there is no apparent association between changes in age structure and in total social spending.

These are findings which once again appear to challenge the orthodoxy of the population ageing thesis. One reason they occur is a little noticed tendency for countries to trade-off pensions spending against other forms of social expenditure. In the period under examination here, Japan, Greece and Italy, the countries which Table 9.1 shows to have been ageing most rapidly, were simultaneously in the vanguard of pensions expansion as shown in Table 9.2 and in the rearguard in respect of the growth of other social expenditure as shown in the first column of Table 9.4. This does not seem to be a particularly new phenomenon. Statistical modelling for total social spending minus pensions for 1965 produces a term for age structure which is both significant and negative. In other words, it seems probable that, in the earlier stages of welfare state development, countries with relatively aged populations may well have concentrated on pensions programs to the detriment of welfare provision in other areas of need.

In other respects, the weakness of the association between population ageing and the non-pension components of the welfare state reflect new forces at work in shaping the welfare state. For many countries, the period after 1960 was one in which there was an increasingly explicit commitment to using the state as a means of promoting greater social and economic equality. Then, in the 1980s and 1990s, as that vision became more and more illusory with declining economic growth, certain countries became increasingly aware of new and more differentiated arenas of social need, most conspicuously those arising from increased degrees of labour market stress (see Castles 2000) and a changing family structure (see Esping-Andersen 1999). The countries with the greatest commitment to equality and with the greatest awareness of changing social needs were those in which the dominant political forces were predisposed to using the welfare state as an instrument of social amelioration. The importance of partisanship in accounting for the growth of post-war social spending is a theme of the comparative literature no less strong than the population ageing theme. The data at our disposal here suggest that, whilst ageing was the single most important factor accounting for change in post-war pensions expenditure, ideology was an even stronger determinant of change in other social spending.[2]

---

2 As already noted, Table 2 shows an adj. R^2 of .50 between change in the aged population 1965-1995 and change in pensions expenditure over the same period. Statistical analysis demonstrates the total absence of any relationship between change in pensions expenditure and

Table 9.4: 1965–1995 Changes in major aggregates and sub-aggregates of public expenditure.

Country	Total Social Spending minus Pensions	Total Social Spending	Total Outlays of General Government	Total Outlays minus Total Social Spending
Australia	8.4	8.2	10.6	2.4
Austria	9.2	8.8	14.6	5.8
Belgium	8.0	11.1	21.3	10.2
Canada	7.8	9.2	17.4	8.2
Denmark	15.2	18.0	28.9	10.9
Finland	16.9	20.9	26.6	5.7
France	10.9	13.7	15.9	2.3
Germany	8.7	9.1	13.1	4.0
Greece	4.4	8.6	27.7	19.1
Ireland	9.2	9.8	4.5	-5.3
Italy	4.2	7.5	18.4	10.9
Japan	4.0	8.3	15.6	7.3
Netherlands	11.7	10.7	12.6	1.9
New	6.7	8.7	•	•
Zealand	16.4	17.5	13.4	-4.1
Norway	16.7	19.8	29.5	9.7
Sweden	10.9	14.2	16.3	2.1
Switzerland	9.2	10.8	8.0	-2.8
UK	7.0	7.9	5.0	-2.9
USA	**9.8**	**11.7**	**16.6**	**4.7**
Mean Adj. R^2	.02	-.05	.25	.33

Sources: Pensions data from Table 9.2. 1965 total social spending from OECD (1994a). 1995 total social spending from OECD, *Social Expenditure Database 1980–1996*, Paris 1998, (CD Rom). 1965 and 1995 total outlays of general government from OECD, *Economic Outlook* (1998 and earlier numbers). **Adj. R^2** indicates the strength of the relationships between changes in the various aggregates and sub-aggregates of public expenditure and change in the population aged 65 years and over.

Turning to changes in total outlays and in total outlays minus total social spending as shown in columns three and four of Table 9.4 reveals seemingly paradoxical findings.

Right incumbency (for data and definitions, see Castles 1998) in these years. By contrast, the adj. R^2 between Right incumbency and change in other social spending over the period 1965-1995 (i.e. the data in column 1 of Table) is -.60, while the relationship with population ageing is quite insignificant.

Contrary to the expectation that the relationship between population ageing and outlays would be weaker than that between ageing and social spending, we actually discover that the relationship is moderately strong and clearly statistically significant. Moreover, and very surprisingly indeed, the apparent association between ageing and change in the non-welfare part of the budget is actually stronger than that for change in the budget as a whole, implying that ageing has a strong influence on precisely that part of the budget which least immediately reflects welfare state concerns.

Here, the theoretical analysis offered by the OECD does provide some initial leverage for greater understanding of what is going on. A possible connection between population ageing and non-welfare outlays might be via increases in net debt interest payments resulting from increased government borrowing to expand pension and early retirement programs in the years of economic stress following the oil crises of the 1970s. Controlling for the impact of increasing financial liabilities of general government[3] since the early 1980s makes the apparent ageing effect on non-welfare outlays disappear completely and reveals a modest but statistically significant relationship between ageing and indebtedness.

However, this latter relationship is far more tenuous than is implied in the OECD analysis. It is only possible to identify two clear cases – Greece and Italy – in which a strong expansion of pensions systems was largely financed through increased borrowing and without Greece's status as a massive debt outlier the relationship ceases to be significant. Other countries experiencing rapid ageing during this period, including Finland, Japan and Switzerland, did not finance their pensions spending through large-scale increases in public indebtedness and did not, therefore, experience disproportionate increases in non-welfare spending. Overall, the comparative evidence suggests that public profligacy in this period was more a matter of financially imprudent choices of government funding strategy and/or of misguided forecasts of future economic growth than of outcomes preordained by demographic forces.

Conclusions

This chapter has utilised a comparative analysis of three decades of OECD public spending change to test propositions concerning the likely consequences of population ageing for public expenditure development in coming years. Its conclusion is quite clear. Apart from the direct impact of pensions spending, there is no unequivocal evidence of direct or indirect ageing effects that need be of serious concern. The ageing effect on pensions spending is real, but any concern this may cause needs to be contextualised by an awareness of the possibility for deliberate policy manipulation of pensions coverage and generosity.

---

3 For data, see OECD (1998a: Annex Table 34).

It is, of course, the case that the countries with the most generous and extensive pensions systems are those which are experiencing the greatest difficulties, and these countries are the primarily the nations of continental, western Europe and Southern Europe. That is why a number of commentators with a more nuanced understanding of national differences than the World Bank have identified the real welfare malaise as one of Eurosclerosis rather than one of population ageing. Eventually, even this view may be too pessimistic. An obvious point, but one sometimes neglected, is that it is the countries with the most expensive pensions systems that have the most scope for pensions reform. The figures in the final column of Table 9.2, which show the declining or stationary trends of pensions spending in countries such as Austria, Germany and the Netherlands, suggest that policy-makers may be better at making such cuts than is often assumed.

The same story emerges from the convoluted history of attempted pension reforms in Italy in the 1990s. Of all the countries in the OECD facing serious difficulties based on the combined effects of population ageing and excessive generosity to beneficiaries, Italy constitutes the most extreme example, with spending on old age and survivors already over 15 per cent of GDP in 2000. Prior to the reforms of 1995 and 1997, pension expenditure projections suggested a pensions bill peaking in 2040 at more than 23 per cent of GDP. After the reforms, the projected spending peak will be 15.8 per cent of GDP in 2032 and will gradually decline thereafter (Ferrera 2000:176–77). The prophets of doom implicitly suggest that democratic politicians are powerless in the face of demographic challenge. The evidence of post-war expenditure development in the area of pensions does not support such a view.

Finally, from the point of view of those countries which are actually low spenders on pensions – and all members of the English-speaking family of nations fall into this category – to read lessons on the potential effects of population ageing from the experience of those countries with the most extensive and generous programs involves a distortion. By almost any criteria, including those of the OECD Secretariat and the World Bank – the existing age structure of the population, recent public expenditure trends and existing levels of public indebtedness[4] – most of these countries are well placed to cope with the public expenditure impact of population ageing in coming decades. To use the spectre of population ageing in these countries as a means of combating the growth of public expenditure is to transform social science analysis into ideological rhetoric.

---

4 We have already noted that the English-speaking nations will maintain more youthful age structures than either the Scandinavian or the continental European countries through until 2030 at least. Table 4 shows that the only English-speaking country in which any of the public expenditure aggregates increased more rapidly than the OECD post-war norm was Canada (in the case of total outlays of government and total outlays minus total social spending). OECD, *Economic Outlook* (1998) indicates that the only English-speaking nation with a high level of public indebtedness in recent decades was also Canada.

Chapter 10

Ageing and Public Pension Reforms in Western Europe and North America: patterns and politics

Karl Hinrichs

Introduction

Since the early 1980s public pension reforms have been on the political agenda in most OECD countries. The expected accelerating rise in the ratio of the elderly to that of the working age population during the decades to come is a common trend in all industrialised nations. It sparked off efforts to keep publicly provided support systems for the elderly financially viable and also to check sharpening intergenerational inequities. At least these are two concerns which figured prominently in legislative processes. In the wake of debates and policy changes, interest was growing almost everywhere in the ways in which old-age social security systems operate in other countries and in the reform strategies pursued elsewhere. To this end, international organisations (such as the ILO, OECD and World Bank) provided additional comparative information and evaluations. A main motivation of policymakers, administrators, media commentators, academics and others for looking beyond their national borders have been 'lessons' which could be drawn for a rational

Jochen Clasen (ed.), *What Future for Social Security?*, 157-178
©2001 Kluwer Law International. Printed in the Netherlands.

reorganisation of pension systems in their own country. The focus has often been on technical aspects and on the search for concrete reform elements which are considered to be worth policy adoption (so called 'best practices'). By contrast, the aim of this chapter is to contextualise pension policy developments during the last two decades in a number of OECD countries. This is confined to a 'family' of countries where similarly structured public pension schemes provide the core of earnings replacement. The selection of countries will be discussed in the following section. Subsequently I will show common developmental trends. In the main part of the chapter I will look into the similar and differing backgrounds of reforms, as well as into patterns of decision-making in public pension policy. 'Lessons' thus mainly relate to the consequences of differing institutional starting points and the modes of compromise-building in the political process of pension reform.

Old and new social insurance countries and the challenges their public pension schemes (will) face[1]

Generally, a number of countries can be identified in which right from the start (or perhaps after a short 'detour') the development of modern social policy was founded on the principle of *social insurance*; the so-called *Bismarck* countries. The 'employment centredness' of social security implies a precedence of status maintenance over poverty prevention. In contrast, the latter objective usually prevailed in *Beveridge* countries. Influenced by the *poor law* tradition, here a universal, tax or contribution-financed basic ('people's') pension system was established. Countries belonging to the *Bismarck* tradition are, in addition to Germany, Austria, Italy, France and Belgium. By legislative decisions of 1935 and 1939, comprising the organisation of the core of retirement provision as social insurance, the United States joined this group. Shortly after, so did Japan, as it gradually enacted a contributory two-tier system consisting of an earnings-related employees' pension insurance and a basic pension scheme (see e.g. OECD 1997b:121-30).

In the course of their development, those social insurance schemes expanded in three dimensions: in terms of benefit levels, the range of entitlements, and coverage of the compulsorily insured. Moreover, all these countries (with the exception of Germany) introduced a floor of minimum protection for elderly whose contribution record led to insufficient benefit entitlement, separate from the general system of social assistance.

Four more countries metamorphosed from originally *Beveridge* into *Bismarck* countries when they topped up their respective basic pension schemes with a second scheme aimed at income continuity during the life course. These countries (which might be called *early birds*) were Sweden (1959) and Finland (1961) and, somewhat later, Canada (1965) and

---

1 For an extended version of this section and for references to background material not explicitly mentioned in this and the subsequent section see Hinrichs 2000b.

Norway (1966). In view of favourable economic and demographic conditions at the time, these countries established a second *public* pillar, which was contribution-based, unfunded (at least in principle), yielded an earnings-related supplementary pension and included redistributive provisions in varying degrees. As these complementary pension insurance schemes matured, the relevance of the 'basic pension' pillar declined in relative or even absolute terms.[2]

Another group of *Beveridge* countries which had not established a mandatory *public* complementary pension scheme until the early 1970s, combined the traditional solidarity principle (minimum pensions, financed out of general tax revenues or tax-like contributions) with the equivalence principle (aimed at status maintenance) by different means. An earnings-related topping-up was attained via *occupational* pension schemes that was either mandated by law (Switzerland, Australia) or arose through collective agreements (Netherlands, Denmark). In the latter case, coverage of nearly all employees was achieved by legal provisions of extension (Hinrichs 2001). In these four countries (which might be called *latecomers*) the second pillar is *funded* and *private*, but publicly regulated and controlled in order to protect employees who adopted strategies of retirement provision based on those benefits. In the Netherlands and Australia the inception *viz.* generalisation of the second pillar was predominantly the result of union pressure, as well as in Denmark after repeated attempts to introduce a true earnings-related public pillar finally failed.

A further *latecomer*, constituting a special case, is the United Kingdom. The introduction of *SERPS* (*State Earnings-Related Pension Scheme*) in 1978 brought the UK into the group of social insurance countries. However, the reforms carried out by the Thatcher and Major governments in 1986 and 1995 reversed this course. The public supplementary scheme's benefits were substantially reduced, rendering *SERPS* unattractive for younger cohorts of employees and increasingly marginal. Presently, it covers no more than about a quarter of all employees. The permitted alternatives to *SERPS* (*contracting out*) – occupational pension schemes and the heavily tax-subsidised private pension plans (*APPs*) – clearly predominate (Davis 1995: 63-4; Liu 1999). New Labour's legislation of 1999 and 2000 following from an earlier Green Paper (Department of Social Security 1998) implied no (further) 'U-turn'.[3]

---

2 These statutory pension *insurance* schemes of comparatively recent vintage (to which, in this case, one might add the USA) are marked by some peculiarities relative to the schemes of the original *Bismarck* countries: from the outset (nearly) the *total* workforce was included in *one* scheme (with the exception of Finland where a kind of 'para-public' system of decentralised funds, controlled by the social partners, was established). There were no, or very high, contribution ceilings (except in Canada), and in Sweden, Finland and Canada reserve funds play(ed) a larger role. However, the schemes in these three countries are far from being fully funded and do not aspire to be so.

3 Thus, from the originally numerous *Beveridge* countries there are only two countries left, namely Ireland and New Zealand, where no comparably complete *topping-up* occurred: in New Zealand, the basic pension is supplemented by *voluntary* private provision and scattered

The examination of patterns of public pension reform in this chapter is restricted to a comparison within the enlarged group of *social insurance* countries since, methodologically, they represent 'most similar cases'. The schemes in these countries are distinct, for public pension expenditure regularly represents the largest single item of their nations' total social spending. They have become the 'grey giants' of their welfare states and, like fully-grown elephants, difficult to move. The most important cause of this immobility is that public pension schemes enjoy particularly high esteem and support among citizens/voters of all ages. However, living up to current and future beneficiaries' expectations of reliable income security poses a difficult challenge for public policy. Whereas tax-financed basic pension schemes in the *latecomer* countries (or those components in *social insurance* countries) might be cut much faster and more discretionary because benefits do not represent *earned entitlements* (Myles and Quadagno 1997), pronounced resistance against reform is a common feature of social insurance schemes. 'Contributory "rights" and privileges, spanning perhaps fifty years, become sacrosanct' (Titmuss 1976:60). Hence, reform considerations of policymakers in this area of social policy are typically shaped by a very long time frame, stretching well beyond one parliamentary period.

This observation has consequences for the research strategy. Focusing exclusively on public pension scheme expenditures (or corresponding GDP ratios) will not suffice – and not merely because monetary figures do not provide an optimal yardstick for international comparisons. More important is that present changes in expenditure are, to a large extent, the result of political decisions reached (very) long ago, and today's reforms sometimes alter the expenditure and revenue situation with an extended time-lag.[4] Moreover, changes in expenditure levels reflect the balance of programme expansions and restrictions in the past as well as current demographic and economic changes so that a 'steady state' will hardly ever be attained. A comparison of old-age security policies, which takes into account these peculiarities, must engage national policies in considerable detail. It has to analyse in depth the institutional set-up, decision-making processes and policy changes.[5] However, these requirements of such a qualitative approach cannot be fully met in a chapter of limited length.

The question I will turn to below therefore is whether, as a result of comparable changes in their environment, old-age security systems in the *social insurance* countries are

---

occupational pension schemes (contributions to both variants are not tax-exempted). In Ireland, complementary, employer-sponsored pension schemes have spread, but are not mandatory. The coverage rate is about 50 per cent.

4 This is also true for the income situation of today's retirees, being the result of institutional arrangements and individual behaviour oriented to those rules, incentives, or obligations when they were at working age.

5 Huber and Stephens (1993: 323), for example, are well aware of the limits of their *quantitative* analysis and demand: '(R)esearchers will have to examine individual pension systems in greater detail ... (and) devote more attention to qualitative aspects of pension systems.'

converging or whether, despite a number of similar policy changes, there are peculiarities in pension reform politics, reflecting certain institutional characteristics of distinct welfare states and different designs of public pension schemes, which constrain processes of convergence. Population ageing, due both to the decline in fertility and to increasing longevity, is a common challenge of all industrialised countries although intensity and timing vary. In addition, concerns about a nation's competitiveness in the face of 'globalisation' is an additional factor putting pressure on (not only) public pension schemes.

Compared with the *social insurance* countries, the *latecomers* (the Netherlands, Australia, Denmark, Switzerland, and the UK) established a different type of welfare state for the elderly by adopting a *private* and *funded* supplementary pillar. Thus, demographic ageing presents itself as a political problem in a different manner as well. Despite the macroeconomic consequences of population ageing, these countries will not have to extract taxes and/or contributions to the same extent as *social insurance* countries in order to fund retirement income. On the contrary, the more those not yet matured 'private' pension systems expand, the more spending on public minimum pensions is contained in a 'natural' way (this is expected to happen in Australia when *Superannuation* benefits grow). Likewise, those schemes' benefits can be scaled back more easily by, for example, stricter targeting (through extended means-testing), cutting supplementary benefits, or modifying indexing procedures. Moreover, increasing the standard retirement age is already underway in several of these *latecomer* countries.[6] Due to the susceptibility of predominantly unfunded pension schemes to demographic shifts, in the 'old' (Germany, Austria, etc.) and 'new' (Sweden, Finland, etc) *social insurance* countries retrenchment policies have been introduced or are in part already effective. By contrast, in the *latecomer* countries a further expansion of old-age security is thoroughly conceivable. Therefore, a convergence of the retirement income schemes between these *two groups* appears most unlikely.

Public pension reforms in social insurance countries

Although the central difference between the *latecomer* and the *social insurance* countries is the *non*-public versus public provision of earnings-related retirement income it does not necessarily imply a marginal or stagnating role of *private* components of income security in *social insurance* countries. Dependent on the standard benefit level and on the extent to which the replacement ratio for employees with above-average wages dropped, additional components of retirement provision have developed, resulting in varying 'public-private

---

6 This does not imply that population ageing will cause no problems for the financing of *latecomer* countries' basic pension schemes. These challenges will vary according to the relative benefit level. Having the most generous basic pension (Hinrichs 2001), the Netherlands already established a reserve fund which is expected to melt away after 2020 in order to maintain the contribution rate to the *AOW* scheme continuously at its present level. Remaining deficits will be covered by subsidies out of general taxation (van Oorschot and Boos 1999).

mixes'. For example, in the USA or Canada the non-public sources of retirement income, especially for formerly high-wage earners, play a much larger role than in Austria, Italy or Germany, where the replacement ratios of public pensions (and, thus, payments as a percentage of GDP) are considerably higher. Obviously, a given institutional design of public pensions gives rise to distinct collective bargaining and individual strategies for supplementing pensions or for compensating missing income replacement through (firm-specific or industry-wide) occupational and private provision. The arrangement and extent of non-public provision itself is also influenced by public policy (tax advantages for individuals and firms, for example, can often be secured only under the condition of adherence to regulatory standards). Nevertheless, none of the countries examined here have a layer of funded occupational pensions which would cover almost all employees over and above the earnings-related public pension scheme. In the USA, for example, coverage is below 50 per cent. Based on collective bargaining, in Sweden occupational pensions are nearly universal but not fully funded in an actuarial sense. I will not elaborate on those differences, past developments and feedback mechanisms here. However, if the public/private retirement income allocation will eventually change as a concomitant, or intended result, of reforming public pension schemes, this might indicate whether reforms as a whole have to be considered as *systemic,* instead of remaining in the realm of *parametric* changes.

Generally, the financial stability of contributory, unfunded pension schemes is threatened from two sides: from the *revenue* side when economic and/or structural developments on the labour market lead to a decrease of covered earnings, or the contribution base does not keep pace with predetermined expenditure. Problems from the *expenditure* side arise if, due to demographic change, there is an increase in the number of insured actually entering retirement and/or the average period of benefit receipt and, thus, the dependency ratio rises. Hence, a doubly destabilising effect follows from growing numbers of early retirees: higher benefit outlays have to be met out of a reduced contributory base. If scheme provisions are not adjusted and if no accumulated reserve funds are available, those changes result immediately in deficits or in the necessity to raise the contribution rate. Presently, the effects of contributory financing, detrimental to achieving higher employment (rates), give rise to demands for restraining the growth of pension expenditures. In the long term, imminent demographic change puts pressure on the schemes' generosity because, if benefit levels were to remain at their current real levels, the unavoidably rising contribution rate would not only intensify present concerns, but would also violate notions of intergenerational fairness, undermining the schemes' legitimacy.

In the case of a current or future 'crisis', there is only a limited repertoire of reform options available for stabilising the expenditure or revenue side of a public pension scheme (Chand and Jaeger 1996). These policy changes can affect either the insured (contributors), the pensioners, or the state's involvement in terms of co-financing or improving the framework conditions (see Table 10.1). Guided by the objective of burdening present or future contributors (much) *less* than under status-quo assumptions, the scope and the mix of adjustment strategies (and thus eventually the allocative and distributional outcome) is determined by the respective institutional design as well as by the interests of the political actors involved, i.e. pension politics. If one studies reforms of public pension schemes which have been initiated since the mid-1980s in view of acute imbalances or long-term threats to the systems' stability, seven broad trends can be identified in all, or at least several, of the *social insurance* countries (for details see also OECD 1996a:17-22, 44-6; Weaver 1998; Gillion et al. 2000:583-97; OECD 2000b:13-61).

First: almost everywhere, reforms have strengthened the *equivalence principle* and thus reduced elements of interpersonal redistribution.[7] The requirements for receiving a 'full' pension, i.e. the target benefit level, were tightened by modifying the respective benefit formula in various ways. For example, reference periods were lengthened, giving more weight to individual equity, or, when computing the individual benefit, earnings of more or all contribution years were taken into account instead of, hitherto, those of a few 'best years' or of the 'last years' prior to retirement. Alternatively, non-contributory periods, which hitherto had increased entitlement, were eliminated or reduced. These various changes have in common that they imply lower pension benefits for those with a less than 'full' employment record and/or whose earnings fluctuate (rise) over the career, or lead to a lower benefit level for all insured if accrual rates were reduced.

In this respect, the most far-reaching changes in benefit calculation will become effective in Sweden and Italy once the transition to a *defined contribution* system has been completed: without factually giving up the pay-as-you-go mode of financing, a funded scheme is mimicked when contributions, paid according to a defined rate, 'earn' an interest rate corresponding to the growth of wages *viz.* gross domestic product. At retirement – the age of entry is optional within a certain range – the benefit is computed as the annuity equivalent to the accumulated 'capital', actuarially adjusted for the age at first pension receipt. The new benefit computation explicitly takes into account the (increasing) life expectancy of every birth cohort when the notional pension capital is converted into a monthly pension payment (in Italy there will be a periodical adjustment of the conversion rate). A post-retirement adjustment of benefits is effected through a combined index of wage and consumer price inflation (Sweden) or according to price inflation alone (Italy).[8]

---

7 It is only in Norway where a weakening of the contribution-benefit link has occurred and which is expected to deliver considerable expenditure savings in the future since the changes of 1992 will result in a lower benefit level with a compressed spread at the upper end.

8 For details on the reforms in Italy and Sweden see Antichi and Pizzuti (2000); Ferrera (2000); Scherman (1999) and Palmer (2000). It has been contested whether it is justified to actually consider this so called 'Notional Defined Contribution' approach (NDC), where all parameters of the scheme are politically determined, as a new paradigm. Cichon (1999) argues that largely the same results can be attained with a linear accrual rate as applied in Germany where each year of covered employment is included in the benefit formula in a similar manner. Moreover, the reformed public pension schemes in Italy and Sweden do not rule out financial instabilities or the need for discretionary modifications in future.

Post-retirement uprating of pension benefits has been changed to the disadvantage of beneficiaries in other countries as well, mostly by linking increases to consumer prices, cutting off the retired from participation in the real wage growth of the working-age generations.[9] Furthermore, indexation as such has been temporarily suspended or, based on discretionary decisions, changed in the USA, Belgium, Sweden, Finland, Italy, Japan, Germany and Austria. Tinkering with adjustment formulas is a subtle, but very powerful instrument that provides immediate and significant long-term savings of expenditure since the 'basis effect' ripples through all subsequent years.

Second: in nearly all of the countries, reforms were implemented which aimed at raising the effective age of entry into retirement, either by gradually raising the standard retirement age or by blocking pathways into early retirement. The hitherto prevailing consensus that the labour market chances of younger workers ought to be improved by providing older employees attractive opportunities to exit working life prematurely has, almost everywhere, been superseded by attempts to reverse the trend of ever lower employment rates in the upper age brackets. Corresponding measures included those of tightening access to disability pensions (e.g. by restricting eligibility to exclusively medical grounds) and of attempts to remove distorting incentives for early retirement. To this end, in a number of places permanent deductions from the benefit level for early retirement were introduced or increased to (almost) actuarial amounts while for those staying in the labour force beyond standard retirement age, a pension bonus was awarded. Sometimes, workers were given the opportunity to combine part-time work with the receipt of a partial pension. Countries with comparatively high employment rates of older workers were as eager in their attempts to raise the actual age of entry into retirement as other countries. At the same time, in those countries where standard retirement ages hitherto differed by gender, reforms were aimed at equalisation, i.e. at raising the retirement age for women.

Third: in almost all countries under consideration, unpaid family work became incorporated in benefit calculation. Raising children and/or taking care of frail relatives now results in (higher) benefit claims in Canada, France, Norway, Austria, Italy, Belgium, Germany and Sweden. The applied procedures and the produced benefit increases differ considerably and cannot be described in detail here. To the extent that these 'family credits' not only compensate for other benefit cuts (e.g. as a result of changed benefit formulas particularly affecting women, or cutbacks of survivors' pensions) they represent the sole expansionary element among the recent reforms. Although the reduction of horizontal disadvantages when performing 'family duties' was the proclaimed objective, at least implicitly pronatalist considerations played as much a role as the issue of gender equity.

---

9 In order to stabilise schemes *implicit* demographic parameters were introduced in the indexation formula in Germany (1992), Austria (1993) and Japan (1994, but terminated in 2000). The technique here was an adjustment of pensions based on preceding *net* (rather than gross) wage growth, so that higher contribution rates (predominantly stemming from the ageing process) slow down pension spending.

Fourth: increased tax-financing of the hitherto exclusively or predominantly contribution-financed public pension schemes can be identified as a further trend. Independent of the various justifications given, the intention combined with these (additional) subsidies out of general revenues to the (fiscally separated) public pension schemes was to contain, or even reverse, increases in the contribution rate – in particular, to relieve employers of non-wage labour costs. Those refinancing strategies were applied in Belgium, Italy, Japan, the USA (in an indirect way), France, Germany, and Sweden.[10] In the three latter countries, the relationship between stronger individual equity on the one hand, and (newly added) redistributional elements aimed at social adequacy and increased fiscalisation on the other, is obvious. Non-contributory components of the benefit package are financed out of taxes, and hence, technically, the demarcation relative to entitlements earned through contribution payments becomes more visible, rendering the schemes more transparent and acceptable.

Fifth: so far as special pension schemes existed for public employees (and workers in publicly owned enterprises), attempts have been made to harmonise them with schemes for employees in the private sector. One strategy pursued has been to gradually reduce privileges of public employees, e.g. with regard to retirement age or replacement level, which formerly had been targets for workers in the private sector. This happened in Austria, Finland and Italy. Another strategy, applied in the USA, made public sector employees increasingly compulsory members of the core scheme. In Germany and France, however, where different rules for public and private employees are strongly pronounced, no such reforms were (successfully) launched. While the first strategy aims at lowering the total wage costs for the state as employer in the long run, the second strategy, at least temporarily, shovels additional contribution revenues into the funds of the social insurance scheme(s). This purpose is also served when certain groups of employees hitherto exempted from insurance become covered on a mandatory basis (such as marginal part-time workers and new types of self-employed in Austria and Germany), or when earned income became more fully subject to contribution payments (e.g. in Canada and Japan).

Sixth: more and more countries which have provided a basic pension regardless of individual need are now fully or partially taking into account other retirement income. While in Canada only the very well-off pensioners have been affected (after plans for elaborate income testing were eventually withdrawn, see McCarthy 1998), in Sweden and Finland the universal, flat-rate 'people's pension' has been abolished and replaced by a 'guarantee pension', tested against other public retirement benefits. It is only Norway that has stuck with a non-targeted basic pension and even raised its level in 1998.

---

10 Since 1993, the revenues of a new energy tax in Belgium have been used to reduce employers' social insurance charges by 1.5 percentage points (largely limited to industrial enterprises in the exposed sector). It preceded a similar approach in Germany where, introduced in 1998, a gradually increasing 'ecology tax' serves to lower the contribution rate to the public pension scheme for both employers and employees. Factually, those indirect taxes reduce the real value of pension benefits (and other transfer payments). This is even more so the case in France where a special tax (*CSG*) is also levied on all transfer income.

Finally: the USA, Japan and Canada have modified their pay-as-you-go mode of financing so that the contribution rate is set higher than is currently necessary for covering annual pension spending, causing trust fund reserves to grow considerably. One goal is to increase the national savings rate so that the economic growth base is enlarged, particularly if the surpluses are not invested (only) in government bonds but, as in Canada, in a more diversified portfolio of securities. Irrespective of whether this strategy succeeds, the second objective is to 'tunnel through' the ageing process, accumulating capital reserves which will then melt away as the population ages during the coming decades, allowing a lower contribution rate to be levied at the then employed than would have been necessary otherwise. To this end, further countries (Norway and France, but also the Netherlands and Ireland) have set up reserve funds fed by various public revenues (e.g. proceeds from privatising public enterprises).

Another change is not directly affecting the public pension scheme but accompanies reforms and leads to comparable results, albeit not with equivalent (re-)distributional consequences. This is the expansion of individual and/or occupational pension schemes, either by mandating participation (Sweden) or by improving incentives, mainly through augmented tax advantages and setting up a regulatory framework, as in Italy, Austria and (very soon) in Germany. Sweetened by the possibility of deducting eligible savings from taxable income, those participating in non-public retirement saving schemes will have thus the opportunity to compensate for more modest public pension benefits resulting from reforms listed above. In contrast, the first strategy, applied in the USA, Canada and elsewhere, amounts to (largely) maintained *public* benefits for future pensioners, 'prepaid' by contributions fixed at a rate which currently generates a surplus in the fund's balance.

Either strategy can attain its respective ends only if the *political* and *economic* contexts provide the chance to translate them into action well before the massive demographic shifts develop; that is, the public scheme's contribution rate has not yet reached a prohibitively high level, a large majority of wage earners can afford additional savings for retirement, or public budgets can currently cope with corresponding tax expenditures.

These two strategies also exemplify that *social insurance* countries with large, matured, unfunded public pension schemes can hardly emulate the *latecomer* countries and create an old-age security system with a predominantly funded component and an absolutely or relatively shrinking public component providing basic security, which is so emphatically demanded by the World Bank (1994) and now also by the OECD (1998b; 2000b). The present generation of pensioners and those of working age who have paid contributions have 'earned' entitlements which they legitimately expect to be honoured by succeeding generations. In view of the virtual impossibility of dismissing these property-like claims, which represent the implicit debt of a public insurance scheme, a 'pareto-efficient' transition of the mode of financing, i.e. without impairing any generation's welfare, is not viable. Members of a number of birth cohorts would have to carry a 'double burden' if they had to save for their own funded retirement income and at the same time redeem claims earned in the unfunded scheme with 'contributions', now bearing an explicit tax character. Such a constellation makes the transition to a *fully* funded old-age security system politically almost impossible.

But also less ambitious shifts in the relative weight of public/private pension components require an extended time frame as can be shown from a projection made by the German government in an enclosure to the reform bill that passed the *German Bundestag (lower House)* in January 2001 (Deutscher Bundestag 2001:7). The estimate takes into account the effects of changes of the public pension scheme and is based on the assumption that contributors to the public pension system follow the recommendation to save an additional (and tax-privileged) 4 per cent of their gross earnings (the final level to be reached by 2008) for a personal pension. If these savings were to yield a constant interest rate of 4 per cent, the personal pension accrual would amount to no more than 11.8 per cent of the standard public pension (after 45 years of covered employment) for a worker retiring in 2030. Since the portion of retirement income presently stemming from funded sources amounts to less than 20 per cent, it is thus unlikely that Germany (or most other *social insurance* countries) will attain the unfunded/funded income mix of *latecomer* countries such as the Netherlands or United Kingdom in the foreseeable future. This assertion is further supported by the fact that reforms of the pension schemes along the lines mentioned above will not prevent a further rise of *public* pension spending (as a portion of GDP). Such a development defines limits on what can reasonably be expected from working-age generations to reinforce their *private* efforts to provide for old-age pensions.

Nevertheless, the inevitably slow process of pre-funding future retirement income from non-public sources in countries with a hitherto high earnings replacement ratio of the public scheme and (almost) negligible non-public pension components, can be regarded as a *systemic* reform introduced alongside *parametric* reforms. Aimed at reducing entitlements, the latter will lower or contain contribution rates so as to obtain more leeway for private provision. Although it will take several decades to catch up with the current retirement income mix in the USA or Canada, the shift which will occur (or is about to happen) in countries such as Sweden, Italy, Austria and Germany implies a departure from the principle of income maintenance through *public* pension benefits (see also below). Moreover, it will be accompanied by distributional consequences. The 'crowding in' of private pension components can be expected to lead to more income inequality in old age – exactly a reversal of what happened when earnings-related public pensions were introduced and thus crowded out more regressive private components of the income package (Jäntti et al. 1996).

Lessons from the public pension reform process

Based on the findings in the preceding section, I will now turn to some conclusions. First, the question of (reduced/revised) diversity will be addressed. The circumstances of reform initiatives and the politics of pension reform policy will then be discussed. Finally, I will look into the implications of recent reforms, particularly, the preconditions of quite substantial retrenchments.

Convergence

Have the reforms initiated since about the mid-1980s in *social insurance* countries reduced the diversity of public pension schemes? No definite answer to this question can be given because 'convergence' can be discussed in relation to several criteria, such as structural design, outcomes, instruments, or goals. If, as for Overbye (1994), the focus is whether a *dual structure* of old-age security, i.e. a poverty-alleviating basic pension supplemented by an earnings-replacing component (or vice versa), has developed as a combined result of risk exposition, political institutions and actor strategies, then convergence is most obvious and also includes the *latecomer* countries. However, this perspective blurs precisely those differences that are crucial for present (and future) problem constellations and political adjustment strategies.

Johnson (1999) examines evidence of convergence in the *outcomes* of public pension schemes. Instead of using (inadequate) expenditure data or indirect outcome measures (like income inequality or poverty rates), he concentrates on the 'pure' impact of the pension scheme's (changed) rules on 'hypothetical individuals'. Apart from the fact that this approach is too 'stylised' (or synthetic) because standard cases are becoming ever less representative and rule changes affect insured persons selectively[11], it cannot adequately grasp the 'final state' when rule changes are fully implemented after (extensive) phasing-in or phasing-out periods. People live through, as Johnson (1999:604) correctly points out, 'both their personal career history and the institutional history of their national pension system'. While he summarises the findings of his simulations on the long-term trends as inconclusive, Johnson (1999:615) states that 'since the mid-1980s ... retrenchment has reversed a trend towards harmonisation and has increased the variance across countries in the level of income provided for similar individuals through the public pension system'.

If one borrows from Hall's (1993:278) distinction of three kinds of policy change (goals, techniques and levels) and reviews the trends discussed above, conspicuously more uniformity of applied *techniques* and *levels* of these instruments can be observed. This applies, for example, to standard retirement ages, pension credits for unpaid family work, or benefit formulas bringing about a tighter relationship between contributions (or lifetime earnings) and benefits. This evolution is less a result of 'emulation' (Bennett 1991) which presumes a transnational diffusion of information about problems and solutions as well as lesson drawing, but stems from a limited set of incremental (or parametric) adjustment options (see Table 10.1), facilitating parallel development. 'There is always a finite

---

11 For example, women in Germany benefit from some of the recent rule changes but lose out due to others, but not in a uniform way across and between birth cohorts.

repertoire of possible responses to emerging policy problems' (Bennett 1991:220). Undoubtedly, a convergence of the profile of the reformed Swedish public pension system with the German approach is discernible if one considers the introduction of (tax-financed) contribution payments covering non-employment periods (child care, unemployment, sickness, military service). What is more, as in Germany, contributions are becoming evenly split between employers and employees (not fully realised yet), benefits calculated on the basis of all years of insurance and there is a reduction of intragenerational redistribution in Sweden. The 'Germanisation' is also true for the Austrian, Finnish and, to some extent, the Italian pension scheme after its latest revisions, which in their central aspects resemble the Swedish reforms. Policy changes may indeed occasionally be borrowed from the 'toolboxes' of others. However, the deliberate sounding out of exemplary policy solutions, eventually leading to a transfer, presumes a high degree of rationality in the policymaking process.[12]

Taking the concept of 'path dependency' seriously, one can expect that *similar* challenges, dealt with in different institutional contexts with a correspondingly different course of issue processing and dissimilar actor coalitions, result in policy changes which, above all, *revise* the original diversity. Insofar, only a very detailed comparison of chosen or accessible reform strategies can inform about changed goals of public pension systems or altered conceptions regarding the future mix of retirement income and its social distribution and, hence, settle the question of whether the level of diversity was actually *reduced*. Obviously, in this respect, again, the reconstruction of the Swedish old-age security system implies the most far-reaching goal shift (or 'third order change'; Hall 1993) towards 're-commodification': The 'citizenship' principle has been replaced with an income test for the new 'guarantee pension' (this is also true for Finland).[13] Furthermore, instead of adhering to distinctive features of the Social Democratic welfare regime, e.g. to 'maximize equality' or to 'minimize ... market dependency' (Esping-Andersen 1999:78-9), the new *inkomstpension* scheme is far less redistributive and will provide benefits which are more differentiated due to its strictly contribution-based formula. Finally, the paramount role of the state in providing retirement income will be reduced when about 14 per cent of the total contribution amount will be diverted into the premium reserve scheme, thus enlarging the weight of private welfare. These shifts away from traditional policy objectives raise serious doubts about the *immutability* of 'regimes' (Esping-Andersen 1999:86-7, 165) and whether the 'regime approach' as such is at all relevant if the focus is on particular policy areas,

---

12 Espina's (1996: 181-2, 201) or Boje's (1996: 14-6) expectations that comparative analysis could be the starting-point for a higher degree of similarity of welfare state programmes seem to be overly optimistic, at least with regard to pension schemes. A 'benchmarking process' that identifies least satisfactory and most dysfunctional elements of each national scheme and replaces them by current 'best practices' applied elsewhere regularly faces hard constraints stemming from the established programme's politics.

13 Esping-Andersen admits that 'this implies a qualitative retreat from the principle of universalism: the notion of solidarity of risks is being rewritten' (1999: 80, see also 88, footnote 16)

given that traits assumed to be crucial to the Social Democratic regime vanished under Social Democratic rule and without social upheaval.

Timing and consensus politics

When examining which governments have initiated predominantly retrenching reforms it is striking to note that they were led by Christian Democratic or Conservative parties (mostly in coalition with liberal parties), 'Grand Coalitions' including Social Democrats, as well as (coalition) governments led by Social Democrats. The 'colour' of the government is obviously of little relevance for the choice of roughly similar adjustment strategies aimed at coping with comparable challenges. Instead it is more interesting to ask *when* reform projects were started and *which* alliances over and above the government party/parties supported the reform.

Weaver's (1998) observation regarding the circumstances of reform initiatives holds true for most countries. Either looming deficits of pension schemes, their impending 'insolvency' (1983 in the USA), growing deficits of the public budget, an unrestrained increase in pension spending, or contribution rates rising due to massive labour-market induced early retirement, represented immediate policy challenges and regularly brought Ministers of Finance into the arena. In addition, and a further explanation why reforms occurred increasingly in the 1990s, pressure was increased because of imminent EU membership (Austria, Finland) or the advancing process of European integration (concerns in Italy and France about meeting the EMU convergence criteria). In the wake of a generally advancing market-liberal ideology, the perception of a need for reform was intensified by a changing assessment of what is affordable (in order not to lose international competitiveness) and efficient (in view of already distorting tax wedges). Of at least equal importance was increased attention towards pessimistic scenarios of ageing, characterised by a preoccupation with rising old-age dependency ratios. However, the actual extent of the predicted demographic shift, and its consequences, hardly affected how much it became a political issue or influenced the intensity of the reform debate. A widely accepted 'crisis' definition therefore provided the necessary thrust to get the reform process going and, in the course of the respective process, not only to tackle acute problems but also long-term challenges. *A priori*, taking a time horizon well beyond urgent 'repairs' cannot be expected from politicians striving for success in the next election. The peculiarities of the politics of public pension policy offer an explanation why politicians dared to burden themselves with even more unpopular decisions, the consequences of which went beyond the current parliamentary period.

Pension policy almost always and everywhere has differed from legislative changes in other areas of the welfare state, in so far as decisions largely came about in a consensual manner. To some extent, this is due to the rather complicated and technical pension law, and thus to experts, representatives of programme administration and special commissions playing a decisive role in preparing reforms. Within those policy communities issues are de-politicised and long-term 'technical' solutions are favoured. On the other hand, taking a long planning horizon is required because present decisions extend far into the future. Bringing the planning period in line with the even longer time horizon of the insured (covering about sixty years – from entering employment for the first time until termination of benefit payments – and with individual capabilities to adjust diminishing to zero at the time of retirement) is all the more important because of the need to convey institutional stability and thus to sustain *institutional trust* on the part of contributors. *Reliable rules,* if supported by a broad majority in parliament and thus not endangered by a change in government, are decisive for the participants in an unfunded pension scheme to be assured of 'security' regarding their life planning and thus for maintaining the institution's legitimacy. In this respect, the 'pension consensus' in Germany, established in 1957 (and lasting until the mid-1990s) and constantly referred to by political parties and the social partners, was not untypical but probably merely more well-developed than elsewhere.

If these conditions were valid (and quite easily met) during the expansionary phase, a consensus appears to be all the more necessary at a time when retrenchments are considered. Governments regularly attempt to win over others for supporting a compromise because this means spreading responsibility for concrete cutbacks affecting large parts of the electorate, or for having caused general insecurity, so that the ability to avoid blame becomes 'a key component of loss-imposition' (Ross 1997:190; Pierson 1996). Obviously, even if they take effect only gradually, far-reaching retrenchments in public pensions become fully implemented and gain acceptance among policy-*takers* if their necessity as such is uncontested, they are perceived as a coherent redesign of the scheme in response to a problem (rather than a systemic rupture), they are negotiated and (broadly) consented to and therefore ensure a socially balanced (fair) distribution of burdens and, last but not least, accrue in small doses when being phased in over a long period.

In almost all *social insurance* countries, where attempts to contain the increase in pension spending were undertaken in order to stabilise public pension schemes, these considerations were politically relevant. The construction of the *Pension Reform Act of 1992* in Germany was guided by the eventually successful endeavour to reach a consensus among political parties and social partners. In the USA, the 1983 reform of *Social Security* was based on a compromise reached by a 'bipartisan commission' which included trade unions and employers. The principles of the Swedish public pension reform, decided upon in 1994, followed the recommendations of a committee composed of members of the four bourgeois parties and the Social Democrats (but not the social partners), which strove for consensual responses to problems identified in a broad political investigation (between 1984 and 1990). Likewise, these five parties supported the subsequent legislation on the details of reform and thus provided for a 90 per cent majority vote in parliament. In Canada, the federal government started the legislation process in 1997 only after an agreement had been reached with most of the provincial governments (of different party compositions). The 'Grand Coalition' in Austria (Social Democrats and the Christian-Conservative party) was successful in integrating both social partners in a multi-stage reform process (in 1997, however, only after intense conflicts with the trade unions). It was thus able to broaden the legitimacy for the resulting sacrifices (Tálos and Kittel 1999:155-60). The same was true in Finland in the 1990s where an oversized coalition government (about 70 per cent of seats in parliament), by and large supported by the social partners, enacted the reforms. In Japan, regularly following from a commission's review every five years legislative changes were approved by opposition parties and the social partners (but this does not apply to the reform in 2000).[14]

Italy, France and Germany provide an interesting contrast. Although beginning already in the 1980s, the 'permanent project' of reforming the excessive Italian public pension system did not make substantial progress until 1992 ('Amato reform') and 1995 ('Dini reform'), under the auspices of a (revived) 'concertation' with the social partners. The changes originally proposed by the Dini government of 'technocrats' were moderated upon consultation with the trade unions before they could pass parliament with the support of the Left parties. In contrast, the previous unilateral attempt of the Berlusconi government largely failed. What is more, the trade unions' fierce struggle against the proposals for an overhaul of the pension system contributed to the eventual fall of the latter government at the turn of 1994/95 (Levy 1999). Again, in 1997 the unions, eager to protect the acquired rights of their predominantly older membership, refused to acquiesce in an accelerated harmonisation of different schemes and harsher phasing-out provisions over and above the 1995 legislation. As a consequence, the Prodi government largely withdrew central parts of its proposal.

The decisive role of trade unions' consent to pension reforms can also be seen in France. Whereas the Balladur government pursued a strategy of consensus – and after making concessions to the trade unions the latter refrained from protests against the reform –, the confrontational approach of the Juppé government two years later failed when it attempted to extend to public-sector employees the measures adopted in 1993 for the private sector and to change the trade unions' role in the management of social insurance schemes (Bonoli 2000:137-49). The succeeding Socialist-led government abstained from putting into practice a law by which funded private pensions would have been established. Aiming to avoid conflicts with the unions, in spring of 2000 it shied away from legislating expenditure-saving changes which were proposed in the *Rapport Charpin* (Mantel and Thomsen 2000).

In Germany, traditional consensus politics, which still characterised the reform act of 1989 (taking effect in 1992), came to a halt when the Christian Democratic-Liberal government unilaterally enacted substantial retrenchments in 1996 and 1997. Although not all elements

---

14 The major reform of the Spanish public pension scheme(s) (which always had some affinity to the *Bismarck* model; Espina 1996: 190-4) also fits the general pattern. The *Toledo Pact* of 1995, converted into law in 1997, not only contained changes corresponding to the trends described above. (particularly the first, fourth and seventh). It also came about as an inter-party compromise, and was approved by the labour unions.

of the reform were controversial, trade unions opposed further cutbacks which affected pensioners and disabled workers. Social Democrats announced that, after the successful election in 1998, they would repeal these parts, and in particular the so-called 'demographic factor' which was designed to take into account increases in longevity in computing *new* and annually adjusting *current* pensions (Hinrichs 1998). Indeed, the new Red-Green government suspended parts of the not yet effective reform implemented by its predecessor and legislated changes to keep in check the contribution rate in the short run (now against the opposition of the former government parties). In January 2001 only the Social Democrats and the Greens voted for another 'structural reform' in the *Bundestag* after negotiations on an inter-party consensus failed. The unions acquiesced in the package because of considerable concessions made by the government.[15]

If there is any 'lesson' to be learned from an international comparison it is not that some highly innovative policy changes can be detected by scanning pension reforms in other countries. The feasible set of incremental changes, as well as the restrictions on non-parametric reforms within a country's given institutional framework, are known and, at least partly, tested (see above). Rather, the first 'lesson' relates to the success of retrenchment in that they trigger no popular discontent and, ultimately, become fully implemented and are not repealed. Successful reforms are contingent upon support reaching well beyond the necessary majority in parliament, i.e. extending to either the main opposition party backing government proposals or to the social partners and here at least to the trade unions agreeing to or tolerating the reform. However, governments may not always be in the position to choose between these alternatives, and if the unions, regularly spearheading the status-quo interests, hold a vested power position they are frequently able to push through only moderated retrenchment.

The second 'lesson' concerns the preconditions for broad support. Establishing a special 'pension reform commission' is a promising political strategy for attaining a consensus, as can be learned from the reforms in the USA (1983), Japan (several reforms), Germany (the 1992 reform act), and also in Finland and Sweden (1990s). If furnished with a clear mandate and authority, supported by the inclusion of social and political interests as well as programme administrators and other experts, such committees provide an opportunity (but not a *guarantee*) for 'de-parliamentarising' conflicts and to internally settle issues. Furthermore, such a scenario helps to manufacture a compromise reform *package* and thus to achieve unanimity otherwise would prove to be more difficult. Consisting of all actors involved in and committed to reform policy, a commission issuing a compromise package which somehow balances desired and critical elements limits possibilities for concerted action by opponents and leaves the less conflict-laden 'fine-tuning' to the subsequent parliamentary process. In contrast, a government which comes forward with a reform

---

15 On some central parts of the reform package the *Bundesrat* (Upper House) has to agree as well. At the time of writing (March 2001) the mediation process between the *Bundestag* and the *Bundesrat* (where the government parties have no majority) had not been completed.

proposal which has not been subjected to prior negotiation is more likely to fail in achieving broad support.

Implications

The welfare landscape is not frozen! Even mature contributory pension schemes can be moved (see also Bonoli 2000). The German public pension reforms of the last decade may serve as an example. Before enacting the reform of 1992, the equally non-acceptable alternatives were either to exempt retirees from any benefit cuts, and then gradually have to increase the contribution rate from about 18 to 36 per cent by 2030, or to cut benefit levels by half while maintaining a stable contribution rate. Including the most recent legislation cumulative reform effects will reduce the increase of the expected contribution rate by more than 14 percentage points (36.4 per cent before the 1992 reform; 22 per cent when the 2001 reform will come into effect – Deutscher Bundestag 2001:7; Sozialbeirat 1998:242). Although one may doubt the accuracy of the projected figures, the difference is astonishing and provides at least two lessons (for other countries' pre- and post-reform scenarios see Franco and Munzi 1996:27-45; Ferrera 2000:177).

First, reforms legislated within one decade and producing such a large financial impact contradict assertions that pension insurance schemes are highly resistant to change. Rather, it is proof of considerable institutional elasticity because, due to the schemes' evolved complexity, a multitude of 'adjusting screws' can be turned without transgressing the boundaries of incremental (or 'system-maintaining') reform. Second, in Germany (and elsewhere), in one way or another, the present and (even more so) future cohorts of pensioners will have to carry the main part of the adjustment burden. By comparison, contributors and general taxpayers will shoulder the smaller (and now reduced) part of the consequences of demographic ageing. Apparently, the fact that one third of the 1998 electorate in Germany was 55 years or older, turns out disproportionately highly at elections and has an immediate interest in pension benefits, represents no insurmountable obstacle to the democratic process and the capacity to carry out substantial retrenchments. This is remarkable given that public pension benefits constitute the predominant or even sole source of income for the large majority of retirees.

It is not surprising that political parties which initiate retrenchments are not punished by voters if their reputation, amongst other things, rests on the perception that they are aiming to pursue foresighted, purposeful policies, and if this is an image which parties are deliberately hoping to reinforce so as to increase their appeal to the electorate. Notwithstanding, the risk of losing voters in subsequent elections is small and, hence, increases the willingness to engage in, ultimately, substantial retrenchment efforts if generous phasing-in/out provisions can be achieved. It requires operating with a long planning horizon (see above) and shows that procrastination does not pay off. Government parties and opposition parties alike might be motivated *not* to postpone 'hardships' since the latter will reappear in form of intensified reform urgency, but with less leeway to spread the burden placed on policy-takers over a longer period. While phasing-in/out stipulations reduce the number of immediate 'losers' of acquired rights and thus the possibility of protest, certain mechanisms or (changed) formulas (such as thresholds triggering certain responses, including the predetermination of which cohorts will be affected by a higher retirement age or by a new mode of benefit calculation) help to de-politicise the actual implementation of reforms. They relieve today's policymakers from being held responsible for retrenchment effects which will occur later. The inclination to engage in a timely and large-scale pension reform should be increased if one can benefit from the 'blessing of intransparency' (Zacher 1987:590, 594-5) which impedes an exact calculation of the individual outcome of rule changes and thus provides another 'blame avoidance' option (Weaver 1986). Taken together, the strategies of gaining reputation (turning 'vice into virtue' – Levy 1999), distributing burdens over time, extending 'automatic government', and lowering the visibility of reform outcomes have been used to enlarge the scope of public pension reforms and to minimise their impact on subsequent elections.

Conclusion

It has been shown that old-age security systems in OECD countries have developed along two different lines. Among the traditional and new *social insurance* countries, as well as among the *latecomer* countries, one finds welfare states that are regarded as belonging to different *regimes*. Substantial path *changes* were thus indeed possible and have occurred. Due to the central significance of old-age security systems for the overall profile of welfare states, these long-term developments should not be underestimated because they have, to varying degrees, remodelled the structural interplay of (labour) markets, state, and private households in producing welfare as well as modified the 'landscape' of political interests.

In the course of sometimes recurrent attempts by *social insurance* countries to stabilise their old-age security systems designs have also been reshaped, although political elites were generally anxious to convey to the public an image of institutional continuity. Despite sometimes producing quite substantial cumulative effects, the *retrenchments* enacted during the last two decades corresponded to the traditional pattern of incremental change (on the 'impossibility' of holistic reforms, see Wiesenthal 2000). Radical (systemic rather than parametric) reform proposals, which might possibly be adequate for an economic and demographic constellation twenty or more years from now, are hardly capable of forging a majority in parliament or consensus among the relevant political actors. The problem here is that such proposals involve considerable insecurity regarding goal attainment and imply 'political rule instability' (Lindbeck 1994) to such an extent that the system's legitimacy could become endangered.[16]

---

16 This points to a *political* dilemma. Far-reaching reforms which aspire to long-term stabilisation in one go are difficult to put through and therefore rarely occur (with the possible exceptions of

The reform of pension systems has not been completed. On the contrary, the intensified debate on the necessity of further action has enlarged the 'window of opportunity' for substantial changes in *social insurance* countries since a once 'coherent policy paradigm' (Hall 1993:210) has been shaken. In view of (over-dramatised) doubts about sustainability, transnational diffusion of experiences with reform policies and advancing reform proposals of market-liberal provenance, the model (or protected 'policy core' – Majone 1991) of a contributory, pay-as-you-go public pension scheme, committed to a balanced blend of individual equity and income adequacy (solidarity), is no longer embedded within a 'politically stable equilibrium' (Heclo 1998:72). This, at least, applies to the USA and Germany (Hinrichs 2000a). No longer does the model function as an uncontested point of reference for actors rallying in this policy arena. Once closed policy communities have lost their 'interpretative hegemony' mainly due to the counter-mobilisation of external actors (coming from mass media, research institutes, the financial services industry etc), who have gained capacity for re-framing pension policy issues (Quadagno 1999). Concomitantly, the focus within public pension reforms has changed. Starting as attempts to maintain the present scheme, increasingly the leitmotiv has become to design a sustainable system with different components of retirement income. It implies that public policy has to become engaged more frequently in shaping the non-public components through regulation in a broad sense, thereby opening up additional arenas of political conflict with hitherto marginal actors.

Sweden, where a seemingly 'complete redesign' was suitable for regaining credibility – Scherman 1999: 44-7; or some 'transition countries' in Middle and Eastern Europe – Müller 2000). In contrast, incremental changes are more likely to achieve a (broad) majority. However, when recurrently put on the political agenda and rule changes are implemented frequently (as in Italy, Austria or Germany during the 1990s), 'security expectations' on the part of the public might be lost. Confidence in the system's reliability should dwindle even more if reform necessity is a permanent issue in the political debate but no decisions are taken (as in the USA).

Table 10.1: Measures to cope with the effects of population ageing on the financing of public pension schemes

I.	*Measures concerning current/future contributors*
1.	increasing the contribution rate
2.	utilizing parts of an increased contribution rate to build up a fund reserve
3.	broadening the contribution base a) making hitherto non-covered employed liable for mandatory insurance b) increasing the ceiling of earnings subject to contributions
II.	*Measures concerning current/future beneficiaries*
1.	changing the benefit formula
2.	suspending automatic benefit indexation and/or changing the indexing formula
3.	raising the standard retirement age
4.	increasing benefit reductions for early retirees up to actuarial level
5.	tightening the eligibility rules for disability pensions
6.	reducing/eliminating derivative/auxiliary benefits
III.	*Measures concerning the state's engagement*
	directly:
1.	increasing/introducing subsidies out of general taxation to public pension schemes
	indirectly:
2.	intensifying population policy (fertility, migration)
3.	increasing the employment ratio (reducing the unemployment level, facilitating higher female labour force participation)
4.	promoting investments in physical and human capital to facilitate higher productivity growth rates

Chapter 11

The Redistributional Impact of a World Bank 'Pension Regime'

Einar Overbye

Introduction

In 1994 the World Bank launched a blueprint for pension reforms in the world (no less). The Bank suggested replace pay-as-you-go based public pensions with funded, mandatory defined contribution-schemes. A shift to funded pensions is supposed to boost savings and economic growth. The proposal has been hugely influential, in particular in Latin America and the new European democracies. However, it has received a less than lukewarm reception from social policy researchers. They often assume that such a shift will reduce or even eliminate redistribution to the poorest. This chapter argues, on the contrary, that although effects on savings and economic growth are debatable, the World Bank pension regime is likely to channel increased government revenues to the poor, in particular to those not living in OECD countries. The first reason is that a World Bank pension regime will limit redistribution toward privileged minorities. The second reason is that the World Bank insists on introducing a bottom

Jochen Clasen (ed.), *What Future for Social Security?*, 179-194
©2001 Kluwer Law International. Printed in the Netherlands.

floor safety net financed from general revenues. Outside OECD, such safety nets are rare.

The changing nature of pension provision

Pension policies are in flux throughout the world. The most dramatic changes take place outside OECD. Beginning with Chile in 1981, many Latin American and some former communist European countries have downsized their former pay-as-you-go based systems and are replacing them with more-or-less funded pension schemes. This change involves, among other things, a closer link between contributions and benefits. In these new 'defined contribution' pension schemes, contributions are typically defined as a percentage of earnings, and benefit levels depend on the number of contributions, plus accrued interests. Peru (1992) Colombia (1993) Argentina (1993) Uruguay (1995) Mexico (1995/6) Bolivia (1996) and El Salvador (1996) have changed their mandatory pension systems inspired by Chile. So have Hungary, Latvia and Khazakstan. Several additional countries, among them Costa Rica, the Czech Republic and Poland, are in the process of redesigning their schemes along somewhat similar lines (Gillian et al.. 2000). The diffusion of what may loosely be labelled 'the Chilean model' has to a large extent been the work of the World Bank, which in its 1994 report 'Averting the old-age crisis' recommended Chilean-type pension reforms to combat poverty, boost savings and develop financial markets. The World Bank 'pension regime' consists of mandatory defined-contribution pension schemes administered by private (competing) financial institutions. Voluntary savings, including occupational pensions, act as a top-up for those dissatisfied with what they get from the mandatory scheme(s). A means-tested or flat-rate minimum scheme financed from general revenues serves those unable to contribute. The World Bank has used both advice and carrots (cheap loans) to advocate this pension regime across the world, in alliance with internal actors (such as Departments of Finance and Treasuries) who tend to support similar ideas.

The World Bank approach, or versions of it, has been more influential outside OECD than among OECD countries. OECD countries maintain pay-as-you-go based pension schemes where 'contributions' are de facto earmarked taxes. These schemes are usually based on the so-called defined benefit principle: the pension level is calculated as a percentage of final or average earnings (or average earnings during the last 5 years); usually between 60 and 70 per cent of the earnings base. In such schemes, the link between formal contributions and benefits is much looser than in defined contribution schemes. With the exception of Denmark, Ireland, the Netherlands, New Zealand and Australia, all OECD countries maintain earnings-related public or mandated pensions (Overbye 1998:210).[1] Sweden, Norway, Canada and the US have installed clear-cut

---

1 The Netherlands is a borderline case. Membership is mandatory in those sectors of the economy where there are collective bargaining agreements concerning pensions. As a consequence, about

public superannuation schemes, where decision-making, financing and administration are solely in the hands of the parliament and state. Continental-European pension schemes more often represent a mix between public and private control, and the social partners are sometimes represented at the Board of Directors. Finally, the UK, Switzerland and Iceland have mandated private (usually occupational) pension provision.

Two OECD countries have redesigned their public pension systems somewhat along the lines of the new defined-contribution schemes emerging in other parts of the world: Sweden and Italy. Both countries have scrapped the defined-benefit principle and introduced schemes that, at least nominally, are tied to the number of contributions an individual makes during his or her entire working career. The Swedish system also includes a small component that is 'genuinely' funded and invested in financial markets (Gillion et al. 2000:476). There are substantial differences between the Chilean and Swedish/Italian models. Nonetheless, the similarities are sufficient that the World Bank referred to Sweden - alongside Chile - as countries to learn from when the Bank's experts were advising Latvia about pension reform.

Changes not only encompass public pensions. Within OECD, an ongoing change in private (voluntary, supplementary) pensions topping up public pensions also indicates a change in pension designs. In Australia, Austria, Belgium, Denmark, Germany, Great Britain, Greece, Ireland, the Netherlands, Spain, Switzerland, Sweden and the US, occupational pensions based on a defined-contribution principle are increasing their market share at the expense of old-style funded defined-benefit plans, which dominated the private pension sector in the past (Dent and Sloss 1996).

Effects on redistribution

A fully funded defined-contribution scheme maintains an actuarial link between contributions and benefits. In principle, the only redistribution that takes place in such schemes is from low to high risks. This type of redistribution is ingrained in any insurance scheme. With reference to old-age pension insurance, this implies redistribution from those who die early to those who die late[2]. By comparison, there

---

70 per cent of the workforce are de facto mandatory members of earnings-related pensions topping up the Dutch minimum pension.

2 In practice, real-life defined contribution schemes can include several additional redistributional features. For example, if minimum contribution periods are required, then employees with short or irregular contribution periods will end up losing money to those with longer contribution records. Further, in the reformed Swedish pension system, parents who stay at home and care for pre-school children are treated 'as if' they contributed certain amounts, although no contributions are actually paid. The point here, however, is what an ideal-type, fully funded pension insurance scheme would look like. In real life, there is always room for additional features.

may be all types of redistribution going on in old-style defined benefit schemes, since there is no formal link between contributions (earmarked taxes) and benefits received. Is there a danger, then, that the present surge in defined contribution schemes (and/or a shift to a defined contribution principle within public plans) will limit or even abolish redistribution to the poorest?

In order to evaluate the likely redistributional effect of a change from status quo to a World Bank-inspired pension regime, we need to clarify the *counterfactual alternative.* What is the redistributional tendency within today's pay-as-you-go based public pensions? Since these schemes can be designed in any number of ways, redistribution may also be in any number of directions. To simplify, however, we can distinguish between three major redistributional trajectories: from both ends of the income distribution to the middle, from the lower to the higher end, or from the higher end to the lower. Let us consider these three possibilities in turn.

Redistribution from both ends to the middle (Director's law)

There is usually a ceiling on the income which 'earns' benefits in a pay-as-you-go based public pension scheme. Ceilings on benefits received (maximum pension levels) reduce the extent to which high-income groups accrue pension rights in such systems. However, there is not always a similar ceiling on the income that is taxed to provide the pension (in the form of earmarked taxes levied on the employee or on the employer on his or her behalf), and/or the scheme is partially financed from general taxes. In countries where there is a ceiling on benefits but no ceiling (or a higher ceiling) on contributions, the scheme redistributes from higher to middle/lower incomes. Lower income groups receive a higher compensation rate (as a percentage of previous income) than higher income groups, relative to how much they pay in the form of general or earmarked taxes.

However, redistribution from higher to middle/lower income groups is not necessarily the only direction of redistribution within a pay-as-you-go based pension scheme. There may also be some degree of redistribution from the poorest income groups toward the middle. The reasons are as follows:

Public earnings-related pensions almost always contain a contribution-requirement. To become eligible for a pension, one must have contributed (paid earmarked taxes) for a number of years, and/or been in regular employment for an extended period of time. Any contribution-requirement implies that some citizens will end up without pension rights. These groups typically include part-time and seasonal workers, the self-employed and homeworkers. Vesting requirements may further imply that short contribution records are not taken into account, limiting pensions for those with limited or interrupted employment records. This is often the situation both within and outside the OECD area. These problems are enhanced to the extent that public pay-as-you-go schemes only cover a limited segment of the workforce in the first place (for example only urban employees, or only employees in large firms). This is the case in many countries outside OECD. As mentioned above, public 'contribution' based pay-as-you-go schemes are often partly financed by the state, through general taxation. This can be part of a formal arrangement (tripartite financing), or the state has to step in to cover a more-or-less unexpected gap between contributions (earmarked taxes) and benefits. If this is the case, those who fail to earn pension rights (part-time workers, workers with short or interrupted contribution records etc.) pay for benefits – through general taxes – which they are cut off from receiving. Hence such schemes do not only redistribute from high to middle income earners: they are also likely to redistribute from the poor to middle income earners.

Redistribution from the lower end to the middle of the income distribution can also be brought about through the elasticity of supply and demand. If a sector of the economy is granted mandatory pension coverage, mandatory earmarked taxes carried by the employees or employer on their behalf will increase the cost of whatever is produced in this sector. If the sector is sheltered from outside competition, these earmarked taxes will to some extent be rolled over into higher prices. Higher prices will affect those who are not covered by mandatory pensions, who indirectly finance some of the earmarked tax - and the poorest segments of a population tend to be among those not covered. To which extent such cost-shifting takes place will depend on the elasticity of demand, plus the availability of substitutes, for the goods and services produced by the pension-favoured sector.

To conclude: In countries where formally contribution-based pay-as-you-go schemes are the *only* public pension schemes around (i.e. no minimum schemes exist), redistribution may well be from both ends of the income distribution toward the middle. The rich lose to the extent that there are ceilings on benefits but no ceilings (or higher ceilings) on contributions. The poor lose if the scheme operates with minimum contribution periods, or if the pension-favoured segment of the economy is sheltered from outside competition.

The above can be tied to an influential theory concerning the likely direction of redistribution within a democracy, first put forward by Aaron Director. Director assumed that redistribution from both tails of the income distribution to the middle is the most common form of redistribution in democratic societies. This assumption has later become known as 'Director's law' (Mueller 1989:448).

What are the arguments behind Director's law? First, since the essence of democracy is majority rule, one should expect ruling politicians to ensure that a majority of voters are at the receiving end of whatever redistribution takes place. To the extent that ruling politicians should host alternative ideas, they are likely - in the long run - to be weeded out of office and be replaced by rulers more receptive to majority preferences. Although short-term deviations may occur, this weeding-out mechanism ensures that, at least in the long run, redistribution will tend to favour a majority at the expense of a minority.

But why redistribution from both ends to the middle? Director assumed that redistribution from both tails of a distribution toward the middle will usually be more stable than redistribution toward one of the tails. Given a choice between taking only from the rich and taking both from the rich and the poor, a majority concerned with maximising its take should collect from both (Mueller ibid.).

Let us, at least for the sake of argument, assume that we are in a country where Director's law holds. How are the proposals of the World Bank likely to affect the direction of redistribution? The ideal-type version of a World Bank scheme implies that no redistribution will take place at all within the earnings-related scheme. This is the case since there is to be an actuarial relationship between contributions and benefits. If so, the result of a shift to a World Bank scheme should be beneficial to the poor and the rich, but not to those in the middle. The shift should be beneficial for the poor since they no longer have to pay, through indirect taxes, for benefits they are cut off from receiving. It should be at the expense of the middle classes (in particular the lower middle classes, who benefit most by benefit formulas tilted toward lower-middle income earners), since they now have to pay exclusively for their own benefits. And it should be beneficial to the upper middle and the wealthy, since they no longer face benefit formulas tilted toward middle-income earners.

In political terms, however, such a shift would demand a 'coalition' between the poorest and wealthiest segments of the population against the middle. If Director's law is valid, this is a very unlikely majority constellation. Hence if this is the case, the fact that the World Bank proposal has actually been implemented in some countries would be difficult to explain. Let us turn, then, to an alternative possibility: that redistribution in today's public pension schemes is mainly from those below the median to those above the median.

Redistribution from lower to higher income groups

Director's law is a theory about redistribution in a democracy. However, most countries in the world are only democracies in a limited sense, or their democratic status is fairly recent. If so, redistribution may follow an autocratic, rather than a democratic, logic.

In autocracies, rulers do not have to compete for votes to stay in power (or, in quasi-autocracies, they can rig elections to avoid defeat). If so, they are under no long-run institutional constraint to satisfy majority preferences in order to stay in office. Unlike democracies, the long-run redistributional tendency in autocracies (or quasi-autocracies) is likely to be from a majority to centrally placed minorities. This minority will first and foremost consist of the ruler and his or her clique or party. Redistribution may eventually be extended to minorities sufficiently powerful that not even an autocratic ruler can afford to neglect them. Thus the armed forces in particular are likely to have privileged access to social security, as is indeed the case in many countries.[3] The loyalty of public employees is also of importance to rulers everywhere, implying that civil servants will usually have their own pension schemes. With particular reference to autocratic rulers in developing countries, they may be more receptive to demands of urban rather than rural workers, and more to employees in large rather than small companies, since urban employees in large companies are better organised and may pose a greater threat to the regime during times of political unrest. In non-democratic countries, then, one should as a general rule expect public pensions to benefit the ruling clique plus powerful minority groups who represent a potential threat to the regime.

The above hypothesis is inspired by Tullock's (1987) view that the preferences of an ideal type autocrat can be reduced to the following: (1) getting into power, (2) hanging on to it, (3) getting some enjoyment while possessing it (see also Mueller 1989:272). Again, it must be stressed that the above concerns a theory about the *long-run* redistributional tendency in an autocracy. Some autocrats, in particular 'enlightened' autocrats, may well have the well-being of a majority in mind. However, enlightened autocrats (and their successors) have less to fear than elected rulers if they should change their preferences across time and pursue more narrowly defined objectives. Since there is no institutional constraint in autocracies to maintain a benevolent attitude across time, there is a larger possibility than in a democracy that the regime will end up serving only entrenched minorities. As in democracies, then, the long-run redistributional tendency in an autocracy should be distinguished from eventual short-term deviations.

At this point it should be emphasised that the above does not imply any moralising on behalf of those groups which are able to get social security from an autocratic ruler. In autocracies, in particular in the non-enlightened kind, the only certain way to be granted favours is through lobbying or by more-or-less subtle threats. To abstain from lobbying or from threats will not make an autocrat more benign toward groups with less lobbying power and/or less ability to muster credible threats. We are dealing with an effect of how the decision-making system is framed, not with any difference between moral and not-so-moral ways to seek political influence.

Is there any empirical backing behind an assumption that autocratic regimes normally offer social security mainly or only to groups that might otherwise threaten their grip on power? In Latin American countries, which have a long tradition of social security plus unstable or imperfect democracies, the general rule appears to be that relatively small groups have generous pension benefits, while the majority of the population is offered only limited protection (Gillion et al. 2000:533 ff.). Because of the large informal sector, many Latin American workers are not covered by public retirement schemes. The same goes for the self-employed. Minimum contribution periods are often long. For example,

---

3 In this context it is worth noticing that the armed forces maintained their privileged pension schemes in Pinochet's Chile, while all other sectors of society were encouraged to adapt funded defined contribution-schemes.

in Argentina, a worker must contribute for 30 years to receive a pension from the defined benefit scheme, although an advanced-age benefit can be received at age 70 on the fulfilment of 10 contribution years (ibid.:537). Arab and Middle East countries also have rather extensive programmes. They are usually financed on a tripartite basis, but typically exclude casual and temporary workers, domestic servants, the self-employed and non-nationals (ibid.:548). Coverage is even more uneven in Africa and Asia, and so is the democratic tradition (ibid:499-531). In China, pension coverage has traditionally been limited to urban employees in state-owned firms (Zhongli 2000).

What is the likely effect of a reform along World Bank lines if present-day social security schemes are partly tax-financed and serve only core segments of the population? Basically, a shift to a World Bank pension regime should be even more beneficial for the poor than if Director's law is in operation. The situation of the poor should be improved simply by limiting, or abolishing, the amount of redistribution going on in today's schemes. Thus whatever weaknesses e.g. the Chilean system possesses, at least it maintains no minimum contributory period in order to be eligible for a pension (Gillion et al. 2000:537).

The uneven coverage of social security outside OECD is perhaps the major reason why the World Bank proposal has been less resisted here than among OECD countries. Since a majority is often left outside social security schemes in the first place, they have little interest in opposing World Bank proposals. A larger segment of the population is likely to be satisfied with status quo within OECD, where decades of democratic rule have ensured that membership in pay-as-you-go based public pension schemes has been widened so as to favour a majority rather than a minority. The popularity of a World Bank pension design outside OECD may at least to some extent be indicative of a process of *democratisation*. Ruling elites might be in the process of becoming more sensitive to the demands of the majority – or at least to the demands of larger minorities. In this context, notice that public pension coverage was also highly uneven in many European countries before democratic rule became firmly established. Baldwin's (1990) analysis of British, French, German and Scandinavian pension reforms between 1875 and 1975 as well as Kolb's (1989) account of the first hundred years of German pension legislation indicate a link between the entrenchment of a democratic decision-making system and broader public pension coverage.

Redistribution from higher to lower income groups (Meltzer-Richard)

The Meltzer-Richard hypothesis is the major contender to Director's law concerning the likely long-run direction of redistribution within well-established democracies (Mueller 1989:448). The Meltzer-Richard hypothesis and Director's law share an assumption that redistribution in a democracy (unlike an autocracy) as a general rule will be from a minority to a majority. But while Director's law assumes that the middle class will benefit from rich and poor alike, the Meltzer-Richard hypothesis assumes that redistribution will usually be from those whose income is above the median to those below the median. There are several arguments behind this assumption. First, although a median voter might ideally prefer to receive transfers from rich and poor alike, there is simply not much to be got from the lower end. Hence wealthier segments are likely to be harder hit by the redistributional interests of a majority than the down-and-out. Second, and perhaps more important, too much poverty in a society creates various types of negative externalities (such as an unsafe 'social space' and risk of epidemics), providing a majority with an incentive not to let the poorest suffer outright deprivation. Third, the majority may feel a normative commitment to ease the lot of the weakest and most destitute.

Politically, the Meltzer-Richard hypothesis presumes some type of 'coalition' between the poorest and the lower middle classes against the upper middle and the wealthy. My hunch is that this is possible to accomplish in particular in countries with a (historically derived) strong egalitarian ethos to begin with, and/or where organisations fostering the interests of rural and urban workers have a tradition of cooperation.[4]

OECD countries: redistribution according to Meltzer-Richard?

A combination of 'contribution' based pay-as-you go schemes (with income ceilings) supplemented by various types of minimum provision financed from general revenues is likely to result in a Meltzer-Richard type of redistribution rather than Director's law. 'Contribution' based schemes ensure redistribution from the upper to the lower middle classes, while tax-financed minimum schemes ensure some net redistribution to those unable to contribute. A mix of contribution-based schemes plus benefits to the poor are found in almost all OECD countries. The scope and level of tax-financed minimum provision varies, however. Nordic and Australasian countries maintain more-or-less flat-rate minimum pensions financed from general revenues.[5] Austria, Belgium, France, Greece, Italy, Portugal and Spain rely on means-tested pension supplements or 'social

---

4 From a theoretical perspective, Director's law as well as the Meltzer-Richard hypothesis may both capture the outcomes of any redistributional game. This is so because redistributional games are essentially games with empty cores, implying that no stable equilibria exist (Mueller ibid.). In the absence of stable equilibria, there may even be cyclic shifts in the direction of redistribution. Thus provided that a majority is at the receiving end, redistribution in a democracy may in principle go in all directions: toward the middle, toward the lower end or toward the higher end. To make specific hypotheses concerning the direction of redistribution we must rely on additional information concerning the social, political and institutional structure of the country we are analysing.

5 The Australian minimum benefit is 'affluence-tested', i.e. it excludes roughly the top 30 per cent of the elderly. Denmark's minimum pension is only earnings-tested, while the Swedish and Norwegian benefits are only tested against income from mandatory public superannuation (Overbye 1998).

pensions'. The US also provides an income-tested pension supplement (SSI), while Germany grants only standardised social assistance alongside mandatory earnings-related systems.

Within OECD, Scandinavia and New Zealand comprise one extreme. In these countries, minimum benefits (if housing benefits are included) are so generous that earnings-related public pensions only provide a rather modest increase for those formally 'contributing' (often to the frustration of those compelled to contribute, since they often complain that they get little value for their money). The rather flat-rate character of the overall pension structure is most pronounced in New Zealand and Denmark, which have no – or next to no – 'contribution' based scheme topping up the minimum scheme in the first place.[6] Italy, Spain and Greece can be considered an opposite extreme within OECD, since earnings-related pensions are very generous for those with full-time employment while tax-financed minimum provision is rudimentary and/or benefit levels low. These countries also maintain minimum contribution periods rather ungenerous to those with short or interrupted careers: 19 years in the former Italian system (now down to five years in the new defined contribution scheme); 15 years in Spain and 4500 days in Greece (MISSOC 2000:306-7).

Depending on the generosity of minimum provision financed out of general revenues, the poorest also benefit from public pension provision. Redistribution through tax-financed minimum benefits offsets whatever redistribution might take place from the poorest to the middle through general taxation to finance formally 'contribution' based pay-as-you-go schemes. Some countries have also watered down the 'contribution' requirement by awarding earnings-related pension rights even to those who do not earn any income. For example, Norway treats children and youth who become disabled before age 26 as if they earned an average income at the time of the event, and grants them unabridged public superannuation. And Germany, Sweden and Norway (among others) grant superannuation credits to parents looking after pre-school children.

If we move outside OECD, however, minimum protection schemes financed from general revenues are far less common than 'contribution' based pay-as-you-go schemes. In former communist countries, minimum protection schemes did not exist.[7] Social

---

6 In Denmark, Norway, Iceland, the UK, Canada, Australia and New Zealand minimum protection during old age was introduced even before the introduction of contribution based public pension schemes. The UK later switched to a minimum benefit with a contribution requirement, while Sweden and Finland went the other way and dropped a contribution requirement in their minimum scheme. Today, a pure flat-rate minimum scheme exists only in Norway and New Zealand. However, in Denmark, Sweden and Finland the degree of means-testing is extremely limited: Minimum benefits are only tested against earnings in Denmark and only against income from mandatory superannuation schemes in Finland and Sweden. The Netherlands also employs a de facto tax-financed minimum scheme since the 'contribution' requirement has been watered down during the decades so that most types of activity now count as 'contribution' periods.

7 The former GDR was an exception to this rule, employing a flat-rate minimum pension scheme.

security consisted of 'contribution'-based pensions, short-term cash benefits (sick pay and the like) and health care. Bottom-line security was provided by guaranteed employment plus heavily subsidised housing, basic goods and services. The perils of not providing bottom-floor safety nets became apparent when the regime shift created massive unemployment. As far as Africa is concerned only Mauritius, Seychelles and South Africa provide basic pensions to the population (Gillion et al. 2000:516-7). Some Latin American countries also provide tax-financed minimum benefits, e.g. Brazil introduced a system for the entire rural population in 1971 that did not require contributions, and granted flat-rate benefits equal to one-half of the highest national minimum salary (Huber 1996:150). In Asia, social insurance schemes tend to be limited to public sector workers and employees in large firms, often with limited vesting rights at that. Minimum protection is left to the family and/or charity (including NGOs). South Korea is a partial exception to this rule, however. After the democratic transition in 1987 most types of social security programmes came into effect (Shin 2000:86). A national pension programme was launched in 1988, to be fully mature by 2008 (ibid. 87). Again, this suggests a relationship between democratisation and a shift toward a Meltzer-Richard (or at least a Director's law) type redistributional profile.

Minimum protection in the World Bank pension regime

To what extent may the World Bank proposal help induce some element of redistribution from the upper to the lower half of the income distribution; in particular to the very lowest? A funded defined contribution scheme, designed along actuarial lines, will not provide this type of redistribution. Its eventual redistributional effect is at best indirect, by replacing present-day pay-as-you-go schemes favouring privileged minorities with a 'neutral' scheme. But the World Bank proposal also includes the introduction of some type of minimum protection scheme financed from general revenues. The reason for this is straightforward: if the funded scheme is based on contributions and allows no room for redistribution, then a separate scheme must be constructed alongside the funded scheme to care for those unable to contribute.

The Bank is rather pragmatic when discussing the ideal institutional design of this minimum scheme. It can be means tested or flat-rate, part of general social assistance or separated out as a minimum scheme only for the elderly (World Bank 1994:117, 239 ff.). The important thing, however, is that the Bank stresses the importance of a bottom-floor safety net financed from general revenues, excluding nobody. This element of the World Bank proposal has gone largely unnoticed by its critics, who tend to focus exclusively on the funded design. Perhaps the neglect is due to the fact that most OECD countries have had such schemes for several decades - beginning with the Poor Law tradition. However, in those countries where the World Bank has been most influential, this part of the proposal is of major importance. It may well be that the main long-run impact of the Bank's proposal will be to stimulate more countries to introduce social assistance-type schemes. The Bank's main influence in this respect has probably been in the former communist countries. At least in Albania and Croatia, the World Bank was a major actor in setting up (and financing) social assistance benefits. Without the Bank, the poorest in these countries might have had greater problems to make their voices heard in the internal competition for scarce public revenues.

Social policy scholars in the West, in particular those socialised in the Titmuss tradition, are raised to believe that means-tested (residual) benefits represent an inferior way of providing social protection. However, some at least might consider that even a stingy, means-tested and mean minimum protection system can be superior to nothing at all. Outside the OECD area, where most of today's poor live, this is the main counterfactual alternative. 'Contribution' based rights cannot reach all the way down to the poorest segments of a population, and in many countries they may not even reach half-way down.

Why have World Bank-type pension reforms been more influential in some countries than others?

The argument so far has been that World Bank-type pension reforms may limit pension privileges for entrenched minorities and introduce a rudimentary minimum protection system for the worst off, thus having a positive redistributional impact. However, redistributive effects have hardly been the major arguments behind today's pension reforms. The motives behind the reforms must be sought elsewhere.

The main reason why the Word Bank pension regime has become popular among policy makers concerns its promise to boost savings and develop financial markets. Compulsory savings may boost the national savings rate, resulting in lower interest rates and more rapid economic growth. Pension fund money may form the core of a larger internal capital market, which may in itself have positive effects on allocation of resources. Many developing countries lack an internal capital market. The argument has less merit in OECD countries, where capital markets are already well developed.

Another reason why World Bank proposals have proven more popular in some countries than in others concerns the degree of administrative efficiency prevailing in today's public pension schemes (including provident funds). For example, administrative costs make up 10-15 per cent of total expenditure in Brazil and Turkey, as compared to 1-2 per cent in most OECD countries (World Bank 1994:149). Administrative inefficiency and/or fraud may take place also within defined-contribution schemes. However, fraud and mismanagement should be easier to deal with under a defined contribution regime. First, a defined-contribution scheme usually provides a clear link between money in and money out. If incoming money should be lost somewhere along the way, individuals can take legal action against the administrators. This is more difficult in pay-as-you-go schemes (as well as in provident finds), where there is no formal link between contributions and benefits – no name tag which follows the money as it moves through the administrative apparatus. Second, if several administrators have to compete with each other, competitive pressure should in theory at least weed out the most fraudulent and/or incompetent.

Yet another reason why the World Bank proposal has enjoyed more popular support in Latin America and the new European democracies than within OECD concerns the traumatic historical experiences these countries, and in particular the new democracies, have had with public pension provision (and with the state-citizen relationship more generally). Hyperinflation combined with inadequate indexing (due to tight government budgets) has eroded confidence in public pension provision. Mistrust in the state is likely to fuel support for private alternatives, at least as long as we deal with countries where the private sector is not (yet) discredited to the same extent as the public sector.[8]

Finally, a defined contribution-type public pension scheme may limit certain types of 'strategic behaviour' prevailing in some defined benefit plans. If a defined benefit scheme is based on final salary and only requires a limited number of contribution years, people may be tempted to work only the minimum number of qualification years and spend the rest of their work life in the informal economy (avoiding contributions and taxes), only to re-enter as full time employees at the very end of their career to maximise final salary. Such behaviour is not possible in defined contribution schemes. Incidentally, it is worth noticing that many OECD countries have reorganised their defined benefit systems during the 1990s to limit this type of strategic behaviour. For example, Spain extended the number of contribution years from 20 to 25 in 1997 and the reference period for benefit calculations from 8 to 15 years (Gillion et al. 2000:585).[9] Similar extensions have taken place in Austria, Finland, UK and Greece (ibid.:585-6, George et. al. 1999:47 ff.). By extending the number of contribution years and using career average rather than final salary as the reference period, defined benefit schemes become more similar to defined contribution schemes as far as the relationship between life-cycle earnings and pension benefits is concerned.

It is an open question if a shift toward a World Bank-inspired pension regime will have positive effects on economic growth and administrative efficiency. Econometric studies of the relationship between pay-as-you-go based pension schemes and savings show mixed results (Hughes 2000:51-6). From a theoretical perspective, it is not obvious why the introduction of a mandatory, funded pension scheme should change individual preferences for savings and consumption over the life cycle. If preferences are not affected, people will respond to mandatory savings simply by reducing other types of savings, or by contribution evasion (a major problem in Latin America and Eastern

---

8 In countries where trust in all formal institutions, be they public or private, is non-existent, there is little left to build social security on - although schemes run by the social partners or by various types of mutuals (eventually tied to the kinship group and village community) may possibly offer alternatives in some countries.

9 Even 25 years is generous by OECD standards. Most countries demand between 30 and 40 contribution years to earn full benefits.

Europe). In any case, the shift toward defined-contribution type public pensions is so recent that any belief in their positive economic and administrative effects must remain largely an article of faith at this stage.[10] Be that as it may. My point, however, is that even if the recent design changes should have no beneficial economic and administrative effects, they are at least likely to have some beneficial redistributional effects, in particular if the World Bank succeeds in getting more countries to introduce residual, tax-financed minimum protection systems. Thus while the standard justification for a World Bank pension design has been that it may be bad for redistribution but is probably good for economic growth, the argument pursued here is that positive economic effects may or may not materialise, but at least there are reasons to expect less redistribution to the upper half and more to the lower half of the population, in particular if we limit our attention to countries outside OECD.

Concluding comment

When the World Bank launched its pension proposal back in 1994, it was criticised by many – including this author – for promoting a one-size-fits-all approach to pensions, without taking into consideration the political and institutional legacies of different countries. Today, however, critics of the Bank, in particular those in OECD countries, may commit a similar fallacy: to assume that the redistributional effects of present-day pay-as-you-go schemes are the same everywhere as in their home country. The problem with an ahistorical attitude is that counter-arguments which may be valid in one national setting may stereotype the World Bank proposal as 'bad for redistribution at all times and in all places', which is highly unlikely. The very different types of pay-as-you-go based public pension schemes around in today's world should sensitise us to the very different counterfactual alternatives to a World Bank system.

Granted, providing adequate resources to the poorest among the elderly is only one of many redistributional issues. Another, though related, issue is how to prevent mandatory pensions – like a young cuckoo – growing so large during the anticipated greying of the population that they push their siblings (other types of welfare spending) out of the nest

---

10 Aaron (1982), among others, assumes that an eventual positive effect on total national savings by switching to a funded pension system is either moderate or nil. However, there is even less reason to suspect a *negative* effect on savings. Hence a shift to a World Bank pension regime may - with luck - have a positive effect on savings, and the worst case scenario is only that nothing happens. Thus if policy makers are risk-averse, then (ceteris paribus) the savings argument suggests that a funded public pensions is preferable. Something similar might be said with regard to administrative efficiency: perhaps private administrators will turn out as inefficient as public administrators in many developing countries. But there are few reasons to assume that they will be even worse, and some arguments suggesting that they might possibly be better. If so, risk-aversion should dictate that private, funded provision by competing managers should be given a try - at least in countries with negative experiences with public pay-as-you-go based 'contributory' plans.

in the process.[11] Whether or not this challenge is best met by an all-out change to a World Bank pension design or incremental changes in existing pay-as-you-go schemes is an issue that cannot be answered without performing specific analyses of the many specific countries in the world. The purpose of this article has only been to call for a more nuanced view of the World Bank proposal as regards one, admittedly crucial, aspect of mandatory public pensions: how to ensure that they not only provide income security for the majority in the middle, but also secure something for the poorest.

---

11. All social security schemes, be they funded or pay-as-you-go, transfer resources from low risks to high risks. This is the case also in systems designed along purely actuarial lines. Old age pension systems secure the population against the risk of longevity, i.e. the risk of living longer than expected. In old-age pension schemes, then, money is transferred from those who die early to those who die late. The risk of longevity is probably the only social risk where a majority of voters are likely to regard themselves as belonging among the high risks. It is also the only social risk where the healthy, powerful and wealthy are likely to be the highest risks. For these reasons, old-age pension schemes are likely to enjoy more widespread popular support than e.g. unemployment schemes, disability schemes and social assistance. Thus if priority conflicts within the public sector should escalate in the future, there are sound theoretical reasons for assuming that a 'young cuckoo' effect will manifest itself.

II C

ACTIVATION REFORMS

Chapter 12

Activating Welfare States.
How social policies can promote employment[1]

Jon Kvist

Introduction

The nexus between the welfare state and the labour market is a classical issue in political economy. Liberals present this as the big trade-off between equality and efficiency; the welfare state is a 'leaky bucket' where redistribution distorts the proper functioning of the market by, for example, providing disincentives to work (Okun 1975). In response, socialists have argued that the welfare state is better conceived of as an 'irrigation system' which often enhances efficiency (Korpi 1985). The contemporary welfare state debate reflects these issues. For example, whether Europe's economic problems were caused by its generous welfare states was widely discussed during the 1980s. Extensive social protection programmes were seen as the main reason why Europe did not replicate the US 'Jobs Miracle'. In the early 1990s, however, numerous empirical studies showed

1 I would like to thank Jochen Clasen, Jan Høgelund, Mads Jæger, Olli Kangas, and Adrian and Dorothy Sinfield for helpful comments on an earlier version of this chapter.

that there was no straight trade-off between social protection and economic flexibility (see, for example, Blank 1994, Atkinson and Mogensen 1993).

Part of the reason why existing research has not established a firm link between welfare states and employment may be too narrow a conception of the dimensions of the welfare state. The latter does not only consist of a redistribution and insurance dimension in providing a safety net and income replacement for people not in work. It also has a caring and human resource dimension, providing, for example, social care for children and elderly, and also education, training, health care and rehabilitation measures (e.g. Sinn 1995, OECD 1999a). Whether or not the welfare state actually hampers employment and economic growth is therefore ultimately an empirical question that must take account both of disincentive effects and the alleviation of market failures (Søndergaard 1999), of constraining as well as enabling mechanisms for people's desire and opportunities to work. Since the disincentive problems are well covered in the economic literature (e.g. Barr 1994), here we will focus only on how the welfare state may promote employment by revisiting some of its core social policies.

It is important to appreciate that there are many policies which may help countries facing ageing populations, low fertility rates, social exclusion, precarious jobs, fiercer competition and budget constraints. High economic activity and flexibility, and thus employment, are crucial to solving such social and economic challenges. This is recognised at the political level - for example by the adoption of activation policies and the gradual expansion of social care programmes (OECD 1998b). In 2000, EU member states agreed to 'raise the employment rate as close as possible to 70 per cent by 2010' as part of the EU's strategic goal of becoming 'the most competitive and dynamic knowledge-based economy capable of sustainable economic growth with more and better jobs and greater social cohesion' (EU 2000).

Besides reducing early exit from the labour market the greatest potential for increasing employment in most countries is to promote the entry and re-entry of women and workers with low skill levels into work. Labour force participation rates rise with educational level in nearly all European countries, and particularly among women (OECD 2000a). What is more, the gender gap in labour force participation decreases with increasing educational attainment. For these reasons we concentrate on social policies that may enhance employment opportunities and improve skill levels.

Several cross-national studies have investigated the relationship between the welfare state and employment or economic growth at the macro-level, although the empirical evidence of a causal link is still inconclusive (Atkinson 1995). Similarly, many national studies have investigated the relationship between different aspects of particular schemes and employment. What is largely missing in the literature, however, are comparative studies that take a whole-system approach in examining mechanisms through which the welfare state may promote employment - in other words, studies that concentrate on the 'black box' in which policy inputs are transformed into employment outcomes. In this chapter we will make a first attempt to open up this 'black box' by examining a range of social policies across half a dozen countries and discuss how these policies may positively influence employment for two population groups: women and lower skilled people.

Social policies and employment

We assume that there is a connection between the ways in which social policies (inputs) affect different socio-economic groups differently (outputs), and, in turn, that this influences the employment prospects for these groups (outcomes). Drawing, amongst others, on the work of Esping-Andersen (1999), we argue that social policies relate to three basic operations and sets of policies that welfare states can undertake to actively promote employment, particularly for women and the less skilled: de-familialisation, de-commodification, and re-commodification. The specific nature and weight placed on these operations reflect a country's political economy, whereas the outcomes of operations relate to the emphasis placed on the redistribution, insurance, caring and human resource dimensions of the welfare state. However, the final result on employment for various socio-economic groups is not only affected by the concomitant economic and institutional factors related to state policies, but also by other contextual factors, not least public attitudes and economic development. Figure 12.1 illustrates the connections between input, outputs and outcomes.

First, welfare states can take on caring tasks from the family, i.e. they have a *de-familialisation* potential (see Esping-Andersen 1999, O'Connor et al. 1999). De-familialisation may increase family members', in particular women's, employment prospects, as persons with caring tasks may enter the labour market more freely compared to a situation where there is no state provision of caring. Vice versa, a low degree of de-familialisation may constitute an obstacle for persons with caring responsibilities wanting to enter or remain in the labour market. In this way a high degree of de-familialisation helps women to enter employment, to become commodified. Investing in the caring dimension of the welfare state may positively influence employment opportunities for groups who would otherwise be constrained by having to look after children or elderly who need care. Widely available and affordable childcare, in addition to extensive elderly care, are the cornerstones of de-familialisation policies. Moreover, enrolment in child day care institutions may also be seen as an investment in human resources that in the longer run may enhance employment. This is because child day care can contribute positively to children's development, in particular children from poorer families, where parents' social problems, including unemployment, could otherwise be passed on to their offspring (Christoffersen 1994; Duncan and Brooks-Gunn 1997).

Second, welfare states may support the flexibility of the labour market by providing easily accessible and relatively generous benefits for persons in periods between employment, and by applying a limited level of employment protection. We denote this operation the *de-commodification* potential of the welfare state (see Esping-Andersen 1990). Neo-classical economists see de-commodification as synonymous with work disincentives, while we argue that it may also enhance employment by stimulating private risk taking (see Sinn 1995). Persons with insurance against loss of income while out of work are more likely to search for the job which best matches their qualifications and are less likely to get stuck with the same employer for security reasons. In short, better benefits in return for less job security may be better overall, both for individuals at the micro-level and the promotion of employment at the macro-level. Employment protection legislation and unemployment compensation are the key policies behind de-commodification. When individuals are not tied to one employer by strict employment protection legislation and can secure accessible, generous social security benefits when out of work, it is more likely that they will take risks such as changing jobs. Individuals in this situation would fear the loss of economic well-being to a much lesser extent than those without recourse to an accessible and generous safety net which helps through temporary periods of unemployment or transition between jobs. It would also discourage 'cuckoo's nests', i.e. jobs filled with overqualified persons, and thus the under-utilization of skills. In short, investments in the insurance dimension of the welfare state may promote employment.

Figure 12.1: Principal illustration of welfare state inputs, outputs, and outcomes.

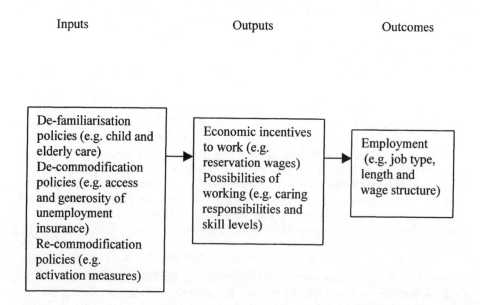

Finally, welfare states may actively try to promote employment by various types of activation or labour market policies for those unlikely to succeed by themselves. We call this operation the *re-commodification* potential of the welfare state. Re-commodification may increase employment by raising human resources, for example by lifting skill levels through active labour market policies with an emphasis on furthering qualifications. The supply and demand of labour may thereby be better matched than without such investments in human resources. Besides these qualification effects of activation, there are also strong motivational effects. Benefits dependent on, for example, accepting activation offers minimize work disincentives potentially associated with benefits.

Two observations should be made at this stage. First, welfare states deliver a series of other policies which, among other things, also impact on employment, such as the provision of health care, employment, housing, tax policies and education. But we also find examples within the realm of traditional social policy. In particular, state subsidised familialisation of caring tasks may in the short term decrease parents' labour market experiences, notably those of women. Parental leave schemes are among the chief policies governments enact to enhance familialisation, and these are more frequently taken up by women than men. At the same time such policies also promote employment, as participation in the labour market is usually a condition for eligibility. Since the overall impact on employment of such policies is uncertain, we have not included them in the cross-national analysis here.

Second, policies do not work in isolation. The complex configuration of social policies stratifies the population in a systematic fashion according to gender, age, class and so forth. The very combination of, and emphasis on, the various operations thus constitute different types of welfare states privileging some groups rather than others. In the comparative welfare state literature it has become commonplace to distinguish between three welfare state ideal types: the Social Democratic, the Conservative and the Liberal (e.g. Titmuss 1974; Esping-Andersen 1999). The state in the Social Democratic model has the largest and most active role in trying to fulfil the promise of (more) employment for all. Male insiders in the labour market are better catered for in the Conservative model, whereas the state has a residual role in the Liberal one. Since our interest is to investigate how welfare states may actively try to promote employment, we compare the Social Democratic model and how its policies may work to the benefit of women and the less skilled, with other types of welfare states. The Social Democratic model combines high degrees of de-familialisation, de-commodification and re-commodification through a wide range of policies. A full account of these three operations is not possible here due to their sheer magnitude and complex impact on the labour market (but see Søndergaard 1999, Atkinson 1999). Instead, we concentrate on a few programmes and their respective key attributes which are at the heart of the three operations and which are, arguably, the most important aspects in terms of the employment prospects for women and the less skilled; i.e. child day care (universality), social care for the elderly (extensiveness), employment protection legislation (strictness), unemployment insurance (coverage, accessibility, generosity, and work requirements) and active labour market policies (scope).

Six European countries are compared here. Denmark, Finland, and Sweden represent the Social Democratic strategy whereas Germany, the Netherlands and the United Kingdom represent alternative strategies. The main objective of the remainder of the chapter is to provide a systematic and holistic cross-national comparison of social policies, and to discuss the mechanisms through which these policies may affect employment.

Child day care and social care for the elderly

The main reason why European women in employment stop working is not a breach or non-renewal of contracts, ill health or marriage but after having children. For example, more than half of all women in Germany, the Netherlands and the United Kingdom state that children were the main cause for stopping paid employment (Eurostat 1997). Reconciling work with family life is thus one of the greatest challenges faced by women with children, and by countries which want women to stay in the labour market.

Although cultural factors and the fact that becoming a housewife is strongly correlated with the level of education in all countries, there are sharp cross-national differences, as shown in Table 12.1, which may at least partly be explained by the existence of different social policies. The more women are expected to care for their children during normal working hours, and the less available and affordable child day care, the less likely it is that such women enter the labour market or, if they do so, that they will not work fewer hours. In the country with the best record in child day care coverage, Denmark, almost no housewives give children as a reason for stopping work. Similarly, among those with two or more children below the age of five almost no Danish women describe themselves as housewives, compared with more than half in the other non-Nordic EU (Eurostat 1997).

Hence, the welfare state can play an active role in facilitating women's employment opportunities whilst having children by providing families with the opportunity to have their children cared for during working hours outside the family, either through nurseries or via various sorts of family day care schemes. Such de-familialisation thus describes the extent to which families do not have to take care of their children due to the existence of state supported schemes. In principle, a high degree of de-familialisation enables adult family members, notably women, to enter the labour market, or, to put it in the terms previously used, fosters the commodification of women.

One measure of the de-familialisation potential of welfare states is the proportion of children aged 3-6 in child day care. From 1990 to 2000 this proportion grew in Scandinavian countries, although most in Sweden (Kvist 1999, Kvist 2000a). Today more than four out of five children in this age group attend day care in Denmark and Sweden, and more than three out of five in Finland (see Table 12.1). This indicates that the demand for childcare has almost been met. Nordic women are thus better able to choose entering the labour market, if they can find a job, than women in countries without extensive child day care coverage. Directly comparable data do not exist, but around two in five British and German pre-school children attend day care and one in four of their Dutch counterparts (see Table 12.1).

Other caring tasks which may potentially obstruct women's employment opportunities relate to the needs of frail elderly relatives. Although not a perfect indicator, the proportion of women looking after relatives is two to three times as high in the United Kingdom, Germany and the Netherlands as it is in Denmark. Equally the amount of care measured by hours per day is significantly higher in the former group of countries (Eurostat 1997). De-familialisation thus also relates to how the state may facilitate the employment of women with frail elderly relatives by providing social care for elderly. Since the extent to which women are expected to take care of relatives may influence their labour market participation, one measure of this aspect of de-familialisation is the proportion of elderly in institutional care or in receipt of home help services. Here the trend in the 1990s was stable in Denmark, whereas the scope of home help contracted in Finland, and Sweden experienced a shift from institutional care to home help (Kvist 1999). Today more than four out of ten elderly in Denmark receive social care (see Table 12.1). In Sweden the figure is one in three and in Finland three in ten. Again, we have no reliable cross-national data on the extent of care for the elderly, but the share of elderly receiving either home help or living in institutional accommodation is about one in five in the Netherlands and one in eight in Germany and Britain.

The care of elderly in the Nordic countries demonstrates the changing nature of the solidarity between generations. Prior to the establishment of care services for the elderly, caring was primarily a task for the family - for which read women. Solidarity between generations was in this way internalised within the family. With the occurrence of care schemes for older people, generational solidarity was externalised and institutionalised by state provision. Workers today show their intergenerational solidarity by supporting the current generation of elderly through employment and the payment of taxes. In return they expect future generations of workers to take care of them in a similar fashion.

Other things being equal, this results in higher employment, both by providing working-age women with relatives needing care better opportunities to take up work and by the creation of jobs in social services, again notably for women. In fact, 30 per cent of all people in employment in the Nordic countries – twice the OECD average – work in the public sector, and about two-thirds or all those employed in social, health and education are women (see also Kolberg 1991).

A further factor contributing to women's labour supply in the Nordic countries is the high degree of individualisation in social and taxation policies (see Dex et al. 1995; Hatland 2001). For example, Danish widower's pensions were abolished in 1984. Although not directly linking up with the idea of de-familialisation of caring tasks, there is little doubt that letting persons be treated as individuals rather than as part of a family unit has a positive impact on the employment of women. Taken together, Nordic countries' extensive social services and their individualisation of tax/benefit systems help to explain their higher employment rate and work intensity among women compared to most other European countries.

Employment protection legislation and unemployment insurance

Historically, the aim of labour movements has been to strike a balance between, on one hand, protecting workers against the vagaries of the market through employment protection legislation and social security benefits, and, on the other, preventing the absolute dependence on their status as workers by either de facto citizens wages or the erosion of the economic basis of jobs. Hence, some, but not complete, de-commodification is a goal for social democrats. This is echoed by one of the Social Democratic architects behind contemporary Danish policies, Mogens Lykketoft. He argues that workers' interests and a flexible labour market in terms of high labour turnover can best be achieved by a combination of relaxed employment protection legislation and easily accessible and relatively generous cash benefits for people who have lost their jobs. Relaxed employment protection legislation enables firms to adjust quickly to new market conditions by laying off staff, thereby creating the basis for economic growth and welfare, whilst social security prevents dismissed workers from experiencing major economic difficulties whilst looking for a new job. The combined result is a high degree of labour turnover which is frequently seen as an indicator for a flexible labour market and an economy, that, in turn, promotes employment as compared to a rigid labour market.

The Anglo-Saxon countries have the most relaxed employment protection legislation. Within the six countries covered here, the UK is followed by Denmark and then by Finland and the Netherlands (Table 12.1; see also OECD 1999a, Table 2.6). In contrast, Sweden and Germany have relatively strict employment protection legislation. Job protection is a double-edged sword. On one hand it may provide employees with a sense of security against losing their jobs. On the other hand, job protection may also work as a barrier to employers intending to hire, particularly low skilled, workers. Employers may be discouraged from taking on new staff if they fear that laying off people is difficult or expensive. In effect, this may cement the position of both insiders and outsiders in the labour market (Lindbeck and Snower 1988). Thus, job protection may work to serve the interests of the well-established in the labour market - typically middle-aged males in stable well-paid jobs - at the expense of the not-so-established - typically young females in precarious low paid and low skill jobs. Whereas there is no evidence that strict employment protection legislation affects overall labour market performance there may be an effect on the distribution of employment and unemployment (OECD 1999a:50). Stricter employment protection legislation is also associated with less economic flexibility in terms of lower turnover in the labour market as both jobs and unemployment spells tend to last longer (ibid:50).

However, a relaxed employment protection policy should not stand alone, but be backed up by easily accessible and generous insurance benefits for those temporarily out of employment. Despite generally stricter conditions to becoming eligible for unemployment insurance in the Nordic countries during the 1990s, such programmes are still generally more easily accessible than similar programmes in Germany and the Netherlands (Table 12.1; see also Clasen et al. 2001; Kvist 2000b). The share of unemployed in receipt of unemployment insurance benefits reflects this. In the 1990s this proportion was 50-60 per cent in Finland, 53-73 per cent in Norway, 68-78 per cent in Denmark, and 71-80 per cent in Sweden (Torp 1999). By comparison, about 30-35 per cent of the unemployed in Germany and the Netherlands received unemployment insurance (Clasen et al. 2001). Fewer than 20 per cent of British unemployed people received the contribution based Job Seeker's Allowance (ibid.) which may also be explained by a comparatively short benefit period. In brief, this means that the role of unemployment insurance and other cash benefits, notably unemployment assistance and social assistance, in the income protection of the jobless varies between countries (see also Group of Seven 1995). Unemployment insurance benefits are typically individualised, although they may have different rates for breadwinners and supplements for children, whereas unemployment and social assistance benefits are normally tested against partner's income. This has implications for work incentives and labour supply where incentives in the latter group of schemes are affected by the economic position of possible partners. Other things being equal, individualised and non-means-tested schemes have fewer work disincentives built into them. More generally, access to unemployment benefits may promote the security necessary to facilitate a proper job search whilst out of work (see also Sinfield 1997).

Importantly, such benefits should also allow people not needing to accept the first job offer on the horizon if it is not optimal in a broader view. If benefits are too low, claimants will be economically constrained from seeking the job best matching their qualifications. Neo-classical economists tend to be more concerned with another aspect though by arguing that generous benefits distort work incentives. Indeed, it can be argued that unemployment insurance should serve two purposes which are at odds with each other. One is to provide insurance against temporary income loss, thus facilitating a proper job search and diminishing mismatch problems. The other purpose is to secure against relative poverty which mainly affects the lower end of the income scale and hence the less skilled, and may thus create work disincentives for this group. Many continental European countries provide just as generous if not higher benefits for middle and high income groups as the Scandinavian countries despite having lower official replacement rates (Hansen 2000). The Scandinavian countries tend to provide more generous benefits for low-income groups (defined at 75 per cent of the Average Production Worker, APW) than the continental European countries (see Table 12.1). This shows two important things. First, national unemployment insurance schemes create different opportunities and incentive problems for the heterogeneous population of unemployed depending on the occupational, income and family situation (see also Grimshaw and Rubery 1997; Kvist 1998, 2000c). Second, and in relation to this latter point, the net replacement rate decreases most rapidly with rising previous income in Denmark and Sweden. On this basis one may argue that the Nordic countries may have latent problems of work incentives for low income groups, and insufficient insurance against income loss for higher income groups which would facilitate proper job search. However, as unemployment falls disproportionately on the shoulders of low-income groups, and in particular the less skilled, this may not be a major problem. The problem is further reduced if families consist of two earners, which has become the norm in Scandinavia.

However, work incentives and the facilitation of job search are not only influenced by the level of benefits, but also the duration of benefits and conditions imposed upon claimants, a point we will return to in the next section. To sum up, we find that Denmark comes closest to the combination of relaxed employment protection legislation (actually the most relaxed non-Anglo-Saxon among the OECD countries) with easily accessible, generous unemployment insurance benefits. Finland also approaches this model. In contrast, Sweden appears to have tougher employment protection surpassing the Netherlands and close to Germany, although Sweden has the most easily accessible unemployment scheme of all six countries. The United Kingdom is unique in the sense of combining the most relaxed employment protection legislation with fairly accessible but low unemployment benefits. Clearly, there are marked differences between the countries in their de-commodifying potential. In the United Kingdom market forces, and hence a low degree of de-commodification, are seen as the most desirable and efficient way of clearing labour markets and fostering economic growth. In Germany, and less so in the Netherlands, insiders in the labour market are well covered through strict employment protection legislation and generous benefits, but outsiders face second-class social and employment protection. Finally, in the Social Democratic model, as represented most clearly by Denmark, employment protection is low, but is combined with a generous social safety net for low-income groups. How the balancing of employment and social protection impacts on employment is an empirical question to be investigated, but there is no doubt that such an analysis should not only include work disincentives, but also the enabling mechanisms of unemployment benefits as well as conditions attached to benefit receipt and the role of active labour market policies.

Conditioning benefits and active labour market policies

Conditions attached to benefit receipt can be seen as a way of linking welfare with work. This is particularly the case if cash benefits are linked to active labour market policies - at least when such policies aim to help the jobless back into the labour market and/or provide meaningful activities. In other words, conditions and activation offers must be of a certain quality, a helping hand and not merely an instrument to police moral hazard which is dominant in the liberal approach to workfare (see also Standing 1990; Gilbert 1992). The combination of work requirements and such active labour market policies provides the re-commodification potential of welfare states and is seen as typical of the Social Democratic model. In this section we will look at how the conditioning of benefits coupled with activation offers may promote employment by eliminating work disincentives and strengthening qualifications.

Eliminating work disincentives is one of the goals of conditioning benefit receipt on accepting job and activation offers, and should be seen in the light of relatively long and generous benefits for low income groups. In this regard, the conditioning of benefits upon accepting work and activation offers is the Social Democratic model's functional equivalent of non-generous benefits in the Liberal model and restrictive access to benefits in the Conservative models. Relatively generous benefits in the Social

Democratic model for low-income groups are thus circumscribed by tough work conditions in order to combat unemployment traps and benefit dependency. In this way conditionality and activation together stimulate the unemployed to seek and get work. This practice of testing work willingness enjoys broad political support in all Scandinavian countries.

Besides eliminating work disincentives the combination of conditional benefits and activation offers also has a qualification goal. They aim to endow participants with more qualifications, be they occupational qualifications such as computer skills, general qualifications such as literacy and language skills, or personal qualifications such as increased self-esteem. Here the conditioning of benefits on activation aims to secure people against marginalisation, against entrapment on benefits or in precarious jobs.

We expect significant cross-national differences in the number of unemployed people actually receiving activation offers, with more participants in countries resembling the Social Democratic model than in countries approaching the Continental European and Anglo-Saxon models as mentioned earlier. This is partially reflected by the share of the labour force entering labour market programmes, i.e. labour market training, youth measures, and subsidised employment. This proportion amounts to 16.6 per cent in Denmark (1995), 12.2 per cent in Finland (1997), 12.4 per cent in Sweden (1997), 3.2 per cent in Germany (1997), 14.1 per cent in the Netherlands (1997), and 2.2 per cent in the United Kingdom (1996-97) (OECD 1999a, Table J). The Netherlands deviates from the expected pattern due to a spectacular increase in the use of subsidies for regular employment from 0.4 per cent to 11.2 per cent of the labour force between 1995 and 1996 (see also Hartog 1999; Oorshot and Engelfriet 1999). Although this represents a qualitative shift in Dutch employment policies, the Dutch reliance on wage subsidies still makes it distinct from the Scandinavian countries where labour market training plays a larger role.

Of course, high rates of participation inflows may indicate relatively short activation periods. Ideally we would therefore need to refer to comparable data on the average proportion of people on activation offers over time or at some point in time. At present we only have comparable data for the Scandinavian countries (see Table 12.1). The scope of Swedish and Finnish activation rose with increasing unemployment during the first half of the 1990s from around 1.5 per cent to 4 to 5 per cent of the labour force (Torp 1999). Then it declined slightly in Sweden, and increased slightly in Finland. In contrast, the scope of activation has remained fairly stable in Denmark after the introduction of the labour market reform in 1994 when unemployment was decreasing. This was also reflected in a growing share of insured unemployed being activated in the latter half of the 1990s, i.e. a doubling from 15 per cent in 1994 to 31 per cent in 1998. Rising levels of unemployment in the early 1990s resulted in a decreased rate of activation in Finland and Sweden, i.e. the share of unemployed people participating in activation dropped in Finland from 34 per cent in 1990 to 16 per cent in 1993, and in Sweden from 46 per cent in 1990 to 30 per cent in 1993. Then the rate picked up again in both countries to a level of 22 per cent in Finland (1997) and 38 per cent in Sweden (1998). Adding social assistance claimants in activation in Denmark, this would mean that today around four out of ten unemployed in both Sweden and Denmark are in activation at any one time, and about one in five in Finland. Coupled with tough requirements regarding the acceptance of job and activation offers there is thus no sign that the Scandinavian countries are giving up their activation line - indeed quite the contrary. In other words, re-commodification can still be seen as an integral part of the Social Democratic welfare state.

Concluding remarks

It should be clear that there is no one welfare state influencing employment in a uniform manner, nor any uniform manner in which welfare states influence employment. We should not assume simple relationships between the existence of welfare state programmes and the workings of the labour market, but appreciate the complex relationship between different types of welfare states and employment. Moreover, we have seen how any type of welfare state acts in different ways for different groups of the population, depending on family and income situation, work record and status. In short there is a multitude of welfare states for different socio-economic groups, and only by appreciating this complexity may we be able to start formulating proper policy recommendations which enhance the employment situation of women and the less skilled.

What can be learned from the Scandinavian experiences with regard to these two groups? The main premise is that access to paid work is the best guarantee against poverty, marginalisation, and exclusion, and a way of securing an economically sustainable welfare state. In the Nordic countries the state plays an active role in serving these goals through three main state operations:

1.   De-familiarisation of caring tasks through extensive social services for children and elderly that contribute to maximising mothers' ability to enter paid employment by enabling them to opt out of caring responsibilities more easily during working hours and by the creation of jobs in social services. De-familiarisation thus suggests an especially interesting employment scenario for lower skilled females.

2.   De-commodification of labour through relaxed employment protection coupled with easily accessible and relatively generous benefits aims to make people secure during interruptions of employment. De-commodification together with re-commodification may thus help towards lowering the structural rate of unemployment by creating a more flexible labour market and by securing a more egalitarian distribution of employment and unemployment risks.

3.   Re-commodification of unemployed people through extensive and individually tailored employment programmes aims to protect them against lifetime entrapment on benefits and in precarious jobs. As unemployment falls disproportionately

on the less skilled, re-commodification has its greatest employment potential for this group.

In total, these social policies may improve the quality and utilization of human capital, in particular among non-privileged groups like women and the less skilled as without any help these groups are less likely to maximise their potential than other groups.

Some of these policies were not originally intended or designed to promote employment. Most notably de-familiarisation of caring tasks was largely motivated by the aim to secure gender equality from the 1960s through to the 1990s. Nevertheless, an important by-product has been that women, including single mothers, have now wide access to gainful employment because they can reconcile employment with having children and caring for older people, and because of the creation of many jobs in social and health services.

However, there are barriers to the wholesale import of Social Democratic style solutions to the challenge of raising employment for women and the less skilled. Dominant cultural values together with the inertia inherent in existing policies provide barriers for the import of such policies to non-Nordic countries. Financial strain may also render the possibilities of policy adoption less feasible. For example, it seems unlikely that European governments in financial distress are likely to greatly expand their social services much. Politically it is easier to introduce and expand programmes at times when everybody is gaining than at times when priorities have to be made and thus conflicts occur. Hence, if non-Nordic policy makers want to change towards a more Social Democratic style of policies, they may enter troubled waters. At the same time, ageing populations, marginalisation and, in some countries, low fertility rates may lead policy makers to revise traditional policies. Change seems inevitable, but policy makers have choices, including the choice to strive for an activating turn in order to secure the economic and social sustainability of their welfare societies.

To the extent that policy-makers want to embark on the latter policies, they may want to consider the lessons which can be drawn from the experience of the qualitative shift in Danish social and employment policies during the 1990s. Besides the positive effects on employment and an increase in participants' self-reported well-being, another lesson is the need to create a common vision for policies, or – in less ambitious terms – a common understanding of the problems at hand and how to start tackling them. In the Danish case, failing policies and the increasing number of people becoming marginalised in the 1980s showed policy-makers and professionals that it was no longer enough or desirable simply to compensate 'losers' in the labour market with cash benefits. Instead it became increasingly recognised that the state had to take on an active role in order to minimise the human and economic costs associated with unemployment in the longer run. The state became obliged to try to prevent and combat marginalisation through benefits in kind, that is social services and labour policies. The broad consensus among political parties, social partners, street-level bureaucrats, and individual participants on the desirability of such a shift in policy bears witness to the existence of such a common understanding.

Table 12.1: Features of employment/population rates and social policies in six European countries

		DK	SF	S	D	NL	UK
1.	Pre-school children in child day care (%)	67	46	66	38	26	42
2.	Elderly in receipt of social care (%)	43	29	34	12	19	11
3.	Employment protection legislation (OECD ranking 1-26)*	8	11	18	20	13	1
4.	Access to unemployment insurance (0 to 1)**	.64	.51	.75	.42	.28	.52
5.	Generosity of unemployment insurance for low paid ***	80	66	80	59	71	26
6.	Generosity of unemployment insurance for well-paid ****	46	50	52	58	69	14
7.	Activated unemployed (%)*****	31	22	38	..	..	..

Source: Kvist (2000c).
Notes: *Weighted average of indicators for regular contracts, temporary contracts and collective dismissals converted into ranking increasing with the strictness of employment protection legislation in 26 OECD countries. **Indicator based on the coverage and allocation criteria as well as re-entitlement requirements for unemployment insurance increasing with easier accessibility. *** Net replacement rate for single person with previous earnings at 75% of the Average Production Worker (APW). **** Net replacement rate for single person with previous earnings at 150% of the APW. ***** Participants in active labour market measures as share of unemployed.

Chapter 13

Welfare to Work and the Organisation of Opportunity:
European and American approaches from a British perspective

Martin Evans

Introduction

The phrase 'welfare to work' describes policies that move people who claim out-of-work social transfers into the labour market. But as use of the phrase has grown its precision has suffered. It is used cross-nationally to refer to schemes but often refers to very differently conceived and targeted programmes. The recent US influence on British policy– both in the adoption of the phrase itself and in policy design (for example, Deacon 1999, Walker 1998, Wilson et al. 1998) has been obvious but there are also European influences. The danger for policy analysis is that the term 'welfare to work' is used rhetorically by policy makers who can portray policy outcomes in simple headline terms, especially in the USA. This means that when their counterparts in other countries look abroad and draw conclusions about foreign policy performance they often do so

Jochen Clasen (ed.), *What Future for Social Security?*, 211-234
©2001 Kluwer Law International. Printed in the Netherlands.

without any requirement to confuse a politically simple message with complexities of fact and context.

Comparing policy design and implementation across different countries must get behind the rhetoric in order to understand what programmes apply to which target groups under what circumstances. This is often difficult because the different national policy contexts often mean that the 'welfare' target groups are not only different in composition but also have very different underlying entitlements to cash transfers. The word 'welfare' only refers to unemployed social assistance claimants in some countries while in others the term is wide enough to encompass social insurance claimants of both unemployment and invalidity benefits. This chapter uses a three-part categorisation of common elements of policy based on the phrase 'welfare to work' itself.

Welfare	The definition of claimant populations that make up the target groups in each country.
To	The active employment programmes
Work	The provision that is made in work through benefits, subsidies, services or through actual employment.

This simple heuristic distinction is often difficult to maintain in practice because policy assumptions overlap. For instance, negative definitions of entitlement - i.e. who is *not entitled* to be a claimant - are seen as an activating measure for employment. A more structural problem in this view of policy is that it assumes much about macro-economic policy and the overall economic climate in job creation and labour market development.

This chapter looks at policy in four countries: the USA, France, Germany and the Netherlands from the perspective of British policy developments. These countries have very differently organised policy regimes with central, local and regional variations in policy design and implementation. Four major urban centres: New York, Paris, Hamburg and Amsterdam are the locations for national policy profiles. Research consisted of national data collection and visits to these locations in 1998 to discuss policy with providers and policy makers on the ground.

WELFARE to work

Welfare to work in Britain

The word welfare is at the epicentre of British reform. It has two meanings. In the term 'welfare reform' it means all cash transfers and is synonymous with the British usage of the term 'Social Security' – i.e. all contributory, universal and means tested benefits. In the term 'welfare to work' it means benefits paid to people of working age who are able to work.

Before 1997 the only claimants put forward for active labour market programmes were the unemployed but under New Labour the target population has expanded to cover lone parents, sick and disabled claimants and others. One reason for this expansion in focus lies in the growth profile of claimants over the 1980s and 1990s. Figure 13.1 shows social assistance and social insurance benefits since 1979 in each boom and trough year of the economic cycle. While the working age population grew by 8 per cent overall the welfare group grew much faster across the economic cycle.

Figure 13.1: Benefit claimants of working age 1979-97 (index 1979=100)

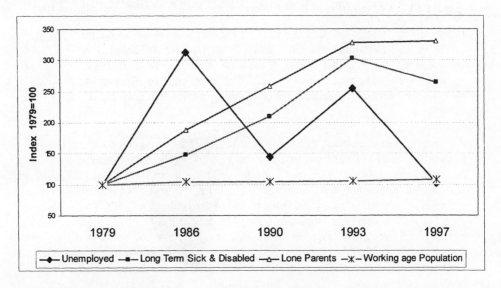

Source: Author's calculations from Evans 1998, DSS 1988 and previous versions
Notes: Claimant totals of Income Support, Unemployment Benefits and Jobseekers Allowance,
      Invalidity and Incapacity Benefits and Severe Disablement Allowance.

A full discussion of the complex explanations of this growth is beyond the scope of this chapter, but the important point for New Labour's policy makers was that they saw some of the growth as endogenous to social security policy. That is that the system of benefits and employment services had contributed to growth. The failure of social institutions to act together in a holistic policy approach and to promote work for all had to be remedied.

The new British definition of populations for welfare to work programmes crosses claimant types (unemployed, lone parents and sick and disabled people) and also crosses the divide between contributory and social assistance provision. This is possible in Britain because of the centralised state-run organisational structure of cash transfers with very high level of coverage by means-tested social assistance. Transferring this conception to the US and European agenda is far more problematic. They just don't see it similarly. The British term 'welfare' when it describes a target group for active labour market programmes is both ideologically loaded and organisationally peculiar. I employ the term *Claimant reservoir* as a more neutral term with no implied organisational basis and more suited to international use. The term implies a more dynamic image of claimant stocks (and inflows and outflows) that is more useful in describing the target groups and their priority in terms of their position in the social transfer systems as part of a direct or indirect pool of unemployed and inactive people.

Figure 13.2: Composition of British working age benefit claimant population 1997

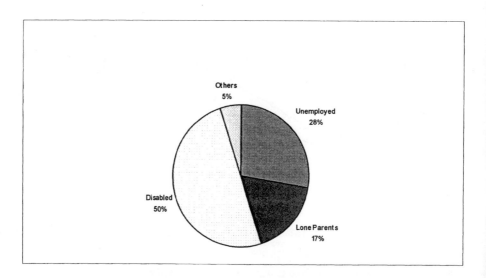

Source: Author's calculations from DSS 1998

The British claimant reservoir still has the unemployed occupying the 'hottest' place in the reservoir because their entitlement to benefits is directly linked to labour market orientated behaviour. The aim of British welfare to work policy epitomised in the New Deals is to both raise the overall temperature for this group and others who do not have that direct link in order to increase outflows into employment. It also aims to expand investment in human capital to ensure that employability is simultaneously improved.

Figure 13.2 shows that in 1997 the claimant unemployed were 28 per cent of the potential claimant reservoir (around 1.3 million people). The new series of British welfare to work programmes, called New Deals, were introduced in 1997 and 1998 to provide active labour market programmes for different groups. The New Deal for unemployed youth, defined as people aged between 18 and 24 and unemployed 6 months or more is called the New Deal for Young People (NDYP). The separate New Deal for the Long Term Unemployed (NDLTU) is for those who are aged over 24 year and unemployed for over 2 years. These target groups represent 25 per cent of the unemployed but only 7 per cent of the total potential claimant reservoir. The New Deal for Lone Parents (NDLP) targets only those lone parents who have their youngest child in school (aged 5¼), around 55 per cent of lone parents or 10 per cent of the potential claimant reservoir. However, the largest *potential* claimant reservoir for welfare to work is for the New Deal for Disabled People (NDDP) for those claiming contributory Incapacity Benefits and/or means-tested social assistance, Income Support. The Labour Force Survey suggests that 42 per cent of these people would like to work (DfEE 1999). This group is around 15-18 per cent of the total claimant reservoir –around double the size of the unemployed. Another new target group is partners of unemployed claimants who have the New Deal for Partners (NDP)– a further 5 per cent. The final target group is any claimant or their partner aged over 50 in the New Deal for the over 50s. (ND50+). This group overlaps with many of the other target groups.

The new policies thus effectively double the claimant reservoir over the pre-1997 position. How does this composition and prioritisation of the claimant reservoir compare to the other countries?

National claimant reservoirs compared

Figure 13.3 provides estimates of the relative size and composition of the other national claimant reservoirs using the expanded British assumptions of a potential claimant reservoir. The four European systems each produce a claimant reservoir of similar size - around 11 per cent to 13 per cent of the 15-64 population. The USA stands out as having an overall smaller reservoir, but one has to remember that only around one third of its unemployed are covered by either UI or social assistance.

The national composition of the claimant reservoirs is also noticeably different with the British system having the smallest proportion in contributory unemployment of any of the five countries and the smallest proportion defined as unemployed among the European countries. Britain and the USA have the largest proportion of lone parents. The size of the discrete contributory invalidity/disability claimant populations is smallest in France and Germany and largest in the Netherlands, Britain and the USA in descending order. However, many claimants with disabilities will be present in non-categorical social assistance populations and in Continental European contributory unemployment populations

The targeting of welfare to work programmes also differs greatly as indicated in Figure 13.3 by the position and size of the arrow indicators. The US has the smallest and most specific target group – lone parents and the few others on social assistance. European levels are higher. In France, Germany and the Netherlands it is primarily the unemployed – which, unlike the US, includes the long-term unemployed and which unlike Britain often includes partially disabled claimants. These three European countries also include lone parents in general social assistance schemes subject to their children being of school/nursery age.

Figure 13.3: Claimant reservoirs and 'welfare to work' target groups - 1997

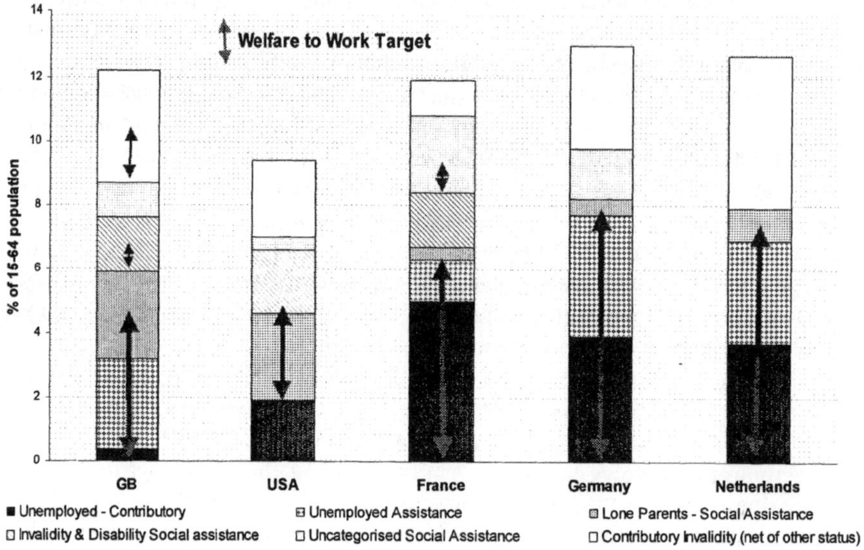

Sources: DSS 1998 and Table 1;US Department of Commerce 1999, unpublished data from US Bureau of Labor Current Population survey, DHHS 2000, unpublished data from US Department of Labor, US Social Security Administration (1998), US Department of Labor unpublished data on UI receipt, UNEDIC (2000) and CNAF (1999) and unpublished data from UNEDIC and CNAF, unpublished data from CNAM, Statistisches Bundesamt (1999), Bundesanstalt für Arbeit (1998), unpublished data from Verband Deutscher Rentenversicherungsträger, Centraal Bureau voor de Statistiek (1998) and Eurostat (2000)

America

The actual term 'welfare' means *only* means-tested social assistance paid either through Federally financed programmes for families with children (formerly Aid for Families with Dependent Children, *AFDC*, but from 1996 called Temporary Aid for Needy Families or *TANF*) or from State funded General Assistance programmes. However, most States no longer have General Assistance for able-bodied people of working and the term is thus for AFDC/TANF programmes primarily. The Federal system of food stamps is part of the TANF package but are also paid to low income working families.

The term *welfare* does *not* include any social insurance or unemployment insurance benefits (UI) in the USA. Indeed, beyond vacancy matching and assistance with job search there are few active employment programmes in the USA directly linked to UI. This means that contributory social security benefits for disabled people, *Disability Insurance*, and its Federally run means-tested non-contributory sister programme *Supplementary Security Income* for disabled people, both run by the Social Security Administration (SSA) are not part of US welfare to work debates. This does not, however, mean that there are no policies to assist such claimants move back to work.

France

The French claimant reservoir is characterised by social insurance and at the heart of the claimant reservoir are the unemployed who claim *Allocation Unique Dégressive' (AUD)* – 5 per cent of the working age population. Additionally, for those who remained unemployed after their contributory benefits ended, there is means-tested unemployment assistance *Allocation de Solidarité Spécifique' (ASS)*.[1]

Additionally, there is the means-tested safety net benefit *Revenu Minimum d'Insertion (RMI)* for people aged over 25 with no contributory entitlement and no right to categorical social assistance (pensioners, lone parents, widows, the long-term sick, and the disabled). Entitlement to *RMI* is posited on economic (employment) and/or social re-integration. *RMI* includes many with chronic poor health and it is thus difficult to identify whom within the RMI caseload could be subject to employment programmes. Lone parents are represented in several places in the French claimant reservoir. French lone parents in general have very high labour market participation and are thus represented in AUD and ASS figures. Other can claim *Allocation Parent Isolé (API)*. For the first year of lone-parenthood and until their youngest child reaches the age of 3. Other lone parents can claim RMI.

Germany

Contributory unemployment benefits (*Arbeitslosengeld*) and means-tested long-term unemployment assistance (*Arbeitslosenhilfe*) dominate the German claimant reservoir. However, there are also considerable numbers of unemployed who have no contributory record and who claim regionally run social assistance (*Sozialhilfe*), around 1.7 million in 1997 or a further 3.2 per cent of the working population. The treatment of the wider group of *Sozialhilfe* claimants varies according to local practice, but municipalities are increasingly asking claimants to register at the employment exchange and encouraging

---

1 However entitlement to ASS is only for those with substantial contributory records.

lone parents with school aged children (or places in *Kindergarten* for younger children) to participate in work search and/or training.

The Netherlands

The Dutch claimant reservoir has a focus on both unemployment and long-term sickness and disablement and social assistance (Blomsma 1999, MSZW 2000). Disability benefits were used during the 1980s as a subsidy for redundancy and were seen to include many who were unemployed or early retired. Dutch social assistance also has fairly strict rules about work participation and hence treats the partners of claimants and lone parents with school aged children or children in nursery as available for work. Indeed the Dutch approach is increasingly to look across the boundaries of benefit entitlement and classify people according to their proximity to the labour market. Unemployed claimants on *Werklooosheidswet* or *WW* make up 390,000 or 3.7 per cent of the working population. A further 438,000 claimants are only social assistance (*Algemene Bijstandswet (ABW)*), 4.2 per cent of the population, around a third of whom are lone parents. The largest potential group in the claimant reservoir is the disabled *WAO* claimants, 615,000 or 5.8 per cent of working age population. Dutch policy towards the majority of the *stock* of contributory invalidity claimants has not placed much emphasis on work despite repeated changes to ensure that new *inflows* into *WAO* are assessed as unemployed and partially disabled wherever possible.

Welfare TO Work: Moving claimants into Work

A more active approach to unemployment is occurring across the EU and OECD countries putting more pressure on preventing long term unemployment by active focus on work and training. What do such policies look like on the ground, how are they implemented and for whom in the claimant reservoir? This section discusses several common themes in activation of benefits.

Removing and altering entitlement to benefits

All five countries have altered entitlement rules for some groups in the claimant reservoir in the late 1990s to encourage movement into work. However, the extent of such change varies greatly.

US social assistance has been hugely cut over the 1980s and 1990s. The majority of states have no cash safety net. Since 1989 the number of States providing any benefits for able-bodied working age people has fallen from 25 to 13 (Gallagher 1999).

Terminating assistance to existing claimants has not ensured universal work participation. Many of Michigan's ex GA cases did not work one year after their benefits ended (Danziger and Kossoudji 1995). The TANF 1996 reforms[2] allowed States to decide what rules of participation would give rise to entitlement to benefits. The impact of this 'no entitlement' rule has been that more conditions have been placed on inflows into benefit and many States have sought to divert claimants away from a claim – into work, to seek assistance elsewhere, or to give one-off help to prevent a claim for regular welfare. This practice of diversion varies widely between states. However, States which follow a strong 'work-first' approach will demand evidence of specific levels of job search (60 hours in 30 days) before entry into benefit is allowed. Evidence from Wisconsin suggests that the new diversion-based entry programmes led to a 53 per cent fall in caseload (Swartz et al 1999). Similar policies introduced in 1998 in New York City led to 75 per cent reductions in welfare inflows.[3]

The 1996 reforms also instituted time limits to support through TANF benefits of 60 months in a person's lifetime. States have discretion to operate different time limits and just under half have implemented tougher rules. Families have thus already reached time limits in 18 states by the summer of 2000. The percentage of the caseload that reaches the time limit ranges widely from over half in Connecticut (55 per cent) to below 5 per cent in five other States. However, the implementation of full termination of benefits has occurred at very high levels in some States. Two states stand out in the size of their time limit impacts. Nearly one quarter of Arizona's claimants reached the State time limit and had benefits terminated while Connecticut cut benefits from of over two thirds of its time-limited claimants, knocking out one third of its total caseload (author's calculations from Havemann and Vobejda 1998).

European approaches have been less extreme but changes to generosity and to entitlement rules and periods have existed in all countries. Removing entitlement entirely has only occurred for the under 18s in Britain. Evidence points to a substantial minority of this age group still not participating in work, training or benefits (Bentley and Gurumurthy 1999). Compulsory employment-based participation for young unemployed people is implemented in Britain and the Netherlands. However, when discussing compulsion and benefit entitlement it is important to remember that France has no entitlement to social assistance at all for single young people (under 25) and that French employment programmes for this group are 'voluntary'. Long-term unemployed have had cuts to inflow entitlement and greater proportions have moved on to social assistance. Entitlement to social assistance has been made more conditional on assessment at the PES.

Great Britain and the Netherlands have accompanied changes to entitlement to a more work-focused claim system for all working age claimants. British lone parents and

---

2 The Personal Responsibility and Work Opportunity Act commonly referred to by the acronym PRWORA.

3 New York Times, December 11th 1998.

disabled claimants must attend a work-focussed interview when they claim (and/or on case-review subsequently) but are not required to engage in job search as a condition of entitlement. In the Netherlands, however, work is a priority applied across all claimant populations and actual job search is required for a larger group – for lone parents with children of school age and partners of claimants and for those partially disabled people who are also defined as unemployed. British policy will move in the near future to the compulsory requirement for partners of young unemployed (under 25s) to register at the Employment Service and to pass the increasingly strict application of actively seeking work.

Increasing focus on work and training

British unemployed claimants have faced increasing pressure on and scrutiny of the status of active job search over the 1980s and 1990s. Most recently, the Jobseekers Allowance regime introduced in October 1996 has made increased and more consistent job-search standard and has increased outflow rates into work (Rayner et al. 2000). Since the introduction of the New Deal programmes, intensive help with job search has begun at 6 months for the under 25s through a specialised *Gateway*. This is followed by four compulsory options – subsidised work placement, full-time education or training, or a job placement in a voluntary organisation or paid environmental project - for those still unemployed. In the NDLTU a similar reactivating facility was introduced after two years, but the system is gradually moving to 18 months and 12 months. However, the period of re-intensification of job search for this group was not viewed as significantly different from previous periodic interventions (Hasluck 2000a). Voluntary programmes of full-time training or subsidised job placements that followed such re-intensification period have been poorly taken up (ibid).

An increase in work focus for the non-unemployed in Britain is obtained in two ways. First, new claimants will have a compulsory interview with a personal advisor who will assess opportunities to work or train. Second, the stock of lone parents and disabled and partners will be approached for similar interviews on a rolling programme under the NDLP and NDDP. Partners of claimants are also being approached for voluntary participation.

France, Germany and The Netherlands have all introduced duration-based interventions for the unemployed in line with the European Employment Guidelines. In France, *Nouveau Depart* interviews will be conducted – for RMI claimants they are planned to occur after two years of claiming. European benefit systems have less frequent registration at the PES and review of job search activity. German unemployment policies have adopted general duration-based intensification measures less than in other countries. However, all unemployed are now provided with an in-depth assessment of problems and needs and access to active labour market programmes has been eased. German social assistance authorities have been incorporating more systematic appraisal of work search and registration at the *Arbeitsamt* (PES). However, the underlying approach of the PES offices is not to enforce job search but to leave it to the claimant. Large caseloads make more regular interviewing difficult and there is little to offer the long-term unemployed or other difficult to serve groups besides a subsidised job in an active labour market programme (OECD 1996b). This has led some local social assistance authorities to invest in their own more activating approach – for instance using specialised intermediaries as discussed below.

The Netherlands already has compulsory training and work opportunities for the under 23-year-olds. All new claimants are immediately assessed for work profiling and training. This comprehensive approach is being extended to all unemployed people as well as to social assistance cases, and to a lesser extent the disabled with an aim to make definite offers of training, work-experience or subsidised work after 12 months of unemployment.

American PES do not have a high work focus for UI claimants. The underlying philosophy has been to leave job search to individual benefit recipients who are faced with a 6-month definite time limit on entitlement. The provision of assistance and counseling was historically low, but since the mid-1990s there have Federal requirements to profile and provide better information and job search assistance. The OECD found that 'it would be worthwhile for the PES to consider examining the registers of job seekers and UI claimants more frequently and systematically than is currently the case' (OECD 1999b:191). The contrast with US 'welfare' is stark. Local State welfare agencies usually have their own employment service with, for example, advisors, jobs clubs and work placement provision (sometimes privatised). Such services are used both to divert and to provide assistance through counseling and intervention. Practice varies but work focus is usually immediate for all claimants with exceptions for those with babies (most often under 1) or substantial disability.

Individual-centered approach

The US approach to individualised assessment comes in two main forms. First the PES has increased the use of individual labour market profiling encouraged by the Federal Department of Labor. This means that claimants for UI are assessed for their risk of long-term unemployment when they apply and are then eligible for re-employment services. However, the effectiveness of such profiling is still largely uncertain. Secondly, there are moves to individualise intensive work orientation of welfare provision. Many States will use a period of individual job search to both test barriers and as a condition of entitlement. The push to get claimants to leave or to divert is also poorly reconciled with individualised help – many fail the inflow test and receive very poor quality of individualised help. However, the individualised caseworker approach stands at the centre of the new welfare system in States like Wisconsin. The Financial and Employment Planner (FEP) has a role that seeks to be *'teacher, preacher friend and cop*'[4] and if the relationship works then results can be rewarding for both parties. The move to casework has also been accompanied by the move towards more individualised service provision in place of simple cash assistance – for instance in the development of childcare places that suit non-standard working hours. Individual casework at its best tends to be carried out in the high quality intermediary organisations that link welfare claimants to work. America Works, a profit making welfare employment service that specialises in placing welfare claimants in clerical work (see Nye 1996), uses attitudinal and psychological and social profiling of all its clients. This is because the organisation receives the majority of its funding on completed successful job placements that have lasted 6 months. If it did not know what the individual problems and preferences to work were it would not be successful. It estimates that one third of its trainees require very detailed personal assistance in order to make a successful transition into work[5].

British welfare to work is dominated by a more flexible approach to individual needs. Personal advisors are the pivotal deliverers of all the New Deals and their quality and the quality of their relationship with claimants has become crucial factors of success (Hasluck 2000b). For the unemployed this New Deal-based approach supplements the individual Jobseeker's Contract.

The French are currently increasing the individualised element of employment service provision. Claimants will have a consistent person dealing with their case and providing support and brokering work. For RMI claimants this could be a social worker rather than an ANPE[6] (PES) employment advisor. Social as well as economic insertion will be considered as a matter of course for RMI claimants. Both types of personalised intervention focus on an individually tailored agreement. ANPE based trajectory agreements include employment insertion as the final activity.

The Netherlands uses labour market profiling to place claimants into four phases according to their distance from the labour market. Individual attention is then focused on economic integration for those who need it (that is phases 2 and 3 who are estimated to be able to get back to work with some help with training or job search assistance). For those with larger social impediments detailed trajectory assistance will then be planned before attempts are made to move them into work.

The German employment services appear to have adopted the least individualised approaches (except that many unemployed are effectively left to their own devices).[7] Social-work casework approach is returning to social assistance (*Sozialhilfe*) but

---

4 Quoted in Jason de Parle, For Caseworkers, helping is a Frustrating Experience, *New York Times*, December 10th 1999.

5 Information from an interview with America Works personnel in New York, May 1998.

6 Agence National Pour l'Emploi.

7 Hamburg *Arbeitsamt* pointed out that their high caseloads and benefit administration task limited their ability to involve themselves heavily in individual cases (March 1998).

practices vary between localities. The individual approach means that discretion is applied to those with barriers to work from childcare needs. For instance, claimants will be helped to arrange appropriate and stable childcare through local *Kindergarten* as part of a return to work plan. Hamburg has greatly increased supervision and counseling approach but has brought in specialised intermediaries to do re-employment work and to teach workers individual employment brokering.

Coordinated administration

The need to draw the separate benefit regimes and organisations together in a coordinated approach has led to the introduction of a single work-focused gateway in Britain, now called the 'ONE service'. The eventual merging of the separate benefit and employment service agencies has also been announced.[8] The coordinated approach is seen as providing a better service at a single point of contact for the claimant and a more efficient and effective administrative approach that cuts down on missing information and fraud as well as providing a work focused assessment for all working age claimants.

Dutch policy has also moved to introduce a single work-focused access to social assistance and social insurance benefits for working age people – Centres for Work and Income (CWI). However the primary aim of the CWI approach appear based on organisational integration under a high-pressure climate for increased efficiency and privatisation of administration. Privatised PES and social insurance administration meant greater co-ordination was required to ensure that dumping and cream skimming were reduced. This is one reason why the 'Comprehensive Approach' - including the 4 phase approach to profiling claimants was introduced – to distribute tasks consistently between the competing and separate administrative interests. Implementation has been planned incrementally on the ground so that each municipality can set up its own working arrangements. All claimants should have access to a CWI site by 2001.

The US move to 'One-Stop' provision was primarily driven to bring together the employment and training programmes that spanned several agencies into single access points. This move has been accompanied by a tightening of administrative budgets that has encouraged efficiency improvements and increasing use of information technology. Customer service has become a greater issue at the same time as private providers of employment services have grown and hence self-service provision for job seekers has also grown. Employment services one-stops are not usually linked directly to welfare reform. Indeed, the whole policy direction of employment and training programmes in the US has been to move towards dislocated workers rather than the disadvantaged (OECD 1999b:198). However, in some States the labour market information side of public employment services has been incorporated into welfare employment services. For State based welfare then the picture of administrative coordination differs hugely

---

8 Prime Minister's announcement to House of Commons 16th March 2000.

between States. The work-first approach has encouraged the positioning of employment services and personal advice together. Wisconsin and New York City have followed similar policies of integrating welfare offices and welfare employment services into a single point of contact – called Job Centers in New York. However, other aspects of claiming, such as verification of identity and address, were separated prior to this in New York – a move seen as a claim deterrence by local advocates. One hugely important issue for coordination in welfare policy is the delivery of Food Stamps and Medicare that have historically piggybacked on AFDC/TANF claims. The move to a coordinated and diversionary approach to TANF has means that administration of Food Stamps and Medicare for the same population has suffered. Indeed, in New York it led to litigation because the new Job Centers were not implementing Federal procedures for claiming and entitlement[9].

France and German cooperation and coordination are not as extensive as in Holland and Britain. Since 1998 the Federally run and financed employment service has been encouraged to set joint goals and programmes in place with municipal social assistance.[10] This has led to specific staff being employed to deal with *Sozialhilfe* claimants in *Arbeitsämter* as well as integrated claimant intakes, for example in Harburg in Hamburg. However, such initiatives do not alter the fundamental financial and structural differences between locally financed social assistance and Federally financed unemployment benefits and employment services. The benefits of employment programmes for the *Sozialamt* are still too often seen as qualifying participants sufficiently to pass over the contributory barrier and onto the Federal bill (Voges, Jacobs and Trickey 2001). ANPE in France is seen as the central agency to the wide range of employment programmes and the central agency for referral. The coordination of these services is the job of the *Prefêt* who overseas Regional plans and agrees local plans for urban renewal, youth employment etc. In practice this means that local ANPE offices have had increased specialised staff complements to take forward specific initiatives and that links between *Mission Locales* and other agencies have been strengthened. However, even those in the system recognise that brokering outcomes across the many agencies and programmes that exist is to push against great bureaucratic inertia.

The use of third party intermediaries

The French concept of social exclusion sees the absence of direct relationship with state and social insurance organisations as fundamental and local organisations have been funded to be entry points for the excluded – for *RMI*stes and for young people especially. These specialised associations thus act both as entry points to French social

---

9 *New York Times* January 23rd 1999. The City admitted that strict diversion procedures violated Federal Law and changed administrative practice – see *New York Times* May 25th.

10 InfoMISEP Policies No 63, Autumn 1998: 28.

policy and as brokers of packages of employment, training and social reintegration programmes. *Objective Emploi* in St. Denis in Suburban North West Paris is an example of such an organisation which works in combined offices with *Mission Locale* for young people.

The use of intermediaries as brokers is very new in Germany and has been seized upon by Hamburg and other North German municipalities as an alternative to Federal employment services for their *Sozialhilfe* clients. *Maatwerk* are a private organisation operating in Helmond in the Netherlands under the Dutch privatised initiative for re-integrating the long-term unemployed. They offer their services for a fixed fee and take on the claimant and find a job in a small to medium sized enterprise for them. They base their approach on finding the right match between employer and client and offer follow up services to ensure the job is of long standing.

This approach matches the practice of many not-for profit and profit making organisations in the USA that have evolved since the mid 1970s in response to the Supported Work initiative for ex-offenders and substance abusers and in the 1980s after the abandonment of urban job creation programmes. The US intermediaries almost all have workers – *job developers* – who contact potential employers and build up a database of contacts for job vacancies. The remainder of the organisation provides training.

Britain has recently recognised the potential of such intermediaries. The vast majority of New Deal provision is run by a public agency, the Employment Service, but with privatised sites as pilots. However, for the New Deal for the Disabled it was recognised that specialised experience was to be found in voluntary groups and charities and these have been funded to adopt and expand employment related services. However, the general nature of Employment Services was seen not to have the individual based employer/trainee advantages of the US style intermediaries. Evidence from the American good practice was collected (Evans and Kazis 1999) and a programme of seed funding has been set up. But the most radical use of intermediaries in Britain has been the adoption of a fixed-fee placement service with private providers in the 15-20 new Employment Zones operating since April 2000. All unemployed over 25 of either 18 or 12 months or more (depending on the site) will compulsory be referred to the private intermediary who will be given a series of subsidies that encourage swift and sustained job placement.

The Dutch use of intermediaries increased after the Dutch government committed itself to an active benefit scheme and increased funding for training and employment schemes over the 1990s. The change in policy direction culminated in consolidation of provision for all long-term unemployed of 12 months or more in 1998. Re-integration of long-term unemployed was effectively privatised. Intermediaries broker work placements of up to 2 years – mostly with private employers. Municipally owned but separate companies have been set up to distribute employment subsidies to employers and to provide placements for the harder to serve claimants. Thus in Amsterdam, a company called *NV Werk Amsterdam* is given the budget for employment based re-integration and it brokers places with employers and distributes the funds. Its original target of providing 10,000 employment places was reached at the end of 1998. Separately, but also receiving subsidies from *NV Werk Amsterdam* is a not-for-profit organisation called *Bureau Maatwerk* that trains and places the hardest to serve (see further discussion below). Under the CWI regime these brokers are used for all long-term unemployed of 12 months or more, but the private employer based subsidies and *Bureau Maatwerk* tend to be separate trajectories with Phase 4 claimants being sent to the latter.

Welfare to WORK: the use of employment and employment subsidies

European Employment Guidelines stipulate that the tax and social security burden on entry level work should be reduced in order to stimulate employment at that level. Such general subsidies are not considered here but such measures overlap with more direct and targeted subsidies linked to welfare to work programmes. This section focuses on three themes: *making work pay* – where specific subsidies paid to low-paid employees; *work subsidies* - paying employers to take on the unemployed/disadvantaged and *work provision* - providing work experience.

Making work pay

Many of the jobs available to long-term unemployed are low paid and present low incentives to move into work, especially if there are children. One solution is to pay benefits in work to raise incomes (see Haveman 1995). Since October 1998 Britain has made such transfers for families with children more generous and shifted them from the benefit to the tax system. *Working Families Tax Credit* is paid weekly to those on a low income who have children and work 16 hours a week or more. The aim of the benefit is not only to improve incentives to work but also to combat working poverty and child poverty more widely and to stimulate employment. In addition to the basic WFTC there is also Child Care Tax Credit, which is an in-work tax credit to offset child-care costs, and a complementary system for disabled people. The new regime may have significant effects on other subsidies for the provision of public and voluntary run childcare and on labour market participation of women in couples (McLaughlin, Trewsdale and McCay 2001). The British government has also suggested extending similar in-work benefits to *all* low paid workers (Treasury 2000). Until such a comprehensive approach is introduced there is a categorical scheme for the over 50s, leaving benefits for their first year of full time work.

The American Earned Income Tax Credit (EITC) pays rebates (which are refundable and hence can be more than tax paid) to low earners when they file taxes at the end of each tax year. The Clinton Administration has raised EITC levels considerably since

1992 and has extended a much less generous scheme to workers without children. Some individual States have introduced their own income tax credit schemes. Additionally, because EITC is paid at the end of the year it is less effective in lifting the transitional income at the margins of benefits and work. States have therefore increasingly moved to allow TANF benefits to continue in employment in order to lower the disincentives to work. Such payments also help States to reach their work participation targets for the federal TANF block grant subsidy. The problem is that in most States such payments count when calculating time limits for welfare receipt and hence will cease when the limit is reached (Greenberg 2000). The USA has also increased health and childcare benefits for low-income families – especially those with children. The problem with these and with the more established in-work benefits of Medicaid and Food Stamps is that take up rates have been disappointing. Only around 13 per cent of eligible families took up childcare in 1998 (DHHS 1999) and many families who are no longer claiming welfare are also not claiming their in work benefit entitlement. The reasons for falling Food Stamp rolls are partly administrative and partly due to raised incomes and claimant ignorance (Zedlewski and Brauner 1999). A major problem for the delivery of in-work benefits in the US is that welfare offices are often no longer adequately set up to provide benefit services in the alternative to welfare because they have moved to a work first model (see discussion above).

Making work pay in continental Europe has more often been based on minimum wages, universal family allowances and, especially in France, pro-family tax systems. Specific provisions for working and combining benefits – and social assistance in particular – have been added more recently. For instance the rules for RMI, API and other social minima were changed in France to allow part-time working in 1998.[11] Most work-based subsidies in France have however been directed at the employer rather than the low paid. Germany has seen less change. The Netherlands has exemptions for disability insurance for part-time workers and there is a move to overall tax credits and taxation in 2001. However, most of the specific action on supporting work in these three countries has been in employer subsidies and employment

Employer subsidies

The French have already invested huge discounts from social security based non-wage costs on jobs at or just above the minimum wage. However, in addition there are a range of subsidised placements in work that also attract specific exemptions from social security costs for temporary and training positions. Many of these subsidies have been targeted at youth employment (and hence mostly outside the claimant reservoir). '*Contrats d'apprentissage*' exempt employers from social security contributions and

---

11 The report by Marie-Therese Join Lambert was published in March 1998 (see InfoMISEP Policies 63 Autumn 1998: 22).

give one-off payments when an apprentice is taken on. The 1980s saw several forms of short-term and permanent job schemes in the private sector *Contrats d'Adaptation, Contrats de Qualification* and *Contrats d'Orientation* which all allowed different forms employment that gave exemptions from minimum wages, and subsidies in cash or social security rebates. In the 1990s minimum wage jobs under '*Aide au Premier Emploi des Jeunes and Contrats Initiative Emploi*' aimed to provide longer placements. The unemployment insurance system also allows benefits to be turned into employer subsidies through the *Conventions de Coopération d'Assurance Chômage* where the employer receives a subsidy calculated at the net rate of benefit received by the unemployed person for up to a maximum of 12 months.

German employers can pay no social security contributions for staff on *Integration Contract*s, which are short-term 'trial jobs'. These are available to the long-term unemployed in the private sector. Other employers who decide to take long-term unemployed workers permanently can claim a wage cost *subsidy* of between 50 per cent and 70 per cent of the average rate of pay. This subsidy is paid out of the annual budget of the *state back-to-work scheme* for the long-term unemployed. The maximum duration of such subsidies is 3 years and the subsidy decreases as the unemployed person remains in the job.

The German PES has been encouraged to experiment by having 10 per cent of their budget freed for innovative programmes. Hamburg used this money to support 1,000 business start-ups and 750 disadvantaged young people and to set up a number of innovative pilot scheme including a voucher system that the unemployed can use to attract employers. Subsidies are also available for newly created enterprises where the *Arbeitsamt* supports an initial phase of business development for one or two unemployed persons to be employed in the new enterprise. These powers were used 2,300 times during the first four months of their operation from April 1997. The *Sozialamt* is also experimenting with employer subsidies called 'wage cost support' and have offered paying direct subsidies based on the benefits of claimants directly to employers for up to two years. These jobs have to be full-time, but there is no compulsion to train the worker taken on. Experience has shown however that many employers are reluctant to accept such an offer

Since 1998 the Netherlands have opened up employment subsidies across the private sector for work experience placements of up to two years for long term unemployed people (12 months or more). These provisions supplement the previous schemes that were based on social employment. Access to job subsidies is usually through intermediaries that are distributing the budgets on behalf of unemployment insurance or social assistance agencies. It is hoped that the move away from public sector employment will result in better flows out of subsidised work into unsubsidised employment. In addition, Dutch policy provides one off hiring grants and also imposes a 'no-risk' policy for sickness pay for employers who employ disabled benefit recipients. If employers have more than 3 per cent of their wage bill paid to such employees they can be exempted from social insurance disability contributions. Indeed, the most recent changes in Dutch policy on the unemployed have seen a move away from job subsidies tied to the social sector and towards private employers.

American Federal Tax Credits are available for hiring TANF ex-welfare and other unemployed and disadvantaged workers. The $2,400 Work Opportunity Tax Credit (WOTC) is payable for employees who work a minimum of 120 hours in a year, and the $8,500 Welfare to Work Tax Credit (WTWTC) is payable to similar client group who work more than 400 hours a year.

Targeted employer subsidies of 6 months are available only for unemployed people from the NDYP and NDLTU in Britain. Take up has been disappointing – especially in the public sector, although this was discouraged at the early stages of implementation - and now funds have been set aside to third party intermediaries to provide employment-based provision.

Providing work

The line between providing work and subsidising employers is not an easy one to draw, but one difference is where the employer is a public or publicly funded organisation. US public community employment is growing because the 1996 changes have actually promoted public employment of hard to serve welfare claimants in community service jobs. Previously it was only possible to provide 'workfare', that is a work commitment on entitlement (Johnson and Savner 1999). This recent change in policy does not mean that workfare has disappeared; New York City still has 36,000 workfare placements. But to give an example of recent developments, New York is also indicative of current policy mood in many large US cities. Despite the stiff opposition by the Mayor and City Welfare Department, New York has now agreed to implement a Transitional Jobs Programme of 7,500 12 month jobs paying $7.50 an hour that also provides for 8 hours training a week.

British provision of work is limited to the NDYP – either in voluntary organisations or in locally-run Environmental Task Forces. However, much of this employment is not based on wages but on benefit rates with a small increase in rates. Other British employment provision has been lined to local provision. Such schemes, usually coming under the name of Intermediate Labour Markets (ILM) received a boost in the six original areas for Employment Zones. However, having invested in setting up such projects all further recruitment to them was cancelled when the government announced the new regime for these Zones described above in Part 2. Evaluation of long-term ILMs such as Glasgow Works has shown very good job retention figures for ex-trainee/employees (Cambridge Policy Consultants 1998).

Continental Europe has had a much longer and stronger commitment to job creation in the social sector. France developed short-term contracts in public organisations for young people and the long-term unemployed in the *Contrats Emploi Solidarité (CES)* in 1990 providing part-time jobs usually for 3 to 12 months. Wages are a proportion of the minimum wage (*SMIC*), 95 per cent of the wage costs are paid from central funds and employers face no social security taxes. Longer-term positions were then established in '*Contrats Emploi Consolidé*' – jobs of 30 hours a week and paid at 120 per cent of the minimal wage to follow on from a *CES* for up to a maximum of 5 years. In 1997 the French government decided to expand public job creation even further for young people and create 300,000 new jobs to provide public goods services that were currently unmet – in schools, police, social housing estates and elsewhere. The jobs are for five years and are set up to stimulate funding for their continuation after this time. This *Emploi Jeunes* scheme is primarily aimed at those who have no work record - including graduates aged up to 30 - but primarily aimed at the under 25s.

German job creation has two separate sources – the Federal unemployment system and local municipal social assistance. Federal unemployment funds have been available for job creation in the third sector (i.e. to avoid substitution). ABMs (*Arbeitsbeschaffungsmassnahmen*) projects provide fixed term temporary jobs jointly financed by the Federal Employment Office and the *Länder* that draw up the local programme of job creation. Federal funds tend to finance the wages for the job and the *Länder* the non-wage costs - around 25 per cent of the gross cost. To qualify one must be unemployed for at least 12 months. Recent changes to eligibility have focused on the harder to serve rather than just the long-term unemployed. Particular to Hamburg is a system of education and qualification that accompanies the ABM schemes. Participants have 20 per cent of their work time set aside for training and qualification and each work placement must agree an element of training and qualification.

Running in parallel but solely directed at social assistance claimants are agencies that put into practice the principles of '*Hilfe zur Arbeit*' – help though work and work experience often provided by *Beschäftigungsgesellschaften* (community businesses). Hamburg has two, the main being HAB (*Hamburger Arbeit Beschäftigungsgesellschaften*). The companies actually produce goods or services and hence the claimants become workers and trainees in a variety of workplace assignments. These could range from metalcraft workshops to a hotel, but all are a response to social needs and should not substitute private employment. The company trades as a normal business and has to win contracts for its goods and services, but is subsidised by the municipality. Training is provided both in-house for work-floor and on the job skills, and by outside trainers.

The Netherlands has had several waves of public employment programmes for the unemployed. Recent changes have moved to create more temporary transitional positions that can either be a stepping stone to an unsubsidised job or can be taken over and fully funded from alternative sources. In moving in this direction policy on employment creation has moved from public and social jobs towards a more rounded market led approach as stated above. Municipalities, and particularly the major cities, have set up publicly funded companies to act as employment pools. These companies operate as system of *Bahnenpool* employing social assistance claimants themselves, providing training and then placing them in work. As with the US intermediary model, one part of the organisation is looking for employment opportunities – especially in areas where public goods employment can be subsidised by the underlying welfare budget of their employees. For instance the local hospital car park was not safe and patients' and staff cars were being vandalised or stolen. The *Bahnenpool* will create the security job with the hospital and provide the staff and continue to employ them but arrange a charge for the service. The position is then reviewed and the potential for a permanent position and its financing assessed. Pay is the minimum wage and the employees continue to be asked to job search.

Conclusions

What are the apparent lessons for British policy? The British extension of target groups for labour market programmes from the unemployed to lone parents and disabled people is opening access to opportunities to train and work. However, it appears that to different degrees European countries were incorporating such groups already through unemployment benefits or on social assistance. Britain's previous policy of defining unemployment strictly, and the rigid categorisation of claimants according to their status rather than through social insurance explains some of such differences.

To what extent does the new expanded vision of target groups reflect widening opportunity? The New Deal budget for re-integration programmes is disproportionately focused on the unemployed, and more so on the young – three quarters of the spending goes to 7 per cent of the population. Early lifetime unemployment has scarring effects on employment and life chances, but does this mean that the needs of the much larger and older group with greater barriers to work should receive so little in comparison? There is a real question of equity here. If we compare the British approach to the Dutch, the latter invest the most in social and work rehabilitation for those with the greatest distance from the labour market. It appears odd to do the opposite. US practice is moving to cope with the reality of long-term hard to serve populations who are increasingly seen as legitimate recipients of cash help and services. German work reintegration programmes are now being refocused on the unemployed with long-term illness and other barriers to work. On the other hand it is true that both the Germans and the French spend huge efforts and sums on youth – but for both countries there is little cost to the government in terms of benefits being spent on these groups which gives a cost-saving incentive to this approach. Investment in youth and remedying the effects of poor schooling and childhood poverty in early adulthood are essential policy aims but should not swallow up funds for the reintegration of long-term unemployed and inactive people.

What is offered as an alternative to 'passive entitlement' to benefits should reflect greater access to opportunities for re-integration. The growing US evidence suggests that a strict 'work first' approach can increase work participation and lower claimant numbers but at a considerable expense to poverty and social exclusion. Tough entitlement rules and diversion has also led to more people falling into poverty both in and out of work.

The increased co-ordination and comprehensiveness of the British approach in the ONE service may lead to greater equity between groups in the claimant reservoir. However, the balance between increased service and improved efficiency in the claiming process and obtaining better outflows of claimants is not yet determined. Spending savings from reducing programme costs from having more claimants leaving more quickly will have to be carefully reconciled against the aims of better service. If the wrong organisational incentives are introduced then it could slip into a US style diversion approach.

Britain is far behind in the use of intermediaries and is trying to catch up. However the approach appears to be one primarily based on improving better matching between employers and claimants and on improving the induction into work by following up the claimant in their workplace. Many of the intermediaries in the USA, Netherlands and Germany actually employ claimants either as trainees prior to placement or as temporary workers to provide soft and hard skills. These approaches seem to be unpopular with policy makers because they fall into the ambit of job creation, which leads to a much larger and obvious difference between British and the other approaches outlined here, the position of public employment.

Where is the employment element in British welfare to work policy? Popular opinion supports government providing work for the unemployed as well as tougher entitlement rules (Hills and Lelkes 1999). There are fairly small programmes of work placements in the NDYP but nothing for the larger groups of older workers or those with limiting illness or disability. The work-based programmes of the original Employment Zones had their central funding withdrawn before their effectiveness could be properly assessed. Britain is apparently reducing the work-based element of re-integration at the same time as the USA and European countries are expanding it. The high cost provision of employment based schemes and their relative cost-effectiveness against interview-based reactivation measures is one reason. Another reason is the economic argument about substitution effects, and about the effectiveness of long-term job placements in obtaining follow-through into employment and the poor reputation of US programmes such as CETA in the 1980s.

But without a transitional work-based programme designed to improve the employability of the hardest to serve, those with multiple barriers to work and little relevant work experience or soft skills, how long will it take for the supply side to reach down to those who are at the back of the queue in the claimant reservoir? This is not to argue that public jobs can solve the problem by themselves but to say that they can provide an essential additional resource to existing welfare to work programmes. Public jobs need not be necessarily be run by public organisations but should provide public goods. There has been a huge disinvestment in public goods in Britain over the past 20 years – for instance parks and public spaces are under-funded and under-supervised (House of Commons Environment, Transport and Regional Affairs Committee 1999) and many communities can identify other needs – such as child care, transportation etc. The provision of transitional employment could then not only be measured in its training and outflows into work but also by the imputed value of the public goods provided. Savings to the benefit budget, revenue charges and an element of subsidy can meet their costs. Substitution effects can be minimised by both careful planning and by letting programmes which become commercially viable to become privately run without subsidy. These transitional job programmes could and should also act as labour market intermediaries where possible. At the moment this employment role is mostly taken up by local ILMs in Britain but they have had streams of unreliable and uncoordinated subsidies and rather capricious treatment by central policy makers.

Britain has preferred to subsidise wages of low paid private workers, but there are good reasons why such subsidies could be used to further socially beneficial employment as well. The move to comprehensive tax credits for all workers makes such work-based approaches easier for a wider population in the future, but there is no reason why the Disabled Persons Tax Credit and Working Families Tax Credit should not be used to help set up schemes in the meantime. Meanwhile, Britain leads the way in income based in-work subsidies that could help sort out structural policy problems in the other countries if adopted.

However, the incentive structures of the British system prioritise the move into work and reinforce the view that 'welfare to work' is a single point transition. Evidence of recidivism (of returning to benefit from work) here and abroad suggests otherwise. Part of the problem is the view that a mixture of duration-targeted and means-tested solutions are optimal. However, this robs the system of any interest in people's history – a factor built in to a contributory approach because contributions reflect work history. The future of British policy, and indeed for the other countries' studied here must reflect more on dynamic profiling. If lifetime learning is to be a compatible aim to 'welfare to work' then policy must learn how to build on training and work experiences and become more welfare to career than welfare to work in its approach.

Welfare, there is that dreaded word again. Americans and Europeans are amazed to hear social insurance programmes and non-contributory disability benefits labelled 'welfare'. In the USA this would be an extreme right-wing point of view. The term 'welfare' has become the lowest common denominator in British policy terminology, tarring the poor and workless with the same brush. British policy makers need to be more discerning and careful before we strip away legitimacy from a system that provides a minimum but inadequate standard of living. People who claim such benefits often have widespread support and a legitimate call on public funds. They are the parents of infants; the carers of disabled people, disabled people themselves. Such people, alongside the frictionally unemployed, have legitimate claims for financial support from the wider community.

Chapter 14

Activating the Unemployed:
the street-level implementation of UK policy

Sharon Wright

Introduction

Having their roots in the welfare to work policies of the USA and being embraced more recently by European member states, active labour market policies have become increasingly popular. A widespread trend towards active labour market policies as a response to unemployment has been identified (e.g. Clasen 1999). Often, the impact of these policies have been evaluated at a macro level. By contrast, with the premise that 'policies cannot be understood in isolation from the means of their execution' (Elmore 1978:185), this chapter provides a micro-level analysis. The emphasis is on how decision-making and service delivery are accomplished in practice, by individuals and through social processes.

Active labour market policies are implemented by front-line staff through their interactions with clients. Accordingly, the chapter adopts a street-level bureaucracy perspective and is based on ethnographic research consisting of direct observation

during 74 visits to one Jobcentre in the UK and on an analysis of interviews between
staff and clients, informal interviews with 48 members of staff and semi-structured
interviews with 35 unemployed people[1]. Documents such as staff guidance materials
were also analysed. In the first part of the chapter, issues of policy implementation will
be outlined and the pressures which front-line Jobcentre staff experience will be
discussed. This is followed by three examples which demonstrate some of the ways in
which Employment Officers re-create official policy. The first example demonstrates
how front-line staff develop routines to deal with the pressures which fortnightly
'Signing On' interviews present. The second illustrates how staff reacted to a new
policy, the New Deal for 18-24 year olds, and the third highlights the way staff
behaviour was modified in response to performance targets for job placements. For each
example the official policy will be outlined, followed by a description of front-line
practice, then an explanation of the pressures which lead to discrepancies between the
two.

Policy implementation and street-level bureaucracy

Traditional understandings of policy implementation have been based on an ideal type,
with perfect implementation as the goal, presenting implementation as a problem rather
than an area of study or a source of understanding (Hill 1997). Although it has been
acknowledged for some time that perfect implementation is unattainable (Hogwood and
Gunn 1984), and might even be undesirable, explanations of the policy process have
continued to be centred around why policy in general, or certain policies in particular,
are not implemented as intended. Barrett and Fudge make an important contribution,
criticising 'top-down' perspectives:

> 'Rather than treating implementation as the transmission of policy into a series of consequential
> actions, the policy-action relationship needs to be regarded as a process of interaction and
> negotiation, taking place over time, between those seeking to put policy into effect and those
> upon whom action depends' (1981:25)

This argument can be taken a step further, viewing implementation of unemployment
policy in a Jobcentre as a process of negotiation, based on the interaction between front
line Employment Service workers and the unemployed clients themselves. Bowe et al
note that 'policy is not simply received and implemented within this arena, rather it is
subject to interpretation and then re-created.' (1992:21-22). Hill adds that 'the
implementation process *is* the policy-making process' (1997:146).

Lipsky's (1980) concept of street-level bureaucracy encompasses this logic and forms
the theoretical framework for this research. Lipsky argues that policy making takes
place as much at street-level as it does through the traditionally accepted top down

---

1 This research is the basis of doctoral work in progress.

approach. He defines street-level bureaucrats as 'public service workers who interact directly with citizens in the course of their jobs, and who have substantial discretion in the execution of their work' (1980: 3). This includes a wide range of public sector workers such as doctors, police officers, social workers and benefit officials. According to Lipsky the dilemmas that these officials experience are centred around conflicts in their goals and are experienced as dilemmas because they have a degree of discretion in their work. The core tension is between serving client-centred goals and organisation-centred goals. Street-level bureaucrats are required to provide a flexible, responsive and caring service but at the same time they are bound by the impersonal and detached rules of the organisational bureaucracy within which they work. The site of this dilemma is in their interaction with, and decisions about, clients. They are also constrained by the lack of resources for the extremely high demand for the services they provide. Street-level bureaucrats therefore organise their work in response to these pressures in three ways: by limiting demand for services; by maximising the use of available resources; and by ensuring client compliance.

Lipsky (1980) argues that people are attracted to working in public services because they want to do a job that they see as socially useful and worthwhile. When they realise that the dilemmas involved in the work mean that they cannot do what they thought they could, they either leave or adapt. He argues that service sector workers adapt by modifying their conception of their jobs, lowering their expectation of what they can achieve and modifying their conception of the clients they work with. In response to this they develop routines and simplifications to make their jobs manageable. Paradoxically these coping mechanisms often develop contrary to the agency's official policy, but are also basic to its survival. It is these processes which are at work when street-level bureaucrats use their discretion in making decisions. Street-level bureaucrats therefore re-create policy through their everyday interactions with clients. In fact policy is co-produced by different social actors through a series of interactions.

The Jobcentre and active labour market policies

In the Jobcentre dilemmas between serving client-orientated goals and organisation-orientated goals are exacerbated for staff because there is a tension between organisational goals themselves. Since 1987 Jobcentre staff have been expected to administer benefits as well as assist clients to find jobs, which means they have to police clients as well as enabling them (Fletcher 1997). The formal goal of the Jobcentre at the time when this research was conducted was: 'to contribute to high levels of employment and growth, and to individuals leading rewarding working lives, by helping all people without a job to find work and employers to fill their vacancies' (Employment Service 1998a:1).

In the UK there have been two main developments in active labour market policies since the mid 1990s. The first step was the change from Unemployment Benefit, an insurance based benefit payable for one year (after which clients could apply for social assistance in the form of Income Support), to Jobseeker's Allowance, which has two forms. Contributions-Based Jobseeker's Allowance is the equivalent of the old Unemployment Benefit but is only available for a maximum of 26 weeks. Income-Based Jobseeker's Allowance is a means-tested benefit and is available for an unlimited period. The introduction of Jobseeker's Allowance brought with it significant changes in the way in which benefits for the unemployed are administered. For the first time clients were required to sign a contract, a Jobseeker's Agreement, stating exactly what they would do to find work, e.g. visiting the Jobcentre twice per week or looking in the local newspaper. Fortnightly re-registering for benefit, more informally known as 'signing on', became more active and clients were required to complete a log of what they had done to look for work since they last signed on. Claiming benefit therefore became much more closely linked to actively seeking work conditions, which were enforced with tougher sanctions. Fletcher (1997) argues that Jobseeker's Allowance also made the Jobcentre's dual role of policing and enabling more apparent.

Jobseeker's Allowance was followed in 1998 by the New Deal, Britain's welfare-to-work scheme (see also Evans in chapter 13 of this volume). The New Deal was first brought in as a compulsory scheme for 18-24 year olds who had been unemployed for six months or more. Clients begin the New Deal with a four-month Gateway period which consists of a series of interviews. Clients must then accept one of four options: a job (for which an employer's subsidy may be available), training, a work placement in the voluntary sector or an Environmental Taskforce placement. Refusal means the application of a special New Deal sanction, i.e. the withdrawal of benefit for between two and four weeks. Since June 1998 it has been compulsory for claimants who are aged 25 and over and have been unemployed for more than two years to participate in the New Deal. This group usually do not have the benefit of a Gateway period (except in some pilot areas) and only have the choice of two options: a job (which may be subsidised for 6 months) or up to 52 weeks of full-time education and training whilst claiming JSA. The 25-plus age group are not subject to the special New Deal sanctions, only the existing sanctions, i.e. there is no benefit withdrawal for refusing to participate in a training option. They will, however, still incur a benefit sanction of two to four weeks for reasons such as having been dismissed from a training option due to misconduct. There are also voluntary New Deal schemes for the over 50s (the most recent New Deal programme, introduced in April 2000), lone parents, disabled people and the partners of those participating in the New Deal.

These active labour market policies have been introduced in a new managerialist context, which has been usefully articulated by Clarke and Newman (1997). During the 1990s the Employment Service came under continuing pressure to reduce its operating costs and obtain better 'value for money'; consequently a tier of management was removed. Market testing, contracting out and cost reviews were among the techniques introduced to help secure efficiency savings and annual performance indicators were set at national, local and even section level (Finn and Taylor 1990). These factors further increase the pressure felt by street-level bureaucrats.

'Signing on'

Official policy

'Signing on' interviews are routine interactions that demonstrate the way in which street-level workers re-create the service which they provide. Clients who have registered for Jobseeker's Allowance must attend the Jobcentre at regular intervals, usually every fortnight, to sign a declaration that they still satisfy the conditions for claiming benefit. These interviews constitute the most frequent interaction that clients have with staff and are therefore crucial to the way in which unemployed people view the Jobcentre. 'Active signing' was introduced as part of the Jobseeker's Allowance regulations in 1996 (CPAG 1996:7). This meant that signing on interviews were made longer and included an assessment of the client's record of what he or she had done to find work in the previous fortnight.

Signing on interviews are formally referred to as 'Fortnightly Interventions'. They are designed to last for at least five minutes (seven minutes for long-term unemployed people) as prescribed by the Jobseeker's Allowance legislation and guidance (CPAG 1996). The official guidelines for signing on detail nine stages that the interviewer is meant to go through (Employment Service 1998b). In brief the stages are:
1. Greeting.
2. Aim/Purpose – an explanation of the purpose of the interview.
3. Access Client Record – a check to make sure clients details are correct and there is no outstanding action.
4. Review Client Jobseeker's Agreement.
5. Evaluate Client Jobsearch Activity – a check what the client has done and follow up on previous submissions, including taking action for 'Refusal of Employment'.
6. Conduct Labour Market System Jobsearch – a computer check for suitable vacancies or a comment if nothing suitable was found.
7. Close Jobsearch Review.
8. Payment Activity – initiating benefit through the computer system.
9. Close intervention.

A system of penalties is in place to enforce client compliance with the regulations. Clients are officially meant to be referred to adjudication, with the possible outcome of a benefit sanction if, for instance, they do not attend their interview at the appointed time.

Front-line practice

The first way in which Jobcentre staff deviated from the official policy was in the terminology they used for these interactions. Rather than using the official term for

'Fortnightly Interventions' staff (as well as clients) referred to the interviews as 'signing on'. This resistance to the use of new terminology was evident from staff at the signing points.

SM 20[2]:   We're called an 'interventionist'. I don't know who dreamt that one up!

The signing on interviews were typically much shorter than the prescribed length, usually lasting around two or three minutes. These interactions were brief and perfunctory for both parties and it was not unusual for the pleasantries of polite conversation to be dispensed with entirely. The following example is of a client signing on.

SM 14   :   Can I help you?

Male Client: I've come to sign on.

SM 14:   (Did something on the computer.) Right. Are you wanting to sign there? (Gave him form to sign.)

Male Client: (Signed it then stood up immediately and left.)

Several of the stages of the interview, such as such as stage two (explaining the purpose of the interview, see above), were completely missed. Other stages were pared down. Stage one, for instance ('Greeting: hello; good morning/afternoon; apologies if kept waiting; good eye contact; smile; ice breaker'; Employment Service 1998b), became 'can I help you?' There was no apology, because being kept waiting was seen as a routine part of signing on, no smile and no 'icebreaker'. Staff acknowledged the discrepancy between official guidelines and actual practice:

SM 8:   ..... You're really not interested in having a long conversation with them, while the queue is up to the door.

SM 17:   Some just come in and throw their cards at you. They don't say anything and they don't even look at you. You speak to the side of their face because they're looking away.

SM 8:   They're like they can't be bothered. I think 'well I can't be bothered either then. Will I just not bother processing your money?'

The 'active signing' prescribed by the Jobseeker's Allowance regulations was administered in a remarkably inactive way by front-line staff. There was a tendency for

---

2 SM1= Staff Member 1 (each research participant was assigned a number code to ensure anonymity).

staff to focus on the necessary parts of benefit administration rather than making efforts to help find people work. Job searches were not conducted during the interview unless clients specifically requested it, which was rare. At times staff conducted job searches in advance of the signing on procedure, which involved making judgements about which clients to check for and which not to. If the job search was not conducted with clients present then they did not know whether it had been done at all. In short, despite the emphasis placed on enabling clients to find work in the formal goals of the Jobcentre and in the official guidance, signing on was much more about administering benefit than helping people to find work.

Pressure

The gap between official policy and implementation by Employment Officers is attributable to the pressures under which staff work. There were complaints from staff of being under 'a lot of pressure' (SM 15) and 'always battling against time and the next person is in' (SM 13). There were time limitations to the interviews, which were tighter when there was not a full complement of staff in the office.

SM 38:   It's very high pressure. . . . There's all sorts that's supposed to get done that doesn't get done.

SM 18:   You've not got enough time to go through everything. You just go through the form and by the time you've done that the next person is waiting.

Time constraints limited the interaction between staff and clients to question and answer sessions (with clients expected to provide very personal information on cue). The main purpose was to complete forms and windows in the computer screen. In fact, many of the interactions in the Jobcentre were shaped by the structure of claims forms and the architecture of the computer programmes used by Employment Officers. It is significant that the part of the work that was most likely to be neglected was the part that was not form-based.

'Signing on' interviews were influenced by the established patterns of interaction with limited time available due to the pressure of other people waiting in the queue. There was usually a constant stream of people waiting in front of the desks, making both staff and clients keenly aware of the need to finish the interview as quickly as possible. More than 22 people had to sign at each desk in each hour of signing. Even if they came in equal time slots, which they did not, this equated to less than three minutes for each interview. One of the Employment Officers at the Signing Points noted:

SM 22:   We need more time. There's not enough time to do it properly. They just come in and sign and then they're away again. We're meant to spend time with them and do a job search but you never get time to do it.

As a response to these pressures staff redefined what it was that they were aiming to achieve during the interview. These goals were more modest than the official purpose and focused on certain aspects of the service delivery while other aspects were either ignored or reduced in scope. One of the primary activities which front-line workers were engaged in was therefore the rationing of services. This took place in terms of limiting time, limiting what was done during interviews (especially neglecting the job search part of the work) and facilitating access to jobs. This finding is in accordance with Hvinden's evidence of welfare service staff concentrating on processing cases rather than assisting people (1994:109).

At signing times those who came late to sign on or who did not demonstrate that they were actively seeking work were, according to the Jobseeker's Allowance regulations, supposed to be referred to adjudication. One reason why this rarely happened was the paperwork required for this procedure. One Front-line worker explained:

SM 33:   There's seven pieces of documentation that you need. You need a copy of the vacancy, their Jobseeker's Agreement. You need statements from the client. You can't just say 'I spoke to them and they wouldn't take it'. You have to have everything in writing. Also it has to be a job that's offering over 24 hours a week for it to be a 'refusal of employment'. So we tell them that and that it'll have to be referred to adjudication and that that might mean that their benefit gets effected. So they're going to get angry or storm out. We would have to tag it for the next time and try to get something in writing, otherwise you're not going to have a chance to get it. That's why not a lot of us are doing it. It's a hassle.

The above examples demonstrate that unemployment policy in practice is as much about what front-line staff do not do as it is about what they do. Blackmore (1999) has criticised policy analysts for being alarmist about the consequences of tighter regulations under the so-called 'Stricter Benefit Regime', which were implemented in the mid 1990s. At street level, he argues, those guidelines were not introduced to the extent which was feared and therefore did not disadvantage clients as much as had been expected (Finn et al, 1998). What is perhaps more concerning is that the procedures which were designed to protect clients' basic rights and those which are designed to enable them to find work were not necessarily implemented either.

The New Deal

Official policy

As an active labour market policy, the New Deal presents a particularly interesting example of policy in practice. In the UK the compulsory New Deal for 18-24 year olds (who have been unemployed and claiming Jobseeker's Allowance for six months or more), was the flag ship of the government's welfare-to-work policy announced in 1997. There was a significant commitment from politicians to the New Deal, which had dedicated resources, funded by a windfall tax on the privatised utilities. Support for the scheme came from the voluntary sector and private employers as well as the Employment Service itself. The New Deal was billed as a new and distinct initiative and was targeted at a specific client group. Many of the conditions necessary for a good fit between policy design and implementation (Hogwood and Gunn 1984) were therefore in place.

The official guidance for the delivery of the New Deal stated that young people 'will receive an initial interview with their Employment Service personal adviser, who will explain the New Deal and remain their point of contact throughout' (Employment Service 1997: 8). The ethos behind the New Deal was to provide personal, client-centred advice and support to enable young people to find work. 'Personal Advisers' were trained and became involved in more 'people-changing' (a term coined by Hasenfeld and Weaver 1996, to describe modifying clients' behaviour). In contrast to many forms of policy implementation (see Hill 1997), the introduction of the New Deal clearly represented more than incremental change.

Front-line practice

When the New Deal was introduced desks were arranged in one corner of the office with a separate waiting area, the walls were painted a different colour and new signs and furniture were used. At first the staff had small caseloads and were able to spend an hour or more on the first in-depth interview with the young client, as they were officially meant to. The personal service which was first introduced was viewed by staff as being productive in establishing relationships with clients. One Personal Adviser described one way in which advisers were able to help young people when the New Deal was first implemented.

SM 26:   If they were going to have to go to the Career's Office we would say 'Oh do you know where you're going? I'll show you where it is'. And also Fiona and I both took them out for interviews. And that worked quite well because if you take them up and they would interview them and take them on the next day. It was great. We never got involved in that before so we were able to go the extra distance, so that we can actually help people.

One of the founding principles of the New Deal scheme, which was praised by staff and policy analysts alike, was the personal service that it would provide. Initially it allowed staff to build a rapport with clients and discuss their backgrounds, problems and aspirations in great detail. However, within a very short time of the scheme running this principle was eroded. As more and more young people were referred to the scheme it was not possible for in-depth personal service to continue. Personal Advisers were not able to accompany young people to visits or job interviews. The initial interviews for people joining the New Deal became group sessions (with approximately 20 people) instead of one-to-one interviews. Group interviews did not provide the opportunity for personal advice and some of the young people who attended group interviews did not participate in the discussion at all. The service provided by New Deal staff was therefore re-created by staff soon after its introduction.

Another example of the application of new policy within the New Deal was for signing on. Here the intended in-depth personal service was again found to be lacking since the signing on interviews were conducted according to a pattern which had previously been established in other areas of the office. This part of the service did not change therefore, with staff being able to retain their existing well established work practices and routines.

Pressure

As the numbers of clients participating in the New Deal increased staff time became more scarce. As a result more limitations were imposed on the length of time which was allocated to each client. Policy therefore was re-created with clients receiving a service which was less personal than had been intended.

What is more, the typical staff reaction to change was to retain existing work practices whenever possible. This was justified in part by the frequency of changes which staff were faced with. Part of this change came in the form of new regulations for claiming benefit or of practices which were encouraged by the management in the particular office. One type of change affected procedures based on new policies or practices. Another source of frequent change was staff turnover, with workers on short-term contracts often coming and going and considerable internal change as staff were moved between sections and transferred to different offices.

Staff resisted change to daily routines that they had developed over time (sometimes for 20 years or more). As the reluctant use of the term 'Fortnightly Intervention' illustrated (see above), changes can take time to be implemented on ground level and some changes will never be implemented at all. Hence, new policy is not made and then simply imposed upon front-line staff, rather it must be accepted and absorbed into daily usage through a series of adjustments. Nor is new policy completely new. It is placed on top of the old practices which in turn are re-created forms of old policies.

Another source of frustration was the insufficient link between a particular policy or scheme and the nature of a problem as perceived by staff who experienced it in their daily work. In the case of the New Deal, Personal Advisers soon found that there were young people who they could not personally advise because their problems were beyond the scope of the new policy and the Employment Service more generally. In other words, some of the young New Deal clients experienced barriers to employment which their Personal Advisers felt they could not help them with.

SM 21: A lot of clients are decent people but a lot of them as well are people with social problems and we're not trained to deal with that. We could do more harm than good if we tried to dabble in it. We've got a lot of sad people.

SM 34: At the end of the day we're not trained to deal with some of the cases that come in. So if we get training on how to deal with difficult situations but we're not trained properly. I mean they're unemployed and along with that they've got other problems. They've got housing problems, or . . . They could be single parents. There's alcoholism. There's debt. Gambling. We're not trained to deal with them psychologically. We're lay people. This is a Jobcentre, a public office. We've not got the time or the medical or psychological expertise to deal with them.

Job matching and performance targets

Official policy

The official goal of the Jobcentre is to enable people to find work and active labour market policies are designed to facilitate labour market entry in a directive way. Matching clients to job vacancies has therefore been prioritised in recent years. Job matching is meant to be carried out as part of the routine interviews with clients. In the particular office where this research was conducted a group of Employment Officers worked in the 'Matching Section', dedicated specifically to this task. This section functioned more along the lines of a private sector job agency than a public service. Employers telephoned in vacancies which were then displayed on the vacancy boards. There was a formal system of validation to ensure that all vacancies were properly administered through the computer system.

Front-line practice

However, it has already been indicated that staff did not always match clients to jobs during routine interviews because of the lack of time and an emphasis on form-based work. The Matching Section was one part of the Jobcentre where job matching was the major concern during interactions with clients. Vacancies, and the good relations with employers necessary to secure them, were particularly valued because they were considered to be 'good business' (SM 24) for the Jobcentre. This framework of understanding fits within a new managerialist model (Clarke and Newman 1997).

Matching clients to jobs implies a process of sifting, screening and 'creaming' the best applicants in the interest of the employer (Anderson 1999). Lipsky (1980) uses the term 'triaging' to describe a form of categorising people into groups according to how easily they can be helped and how likely it will be that they will benefit from the service provided. Matching staff therefore served first and foremost the interests of the employer rather than the interests of the majority of clients. For example, for certain vacancies information was strictly controlled through an informal system so that only a few clients of a 'high calibre' (SM 34) were given information about the vacancy, which was not advertised on the vacancy boards. These vacancies bypassed the formal system of notification (to other offices and even to other staff within the same office) until certain clients had been submitted for the position. The timing of information being entered into the computer system was crucial here. It could imply that staff in other sections of the Jobcentre, and staff at other Jobcentres, were prevented from submitting clients to these undisclosed vacancies. Such a creaming of clients was considered to be desirable because it 'cuts down on unnecessary candidates' (SM 34). Staff were aware that they were acting against official policy because 'we shouldn't restrict applicants, but we want to do what the employer wants' (SM 34).

The Matching staff held hand-written lists of clients who they would put forward for certain vacancies. These vacancies were often for trades people, with employers being keen to have someone ready to start work as soon as possible.

SM 34:   It's an occupation whereby, particularly construction, joiners, brickies, something like that. They phone up and they want someone to start immediately, yesterday. And that would go straight to Matching before going to the computer or the vacancy going up, because they might have people waiting. . . . So that's usually hand written and given over to Matching. It's not printed up. Once they start getting subs we put them on. Because of validation we shouldn't put them on retrospectively so as soon as they start coming in I put them up on the system.

The office mainly advertised vacancies which had been notified to them directly, rather than from other offices. This was because they did not want other vacancies 'to compete with our own' (SM 24). Employers were also discouraged from advertising vacancies by other means, in local newspapers or through agencies. The office held a few copies of the local newspaper. This was the only source of vacancies other than those advertised on the boards which was available to clients. There was not a range of newspapers or recruitment magazines to consult and there was no Internet access. This meant that Jobcentre staff were restricting the applications to those which they could control, thus preventing some people from applying for jobs.

Staff targeted clients to be submitted for vacancies. One adviser described why he would not submit a man who had been unemployed for 10 years for a vacancy.

SM 10:   You wouldn't be fair to the employer subbing someone like that for a job. I mean we're providing a service to the employer as much as to the unemployed person.

In this case the member of staff was re-creating policy to provide more of a service to the employer than to the unemployed client. In this way staff action could actually contribute to certain types of clients remaining inactive in the labour market.

Pressure

Clearly, staff members act in these ways because of the pressure resulting from performance targets for job placements which seemed to have a greater influence on staff behaviour than official guidance documents. Blau (1963) views such performance records as a bureaucratic mechanism to control workers. 'Bureaucratic emphasis on statistical records of operations, designed as a means to improve performance, induced officials to view making a good showing on the record as an end-in-itself.' (Blau 1963:294). This observation of a state employment agency in the 1950s appears to be just as appropriate in describing the activities of Jobcentre workers in the UK in the late 1990s. The incentive of the job placement targets changes behaviour, but not necessarily in ways which improve service delivery. In fact the greater the emphasis on specific targets, the more effort staff will make to meet that target, which consequently means that they will neglect other parts of the service because of the limitations of time.

As Lipsky (1980) argues, evaluation of street-level bureaucracies is very difficult because of the level of discretionary decision making. Numerical targets are inappropriate in measuring performance because 'the behaviour of workers comes to reflect the incentives and sanctions implicit in those measurements' (Lipsky 1980:51). Lipsky argues that 'surrogate measures then become reified and guide future performance' (1980:52). Staff make efforts to meet targets but these efforts are not necessarily of the kind intended by those who design the targets.

Each Jobcentre office has placement targets for getting people into work. These are broken down into targets for each section of the Jobcentre, introducing competition between different offices and different sections. What is more, placement targets in the Jobcentre lead staff not to be interested in just getting people into work, but getting certain people into certain jobs. One staff member noted:

SM 19:   We're primarily here for the registered unemployed. We do keep the
            employed on file. Preference goes to the registered unemployed. If there's no
            one suitable then Matching will put an employed person forward.

Performance targets made disregarding the rules more acceptable, even to senior members of staff. The goal of assisting people to find work conflicts with serving employers' needs in filling vacancies. This has serious consequences for unemployed people who are not put forward for jobs. Even the smallest technicality of vacancy placement, advertising of jobs and matching can influence a client's chance of a job. Staff found it very difficult to meet targets, which they considered to be set too high, and the target system is not necessarily in the interests of employers either. The vacancies which were advertised in the Jobcentre were those which had been vetted by staff in that particular office. The staff in a particular office can only fulfil their targets if an unemployed person gets a job which has been notified to them. There is therefore no incentive for offices to display vacancies from another office. In other words, if an employer requests his or her vacancy to be advertised in every Jobcentre in the UK, for example, this will not necessarily happen. The staff in the Jobcentre which the employer contacted directly might choose not to refer it to other offices, or other offices might choose not to display it.

Targets can operate in a way which prevents staff from doing their day to day client work and even in ways which are contrary to the general goal of the Jobcentre, i.e. to get people into work. The Employment Service targets put an extra weighting onto placing long-term unemployed people into work. In the Jobcentre where this research was conducted one of the strategies for meeting this target was the issue of 'caseload' lists of 10 clients who had been unemployed for two years or more (caseload matching). Staff were required to make extra efforts to find work for these clients, calling them in for an interview to discuss what kind of work they were looking for. All front-line staff were given this task, including the receptionists. This meant that staff who were already working under significant time pressures had to neglect other clients who had been unemployed for shorter periods of time or who did not happen to be on their caseload. One of the signing staff was frustrated by this counterproductive situation. Asked whether targets influenced her work she replied:

SM 44:   They're meant to. Now with all the (caseload) matching you're meant to get
                them done, but you can't because you have to help someone. It's like taking
                away what you're here for. We're here to help the public and it's taking you
                away from it. And that's not what it's about. Like if a punter comes in you
                can't blame them if they don't want to come back if somebody's not giving
                them the time because somebody's working on their targets. If you want to
                give out the right image you have to have a caring attitude all the time.

This relates to Lipsky's observation that people are transformed into 'clients' by being reduced to a set of qualifications or categories in order for them to be processed by the bureaucratic organisation. Ultimately this means discriminating against some clients in favour of others, because time and resource constraints mean that clients cannot all be given the maximum service.

Conclusion

Jobcentre staff experience various pressures in their everyday work. They respond to these pressures by redefining what it is they are aiming to achieve during their interactions with clients and in this way they re-create unemployment policy. The first example showed how staff involved in 'signing on' responded to the pressure of time by conducting interviews in a much shorter time than the official policy dictated, and by focussing on form and computer based work which was necessary for benefit administration rather than primarily helping clients to find work. The second example highlighted the way in which staff reacted to change. The initial New Deal interviews were personal in-depth interviews when the scheme was first introduced, but as demand for the service grew it meant having to shift to group interviews. Since signing on was done in the New Deal section the same way as it was at signing points, staff retained existing work patterns when possible. The third example demonstrated how performance targets influenced staff behaviour, leading to control access to vacancies. In this way Matching Section staff were serving the needs of employers rather than those of the majority of clients. When the overall goal of placing people into work was broken down into specific targets, getting certain people into certain jobs became priority. The work done by front-line staff was therefore structured more by pressures of time, forms, computer systems and performance targets than by statements of official policy or guidance. Front-line workers therefore re-formulated policy in their everyday work, through interactions with clients. As a result, active labour market policies, re-created by front-line staff, became much less 'active', and in some cases even had the opposite effect of ensuring that certain groups of clients remained inactive in the labour market.

As welfare states converge towards active labour market policies, issues around job matching are entering centre stage. Placing emphasis on the links between welfare and work by making claiming benefits conditional upon looking for work is a policy trend which is now firmly established in the UK. The most recent development along this line is the piloting of ONE, the single work-focussed gateway, under which clients applying for a wide range of benefits are required to participate in an interview which not only establishes their claim for benefit, but also discusses their work availability. The crucially important aspect of this reform is that it represents a redefinition of who can be expected to seek employment (although clients are not compelled to take particular action unless they are claiming JSA), including groups such as lone parents and those with disabilities who would ordinarily claim social assistance without any work-related conditions. Encompassing a wider range of clients within the activation aim is likely to bring the pressures on staff time and tension more sharply into focus as more and more clients chase a limited number of vacancies. One consequence is likely to be increased competition for staff to meet placement targets, exerting more pressure rather than relieving the need for vacancy rationing as a practical solution. This, in turn, may actually lead to greater inequalities of opportunity within the client group, disadvantaging those with the least chances of attaining bureaucratically defined success. These issues highlight the need for active labour market policies to be understood in a way which recognises the social processes by which implementation is accomplished at street level.

Bibliography

Aaron, H. (1982) *Economic Effects of Social Security*, Washington: Brookings Inst.

Abberley, P. (1993) 'Disabled people and 'normality'', in J. Swain, V. Finkelstein, S. French and M. Oliver (eds*) Disabling Barriers – Enabling Environments*, London: Sage in association with The Open University.

Abrahamson, P. (1997) 'Combating Poverty and Social Exclusion in Europe' in W. Beck, L. van der Maesen and A. Walker (eds) *The Social Quality of Europe*, The Hague: Kluwer Law International.

Adler, M. Bell, C., Clasen, J. and Sinfield, A. (eds) (1991) *The Sociology of Social Security,* Edinburgh: Edinburgh University Press.

Aguilar, R. and Gustafsson, B. (1988) 'Public Opinion about Social Assistance in Sweden', *European Journal of Political Research,* vol 16, pp 251-276.

Alber, J. (1995) 'A Framework for the Comparative Study of Social Services', *Journal of European Social Policy*, vol. 5, no. 2, pp. 131-149.

Albrecht, G.L. and Levy, J.A. (1981) 'Constructing disability as social problems', in G.L. Albrecht (ed) *Cross-national Rehabilitation Policies: A Sociological Perspective,* London: Sage.

Anderson, L. (1999) 'Witcraft in a State Employment Office: Rhetorical Strategies for Managing Difficult Clients', *Perspectives on Social Problems*, vol. 11, pp. 219-238.

Antichi, M. and Pizzuti, F.R. (2000) 'The Public Pension System in Italy: Observations on the Recent Reforms, Methods of Control and Their Application', in E. Reynaud (ed), *Social Dialogue and Pension Reform*, Geneva: International Labour Office, pp. 81-96.

Arthur, J. and Shaw, W. (1991) *Justice and economic distribution*, New Jersey: Prentice Hall.

Atkinson, A. (1995) 'The Welfare State and Economic Performance', *National Tax Journal*, vol. 48, no. 2, pp. 171-98.

Atkinson, A. (1999) *The Economic Consequences of Rolling Back the Welfare State*, Cambridge, Mass.: The MIT Press.

Atkinson, A. and Mogensen, G. (eds) (1993) *Welfare and Work Incentives. A North European Perspective,* Oxford: Clarendon.

Baldwin, P. (1990) *The Politics of Social Solidarity. Class Base of the European Welfare States 1875 - 1975*, Cambridge: Cambridge University Press.

Barnes, C., Mercer, G. and Shakespeare, T. (1999) *Exploring Disability,* Oxford: Blackwell.

Barr, N. (1994) *The Economics of the Welfare State*, Oxford: Oxford University Press, in S. Barrett and C. Fudge (eds) (1981) *Policy and Action*, London: Methuen.

Beck, U. (1986) *Risk Society*, Cambridge: Polity Press.

Beck, U., Giddens, A. and Lash, C. (1994) *Reflexive Modernisation*, Cambridge: Polity Press.

Bengtsson, S. (2001) 'A truly *European* type of disability struggle: disability policy in Denmark and the EU in the nineties', *European Journal of Social Security*, (forthcoming).

Bennett, C.J. (1991) 'Review Article: What Is Policy Convergence and What Causes It?', *British Journal of Political Science* 21, pp. 215-233.

Bentley, T. and Gurumurthy, R. (1999) *Destination Unknown: Engaging with the problems of marginalised youth*, London: Demos.

Berthoud, R. (1995) 'The "medical" assessment of incapacity: a case study of research and policy', *Journal of Social Security Law*, vol. 2, pp. 61-85.

Beveridge, W. (1942) *Social Insurance and Allied Services*, Cmd 6404, London: HMSO.

Bichot, J. (1997) *Les Politiques Sociales En France Au 20ème Siècle*, Paris: Armand Colin.

Bickenbach J., Chatterji, S. Bradley, E.M. and Ustun, T.B. (1999) 'Models of disablement, universalism and the ICIDH', *Social Science and Medicine*, vol. 48, no. 9, pp. 1173-87.

Bimbi, F. (1997) 'Lone Mothers in Italy: A Hidden and Embarrassing Issue in a Familist Welfare Regime', in J. Lewis (ed.) *Lone Mothers in European Welfare Regimes*, London: Jessica Kingsley.

Birch, A.H. (1984) 'Overload, Ungovernability and Deligitimation: The Theories and the British Case', *British Journal of Political Science*, vol.14, pp. 135-60.

Björklund, A. and Freeman, R.B. (1997) 'Generating equality and eliminating poverty, the Swedish way', in R.B. Freeman, R. Topel and B. Swedenborg (eds) *The Welfare State in Transition: Reforming the Swedish Model*, Chicago: The University of Chicago Press.

Blackmore, M. (1999) 'Mind the Gap: Exploring the Implementation Deficit in the Administration of Stricter Benefits Regime', presented at the Social Policy Association Conference, Roehampton Institute, London, 20-22 July.

Blank, R. (ed.) (1994) *Social Protection versus Economic Flexibility – Is there a trade-off?*, Chicago: University of Chicago Press.

Blau, P. (1963) *The Dynamics of Bureaucracy: A Study of Interpersonal Relations in Two Government Agencies*, Second Edition, Chicago: The University of Chicago Press.

Blomsma, M. (1999)*(Re-)integration of the long term unemployed and the disabled into employment*, The Hague: SZW International Affairs Directorate.

Bock, G. and Thane, P. (eds) (1991) *Maternity and Gender Policies: Women and the Rise of the European Welfare States. 1880s-1950s*, New York: Routledge.

Boje, T. (1996) 'Welfare State Models in Comparative Research: Do the Models Describe Reality?', in B. Greve (ed.) *Comparative Welfare Systems*, Basingstoke: Macmillan, pp. 13-27.

Bolderson, H. (1991) *Social Security, Disability and Rehabilitation: Conflicts in the Development of Social Policy*, London: Jessica Kingsley

Bolderson, H. and Hvinden, B. (1999) 'European disability policy: a background paper', Third European Science Foundation Workshop, London: City University.

Bolderson, H. and Mabbett, D. (1991) *Social Policy and Social Security in Australia, Britain and the USA*, Aldershot: Avebury.

Bolderson, H. and Mabbett, D. (1997) *Delivering Social Security: A Cross-National Study*, Department of Social Security Research Report, no. 59, London: The Stationery Office.

Bonoli, G. (2000) *The Politics of Pension Reform. Institutions and Policy Change in Western Europe*, Cambridge: Cambridge University Press.

Bonoli, G. (2001) 'Political Institutions, Veto Points, And The Process Of Welfare State Adaptation', in P. Pierson (ed.) *The New Politics of the Welfare State*, Oxford: Oxford University Press.

Bonoli, G. and Palier, B. (1996) 'Reclaiming Welfare. The Politics of Social Protection Reform in France', in M. Rhodes (ed.) *Southern European Welfare States*, London: Frank Cass, pp. 240-259.

Bonoli, G. and Palier, B. (1998) 'Changing the politics of social programmes: innovative change in British and French welfare reforms', *Journal of European Social Policy*, vol. 8, no. 4, pp. 317-330.

Bonoli, G. and Palier, B. (2000) 'How Do Welfare States Change? Institutions and their Impact on the Politics of Welfare State Reform', *European Review*, vol. 8, no. 2, pp. 333-352.

Bonoli, G., George, V. and Taylor-Gooby, P. (2000) *European Welfare Futures. Towards a Theory of Retrenchment*, London: Polity Press.

Bos, E., Vu, M. T., Massiah, E and Bulateo, R. (1994) *World Population Projections, 1994-95*, New York: The World Bank.

Bowe, R., Ball, S. J. and Gold, A. (1992) *Reforming Education and Changing Schools*, London: Routledge.

Bradbury, B. and Jäntti, M. (1999) Child Poverty across Industrialized Nations, *Occasional Papers EPS* 71, Florence: UNICEF.

Brittan, S. (1977) *The Economic Consequences of Democracy*, London: Temple Smith.

Brocas, A.-M., Cailloux, A.-M. and Oget, V. (1990) *Women and Social Security*, Geneva: International Labour Office.

Browne, M.W. and Cudeck, R. (1993) 'Alternative Ways of Assessing Model Fit', in K.A. Bollen and J. Scott Long (eds) *Testing Structural Equation Models*, Sage Focus Edition 154, Newbury Park: Sage Publications.

Bundesanstalt für Arbeit (1998) *Amtliche Nachrichten der Bundesanstalt für Arbeit*. 46. Jahrgang. Sondernummer. Arbeitsstatistik 1997, Nuremberg: Bundesanstalt für Arbeit

Burchardt, T. (1999) 'The evolution of disability benefit in the UK: re-weighting the basket' CASE paper 26, London: London School of Economics.

Burchardt, T. and Propper, C. (1999) 'Does the UK have a Private Welfare Class?', *Journal of Social Policy*, vol.28, no. 4, pp. 643-665.

Bussemaker, J. and van Kersbergen, K. (1994) 'Gender and Welfare States: Some Theoretical Reflections.' in D. Sainsbury (ed) *Gendering Welfare States*, Thousand Oaks, CA: Sage.

Cambridge Policy Consultants (1998) *Durability of Glasgow Works' Outcomes: Follow up Research*, Cambridge: CPC.

Carey, K. (1999) 'Design for life', paper presented at Department for Education and Employment, NDC/ DEMOS Seminar, Business Design Centre, London, April 29th.

Cass, B. (1994) 'Citizenship, Work and Welfare: The Dilemma for Australian Women', in *Social Politics* 1, pp. 106-24.

Castles, F.G. (1994) 'The Wage-earners' Welfare State Revisited', in *Just Policies* (May), pp. 12-15.

Castles, F.G. (1998) *Comparative Public Policy: Patterns of Post-war Transformation*, Cheltenham: Edward Elgar.

Castles, F.G. (2000) 'The Dog That Didn't Bark: Economic Development and the Post-war Welfare State', *European Review*, vol. 8, no.3, pp. 313-32.

Castles, F.G. and Mitchell, D. (1993) 'Worlds of Welfare and Families of Nations'. in F.G. Castles (ed.) *Families of Nations: Patterns of Public Policy in Western Democracies*, Aldershot: Dartmouth.

Centraal Bureau voor de Statistiek (1998) *Sociaal-Economische Maandstatistiek Jaargang 15*, Voorburg/Heerlen Netherlands, CBS.

Chand, S.K. and Jaeger, A. (1996) Aging Populations and Public Pension Schemes, International Monetary Fund, Occasional Paper, No. 147, Washington, D.C.: IMF.

Child Poverty Action Group (1996) 'The introduction of Jobseeker's Allowance – what it will mean for claimants and advisers', *Welfare Rights Bulletin*, No. 134, October, pp. 5-15.

Chomsky, N. (1994) *World Orders, Old and New*. London: Pluto.

Christoffersen, M. (1994) 'A Follow Up Study of Long Term Effects of Unemployment on Children: Loss of self-esteem and self-destructive behaviour', *Childhood*, vol. 2, no. 4, pp. 213-20.

Cichon, M. (1999) 'Notional Defined-Contribution Schemes: Old Wine in New Bottles?', *International Social Security Review*, vol. 52, no. 4, pp. 87-105.

Clarke, J. and Newman, J. (1997) *The Managerial State*, London: Sage.

Clasen, J. (1999) 'Unemployment Compensation and Other Labour Market Policies', in J. Clasen (ed), *Comparative Social Policy: Concepts, Theories and Methods*, Oxford: Blackwell Publishers Ltd.

Clasen, J. (2000) 'New Social Democracy and Old Welfare States: A European Comparison', mimeo, Stirling University.

Clasen, J. (ed), (1999) *Comparative Social Policy: Concepts, Theories and Methods*, Oxford: Blackwell Publishers Ltd.

Clasen, J., Kvist, J. and van Oorshot, W. (2001) 'On condition of work: increasing work requirements in unemployment compensation schemes', in M. Kautto et al. (eds) *Nordic Social Policy in the European Context,* London: Routledge.

CNAF (Caisse Nationale des Allocations Familiales) (1999) *1998 Statistiques Nationales*, Paris, CNAF.

Cohen, M.D., March, J. and Olsen, J.P. (1972) 'A Garbage Can Model of Organizational Choice', *Administrative Science Quarterly,* vol.1, pp.1-25.

Commission of the European Communities (1996) 'A new European disability strategy', COM (96) Final, Brussels.

Commission of the European Communities (1999) 'A Step Forward for the EU - empowering victims of discrimination', 1/P99/895, Brussels.

Commission of the European Communities (2000) *Shaping the New Europe*, Strategic Objectives 2000-2005. Brussels: COM(2000) 154 final.

Conroy, P. (1997) 'Lone Mothers: the Case of Ireland,' in J. Lewis (ed.) *Lone Mothers in European Welfare Regimes,* London: Jessica Kingsley.

Corrigan, C. (1985) 'Borderline incapacity: a study of the characteristics and problems of claimants to incapacity benefits considered to be fit for work within limits', MA dissertation, London: Brunel University.

Coughlin, R. (1980) *Ideology, Public Opinion and Welfare Policy. Attitudes towards Taxes and Spending in Industrialized Societies*, Berkeley: Institute of International Studies.

Coughlin, R. (1991) 'The Economic Person in Sociological Context', in A. Etzioni and P. Lawrence (eds) *Socio-economics: Toward a New Synthesis*, New York: Sharpe, Armonk.

Cousins, C. (1995) 'Women and Social Policy in Spain: The Development of a Gendered Welfare Regime', *Journal of European Social Policy*, 5, pp. 175-97.

Cox, R.H. (1997) 'The Consequences of Welfare Retrenchment in Denmark', *Politics & Society*, vol.25, no. 3, pp. 303-326.

Crozier, M., Huntington, S. and Watanuki, J. (eds) (1975) *The Crisis of Democracy*, New York: New York University Press.

Danziger, S. K. and Kossoudji, S. (1995) *When Welfare Ends: Subsisitence Strategies of Former GA recipients*, Ann Arbor: University of Michigan.

Davis, E.P. (1995) *Pension Funds: Retirement-Income Security and Capital Markets. An International Perspective*, Oxford: Clarendon Press.

Deacon, A. (1999) L'influence des idées européennes et américanes sur la pensé du "new labour" en matière de réformes de la protection social, *Revue Française des Affaires Sociales*, no. 34, pp. 189-206.

Deacon, B. (1999) 'Eastern European Welfare States: The Impact of the Politics of Globalisation.' Paper presented at the workshop on 'Globalization and Social Dumping,' European Forum, European University Institute, Florence, Italy, March.

Deitch, C. (1988) 'Sex differences in support for government spending', in C. Mueller (ed) *The politics of the gender gap*, Thousand Oaks: Sage.

Dent, K. and D. Sloss (1996) 'The global outlook for defined contribution versus defined benefit pension plans', *Benefits Quarterly*, First Quarter: pp. 23-8.

Department of Social Security (1998) *A New Contract for Welfare: Partnership in Pensions*, Cm. 4179, London: The Stationery Office.

Deutscher Bundestag (2001) *Beschlussempfehlung des Ausschusses für Arbeit und Sozialordnung (11. Ausschuss)*, Deutscher Bundestag, 14. Wahlperiode, Drucksache 14/5146 (v. 24.01.2001), Berlin.

Dex, S., Gustafsson, S., Smith, N. and Callan, T. (1995) 'Cross National Comparisons of the Labour Force Participation of Women Married to Unemployed Men', *Oxford Economic Papers*, pp. 611-35.

DfEE (Department for Education and Employment) (1999) *Disability Briefing*, February 1999.

DHHS (US Department of Health and Human Services) (1999) *Temporary Assistance for Needy Families (TANF) Programme – Second Report to Congress*, Washington: DHHS.

DHHS (US Department of Health and Human Services) (2000)*Temporary Assistance for Needy Families (TANF) Program - Third Annual Report to Congress*, Washington: DHHS.

Diller, M. (1996) 'Entitlement and exclusion: the role of disability in the social welfare system', U.C.L.A *Law Review*, vol. 44, pp. 261-465.

Dobbelaere, K. (1995) 'Religion in Europe and North America', in R. de Moor (ed) *Values in Western Societies*, Tilburg: Tilburg University Press.

Drake, R. F. (1996) 'A critique of the role of the traditional charities' in L. Barton (ed) *Disability and Society: Emerging Issues and Insights*, London: Longman.

DSS (Department of Social Security) (1998) *Social Security Statistics 1998*, Leeds: Corporate Document Services.

Duncan, G. and Brooks-Gunn, J. (eds) (1997) *Consequences of Growing up Poor*, New York: Russel Sage.

Duncan, S. and Edwards, R. (eds) (1997) *Single Mothers in an International Context: Mothers or Workers?* London: UCL Press.

Durkheim, E. (1966/1893) *The Division of Labor in Society*, (translated by George Simpson), New York: The Free Press.

Dwyer, D. and Bruce, J. (eds) (1988) *A Home Divided: Women and Income in the Third World*, Stanford, CA: Stanford University Press.

Eardley, T., Bradshaw, J., Ditch, J., Gough, I. and Whiteford, P. (eds) (1996) *Social Assistance in OECD Countries: Synthesis Report*. London: HMSO.

Economic Council (1998) *Dansk Økonomi. Efterår 1998*. Copenhagen. Det økonomiske Råd.

Eitrheim, P. and Kuhnle, S. (1999) 'The Scandinavian Model: Trends and Perspectives', Seminar Paper WS/3, Florence: European University Institute.

Elmore, R. (1978) 'Organisational models of social program implementation', *Public Policy*, pp. 185-228.

Elster, J. (1990) 'Selfishness and Altruism', in J. Mansbridge (ed) *Beyond Self-interest*, Chicago: University of Chicago Press.

Employment Service (1997) *Design of the New Deal for 18-24 year olds*, London: Department for Education and Employment/Welsh Office/Scottish Office.

Employment Service (1998a) *Annual Performance Agreement 1998-99*, London: Department for Education and Employment.

Employment Service (1998b) 'Fortnightly Jobsearch Reviews – Structure', internal Employment Service guidance, unpublished.

Erie, S. and Rein, M. (1988) 'Women and the Welfare State' in C. Mueller (ed) *The Politics of the Gender Gap*, New York: Sage.

Espina, A. (1996) 'Reform of Pension Schemes in the OECD Countries', *International Labour Review* 135, pp. 181-206.

Esping-Andersen, G. (1990) *The Three Worlds of Welfare Capitalism*. Princeton, NJ: Princeton University Press.

Esping-Andersen, G. (1993), 'The Comparative Macro-Sociology of Welfare States', in L. Moreno (ed.) *Social Exchange and Welfare Development*. Madrid: CSIC.

Esping-Andersen, G. (1996a) *Welfare States in Transition. National Adaptions in Global Economies*, London: Sage.

Esping-Andersen, G. (1996b) 'After the Golden Age? Welfare State Dilemmas in a Global Economy', in G. Esping-Andersen (ed.) *Welfare States in Transition. National Adaptations in Global Economies*, London: Sage.

Esping-Andersen, G. (1996c) 'Welfare States without Work: the Impasse of Labour Shedding and Familialism in Continental European Social Policy,' in G. Esping-Andersen (ed) *Welfare States in Transition: National Adaptations in Global Economies*, London: Sage.

Esping-Andersen, G. (1997) 'Welfare States at the End of the Century.' *OECD Social Policy Studies, No. 21, Family, Market and Community.* Paris: OECD.

Esping-Andersen, G. (1999) *Social Foundations of Postindustrial Economies*, Oxford: Oxford University Press.

Esping-Andersen, G. and Korpi, W. (1984) 'Social Policy as Class Politics in Postwar Capitalism: Scandinavia, Austria and Germany', in J.Goldthorpe (ed.) *Order and Conflict in Contemporary Capitalism*, Oxford: Clarendon Press.

Esping-Andersen, G. and Korpi, W. (1986) 'From Poor Relief to Institutional Welfare States: The development of Scandinavian social policy', in R. Erikson et al. (eds) *The Scandinavian Model. Welfare States and Welfare Research*, Armonk: Sharpe.

Etzioni, A. (1993) *The Spirit of Community. Rights, Responsibilities, and the Communitarian Agenda*, New York: Crown.

EU (2000) Main Conclusions of the Lisbon Summit by the Portuguese Presidency of the EU, 23-24 March 2000.

Eurostat (1997) 'Family responsibilities – how are they shared in European households?', *Statistics in Focus: Population and social conditions*, 1997:5.

Eurostat (1998) 'Lone-parent families: A growing phenomenon', *Statistics in Focus: Population and social conditions*, 1998:5.

Eurostat (1999) *Labour Force Survey. Results*, Luxembourg: European Communities.

Eurostat (2000) *Labour Force Survey Results*, Brussels: Eurostat.

Evans, C. and Kazis, K. (1999) *Improving The Employment Prospects of Low Income Job Seekers: The role of labour market intermediaries*, London, New Deal Task Force Department for Education and Employment.

Evans, M. (1998) Social Security: Dismantling the Pyramids? in H. Glennerster and J. Hills (eds) *The State of Welfare – the economics of social spending*, 2nd edition, Oxford: Oxford University Press.

Ferge, Z. (1999) *In Defence of Hazy or Multiple Principle Contracts*. Paper for the Sixth International Research Seminar of FISS, June 1999, Sigtuna, Sweden.

Ferrera, M. (1993) *EC Citizens and Social Protection*, Pavia: University of Pavia.

Ferrera, M. (1996a) 'The "Southern Model" of Welfare in Social Europe', *Journal of European Social Policy*, vol. 6, no. 1, pp. 17-37.

Ferrera, M. (1996b), 'A New Social Contract? The Four Social Europes: Between Universalism and Selectivity', EUI Working Paper RSC 96/36, Florence: European University Institute.

Ferrera, M. (1996c) 'Modèles de solidarité, divergences, convergences: perspectives pour l'Europe', *Swiss Political Science Review*, vol. 2, no. 1, pp. 55-72.

Ferrera, M. (2000) 'Reconstructing the Welfare State in Southern Europe', in S. Kuhnle (ed.), *The Survival of the European Welfare State*, London: Routledge, pp. 166-181.

Ferrera, M. and Rhodes, M. (2000a) 'Building a Sustainable Welfare State', in *West European Politics*, vol. 23, no. 2 pp. 257-82.

Ferrera, M. and Rhodes, M. (eds) (2000b) 'Recasting European Welfare States', *West European Politics* (special issue), vol. 23, no. 2.

Fineman, M. (1995) *The Neutered Mother, the Sexual Family, and Other Twentieth Century Tragedies*, New York, Routledge.

Finkelstein, V. (1981) 'Disability and the helper/helped relationship: an historical view' in A. Brechin et al. (eds) *Handicap in a Social World*, London: Hodder and

Stoughton.

Finkelstein, V. (1991) 'Disability: an administrative challenge?' in M. Oliver (ed) *Social Work: Disabled People and Disabling Environments* London: Jessica Kingsley.

Finn, D. and Taylor, D. (1990) The Future of Jobcentres: Labour Market Policy and the Employment Service, Employment Paper No. 1, London: IPPR.

Finn, D., Blackmore, M. and Nimmo, M. (1998) *Welfare-to-Work and the Long-Term Unemployed*, London: Unemployment Unit and Youthaid.

Fletcher, D. R. (1997) 'Evaluating Special Measures for the Unemployed: some reflections on the UK experience', *Policy and Politics*, vol. 25, no. 2, pp. 173-184.

Flora, P. (ed.) (198687) *Growth to Limits. The Western European Welfare States since World War II*, Vol. 1-4. Berlin: De Gruyter.

Flora, P; Kuhnle, S. and Urwin, D. (eds) (1999) *State Formation, Nation-Building and Mass Politics in Europe. The Theory of Stein Rokkan*, Oxford: Oxford University Press.

Folbre, N. (1994) *Who Pays for the Kids?* New York: Routledge.

Franco, D., Munzi, T. (1996) 'Public Pension Expenditure Prospects in the European Union', in European Commission, *Ageing and Pension Expenditure Prospects in the Western World*, European Economy, Reports and Studies, No. 3/1996, Luxembourg: Office for Official Publications of the European Communities, pp. 1-126.

Fraser, N. (1994) 'After the Family Wage: Gender Equity and the Welfare State.' *Political Theory* 22, pp. 591-618.

French, S. (ed.) (1994) *On Equal Terms: Working with Disabled People*, Oxford: Butterworth-Heinemann.

Gal, J. (2000) 'The perils of compensation: disability policy in Israel', paper for conference *Social Protection in the new era: what future for welfare?* Research Committee on Poverty, Social Welfare and Social Policy, International Sociological Association (RC 19), Tilburg University, August.

Galbraith, J. (1992) *The Culture of Contentment*, Harmondsworth: Penguin.

Gallagher, J. (1999) *A Shrinking Portion of the Safety Net: General Assistance from 1989 to 1998*, Washington: The Urban Institute.

Ganzenboom, H. (1988) Leefstijl en -patronen in Nederland (Lifestyles and Patterns in The Netherlands), Rijswijk: Social and Cultural Planning Office.

Garrett, G. (1998) *Partisan Politics in the Global Economy*, Cambridge: Cambridge University Press.

Gauthier, A.H. (1996) *The State and the Family : a Comparative Analysis of Family Policies in Industrialized Countries,* Oxford : Clarendon Press.

Gaxie, D. (et al.) (1990), *Le «Social» Transfiguré*, Paris: PUF.

George, V. and Taylor-Gooby, P. (eds) (1996) *European welfare policy - Squaring the welfare circle*, London: Macmillan.

George, V., P. Stathopoulos and J. Garces (1999) 'Squaring the welfare circle and government ideology: Greece and Spain in the 1990s', *International Social Security Review*, vol. 52, no. 4, pp. 47-68.

Gilbert, N. (1992) 'From Entitlements to Incentives: The Changing Philosophy of Social Protection', *International Social Security Review*, vol. 45, no. 3, pp. 5-18.

Gilbert, N. (2000) 'Renegotiating Social Allocations: Choices and Issues', in N. Gilbert (ed.) *Targeting Social Benefits. International Perspectives and Trends. International*

Social Security Series vol 1, New Brunswick: Transaction Publishers.

Gillion, C., J. Turner, C. Bailey and D. Latulippe (2000) *Social security pensions. Development and reform,* Geneva: ILO Labour Office.

Giner, S. (1986), 'Political Economy, Legitimation and the State in Southern Europe, in G. O'Donnell and P. Schmitter (eds) *Transitions from Authoritarian Rule: Prospects for Democracy,* Baltimore: John Hopkins University Press.

Glennester, H. (1995) *British Social Policy Since 1945,* Oxford: Blackwell.

Goldberg, G. and Kremen, E. (1990) *The Feminization of Poverty: Only in America?,* New York: Praeger.

Goodin, R. (1988) 'Reasons for Welfare', in J. D. Moon (ed) *Responsibility, Rights and Welfare,* London: Westview Press.

Goodin, R. and LeGrand, J. (1987) *Not Only the Poor. The Middle Classes and the Welfare State,* London: Allen and Unwin.

Goodin, R.E., Hedey, B., Muffels, R., and Dirven, H-J. (1997) 'Welfare over time: Three worlds of welfare capitalism in panel perspective', *Journal of Public Policy,* vol. 17, no. 3, pp. 329-359.

Goodin. R.E., Hedey, B., Muffels, R., and Dirven, H-J (1999) *Real Worlds of Welfare Capitalism,* Cambridge: Cambridge University Press.

Goodman, R. and Peng, I. (1996) 'The East Asian Welfare States: Peripatetic Learning, Adaptive Change, and Nation-Building'. in G. Esping-Andersen (ed) *Welfare States in Transition,* London: Sage.

Gornick, J., Meyers, M. and Ross, K. (1997) 'Supporting the Employment of Mothers: Policy Variation Across Fourteen Welfare States.' *Journal of European Social Policy* 7, pp. 45-70.

Gottschalk, P. and Smeeding T. (1997) 'Cross-National Comparisons of Earnings and Income Inequality', *Journal of Economic Literature,* XXXV (June), pp. 633-687.

Gough, I. (1996) 'Social Assistance in Southern Europe', *South European Society & Politics,* vol. 1, no. 1, pp. 1-23.

Goul Andersen, J. (1988) *Vælgermosaik.* Småartikler om valg og vælgere 1986-88, Working Paper, Center for Kulturforskning, University of Aarhus.

Goul Andersen, J. (1993) *Politik og samfund i forandring.* København: Columbus.

Goul Andersen, J. (1998) 'Velfærdens veje i komparativt perspektiv', *Den jyske Historiker* 82, pp. 114-38.

Goul Andersen, J. (2000a) 'Welfare Crisis and Beyond: Danish Welfare Policies in the 1980s and 1990s', in S. Kuhnle (ed.) *Survival of the European Welfare State,* London: Routledge.

Goul Andersen, J. (2000b) 'From Citizenship to Workfare? Changing Labour Market Policies in Denmark, 1975-2000', *Jahrbuch,* Bremen.

Goul Andersen, J. (forthcoming) *Velfærdens værdier* (book manuscript).

Goul Andersen, J. and Christiansen, P. M. (1991) *Skatter uden velfærd. De offentlige udgifter i international belysning.* Copenhagen: Jurist- og Økonomforbundets Forlag.

Goul Andersen, J. and Jensen, J.B. (forthcoming) Employment and Unemployment in Europe.

Government (1989) Hvidbog om arbejdsmarkedets strukturproblemer. Copenhagen: Government.

Grimshaw, D. and Rubery, J. (1997) 'Workforce Heterogeneity and Unemployment Benefits: The Need for Policy Reassessment in the European Union', *Journal of European Social Policy*, vol. 7, no. 4, pp. 291-318.

Group of 7 (1995) Unemployment Benefits and Social Assistance in Seven European Countries, *Working Document No. 10*, The Hague: SZW.

Haas, L. (1992) *Equal Parenthood and Social Policy: A Study of Parental Leave in Sweden,* Albany: State University of New York Press.

Hall, P. (1993) 'Policy Paradigms, Social Learning and the State: The Case of Economic Policy-Making in Britain', *Comparative Politics,* vol. 25, pp. 275-96.

Hall, P. and Taylor, R. (1996) 'Political Science and the Three New Institutionalisms', pp. 15-44 in E.M.Uslaner and V. Haufler (eds) *Institutions and Social Order*, Ann Arbor: University of Michigan Press.

Haney, L. (1997) "But We are Still Mothers': Gender and the Construction of Need in post-socialist Hungary', *Social Politics,* vol. 4, no. 2, pp. 208-44.

Hansen, H. (2000) *Elements of Social Security*, Copenhagen: The Danish National Institute of Social Research.

Hartog, J. (1999) 'The Netherlands: So what's so special about the Dutch model?', *Employment and Training Papers*, No. 54, Geneva: International Labour Office.

Hasenfeld, Y. (1985) 'Citizens' Encounters with Welfare State Bureaucracies', *Social Service Review*, vol. 59, no. 4/December, pp. 622-635.

Hasenfeld, Y. and Rafferty, J. (1989) 'The Determinants of Public Attitudes toward the Welfare State', *Social Forces*, vol 67, no 4, pp 1027-1048.

Hasenfeld, Y. and Weaver, D. (1996) 'Enforcement, Compliance, and Disputes in Welfare-to-Work Programs', *Social Science Review*, vol. 70, no. 2, pp. 235-256.

Hasluck, C. (2000a) *The New Deal for the Long-term Unemployed: A Summary of Progress*, Employment Service Research and Development Report ESR46. Sheffield: Employment Service.

Hasluck, C (2000b) *Early Lessons from the Evaluation of New Deal Programmes*, Employment Service Research and Development Report ESR49, Sheffield: Employment Service.

Hatland, A. (2001) 'Changing Family Patterns – A Challenge to Social Security', in M. Kautto et al. (eds) (2001) *The Nordic Welfare States in the European Context*, London: Routledge.

Havemann, J. and Vobejda, B. (1998) The Welfare Alarm that Didn't Go Off, *Washington Post* October 1, 1998.

Hechter, M. (1987) *Principles of Group Solidarity*, Berkeley: University of California Press.

Heclo, H. (1974) *Modern Social Policies in Britain and Sweden.* New Haven: Yale University Press.

Heclo, H. (1998) 'A Political Science Perspective on Social Security Reform', in R.D. Arnold et al. (eds), *Framing the Social Security Debate*, Washington, D.C.: Brookings Institution Press, pp. 65-89.

Heinen, J. (1999) 'East European Transition, Labour Markets, and gender in the Light of Three Cases: Poland, Hungary and Bulgaria', paper presented at the 5th TSER Seminar of the European Network 'Gender and Citizenship', Georg-August Universität, Göttingen, Germany, February.

Henderson, A. and Parsons, T. (1964) *Max Weber. The Theory of Social and Economic Organization*, New York: The Free Press.

Hernes, H. (1987) *Welfare, State and Women Power. Essays in State Feminism*, Oslo: Oslo University Press.

Hill, M. (1997) *The Policy Process in the Modern State*, Third Edition, London: Prentice Hall.

Hills, J. and Lelkes, O. (1999) 'Social Security, Selective Universalism and Patchwork Redistribution', in R. Jowell (ed.) *British Social Attitudes, 15th Report*, Aldershot: Ashgate.

Hinrichs, K. (1996) *Social Insurances and the Culture of Solidarity. The Moral Infrastructure of Interpersonal Redistributions*, paper presented at the ISA RC19 conference 'Comparative Research on Welfare State Reforms', 19-23 August, Canberra.

Hinrichs, K. (1998) Reforming the Public Pension Scheme in Germany: The End of the Traditional Consensus?, Universität Bremen, Zentrum für Sozialpolitik, ZeS-Arbeitspapier Nr. 11/98, Bremen.

Hinrichs, K. (2000a) 'Auf dem Weg zur Alterssicherungspolitik. Reformperspektiven in der gesetzlichen Rentenversicherung', in S. Leibfried and U. Wagschal (eds), *Der deutsche Sozialstaat*, Frankfurt/New York: Campus, pp. 276-305.

Hinrichs, K. (2000b) 'Rentenreformpolitiken in OECD-Ländern. Die Bundesrepublik Deutschland im internationalen Vergleich', *Deutsche Rentenversicherung* No. 3-4: 188-209.

Hinrichs, K. (2001) 'Armutsfeste Grundsicherung im Alter. Ausländische Modelle und die jüngste Rentenreform in Deutschland', *Zeitschrift für Sozialreform*, vol. 47, no. 4 (forthcoming).

Hirst, P.A. and Thompson, G. (1997) 'Globalization in Question: International Economic Relations and Forms of Public Governance', in J.R. Hollingsworth and R. Boyer (eds) *Contemporary Capitalism: The Embeddedness of Institutions*, Cambridge: Cambridge University Press, pp. 337-60.

HM Treasury (2000) *Tackling Poverty and Making Work Pay – Tax Credits for the 21st Century*, The Modernisation of Britain's Tax and Benefit System No 6, London: Her Majesty's Treasury.

Hobson, B. (1990) 'No Exit, No Voice: Women's Economic Dependency and the Welfare State', *Acta Sociologica* 33, pp. 235-50.

Hobson, B. (1994) 'Solo Mothers, Social Policy Regimes and the Logics of Gender', in D. Sainsbury (ed.) *Gendering Welfare Regimes*, Newbury Park, CA: Sage, pp. 170-87.

Hobson, B. (1999) 'Gender and Economic Citizenship: Reflections Through the European Union Policy Mirror', in B. Hobson (ed.) *Gender and Citizenship in Transition*, London: Macmillian.

Hobson, B. and Takahashi, M. (1997) 'The Parent-Worker Model: Lone Mothers in Sweden,' in J. Lewis (ed) *Lone Mothers in European Welfare Regimes*, London: Jessica Kingsley, pp. 121-139.

Hofstede, G. (1998) *Masculinity and Femininity. The Taboo Dimension of National Cultures*, Thousand Oaks: Sage.

Hogwood, B. W. and Gunn, L. (1984) *Policy Analysis for the Real World*, London:

Oxford University Press.

Hort, S. E. O. and Kuhnle, S. (1999) 'Recent Changes in Emerging east and Southeast Asian Welfare States', paper presented at the workshop on 'Globalization and Social Dumping,' European Forum, European University Institute, Florence, Italy, March.

House of Commons Environment, Transport and Regional Affairs Committee (1999) *Town and Country Parks,* 20th Report, HC477-1, London: The Stationery Office.

Huber, E. (1996) 'Options for Social Policy in Latin America: Neoliberal versus Social Democratic Models', in G. Esping-Andersen (ed.) *Welfare states in transition. National Adaptations in Global Economies,* London: Sage Publications.

Huber, E. and Stephens, J.D. (1993) 'Political Parties and Public Pensions: A Quantitative Analysis', *Acta Sociologica* 36, pp. 309-325.

Huber, E. Ragin, C. and Stephens, J. D. (1993) 'Social Democracy, Christian Democracy, Constitutional Structure and the Welfare State', *American Journal of Sociology,* vol. 99, no. 3 , pp. 711-49.

Huber, E. and Stephens, J.D. (2001) *Political Choice in Global Markets: Development and Crisis of Advanced Welfare States,* Chicago: University of Chicago Press.

Hudson, B. (1993) 'Michael Lispky and street-level bureaucracy: a neglected perspective', in M. Hill (ed.) *The Policy Process: A Reader,* London: Harvester Wheatsheaf.

Hughes, G. (2000) Pension Financing, the Substitution Effect and National Savings', in G. Hughes and J. Stewart (eds) *Pensions in the European Union: Adopting to Economic and Social Change,* Dordrecht: Kluwer Academic Publishers.

Hvinden, B (1994) *Divided Against Itself: A Study of Integration in Welfare Bureaucracy,* Oslo: Scandinavian University Press.

Ibsen, F. (1992) 'Efter Zeuthen-rapporten', *Samfundsøkonomen* 1992:6.

Illich, I. (1973) *Deschooling Society,* Harmondsworth: Penguin.

Inglehart, R. (1977) *The Silent Revolution. Changing Values and Political Styles among Western Publics,* Princeton: Princeton University Press.

Inglehart, R. (1990) *Culture Shift in Advanced Society,* Princeton: Princeton University Press.

Jackson, P. C. (1993) 'Managing the Mothers: The Case of Ireland.' in J. Lewis (ed.) *Women and Social Policies in Europe. Work, Family and the State,* Cheltenham: Edward Elgar, pp. 72-91.

Jäntti, M., Kangas, O. and Ritakallio, V.-M. (1996) 'From Marginalism to Institutionalism: Distributional Consequences of the Transformation of the Finnish Pension Regime', *Review of Income and Wealth* 42, pp. 473-491.

Jäntti, M. and Ritakallio, V.-M. (2000) 'Income Poverty in Finland 1971-1995', in B. Gustafsson B. and P. Pedersen (eds) *Poverty and Low Income in the Nordic Countries,* Aldershot: Ashgate, pp. 63-99.

Jenson, J. (1986) 'Gender and Reproduction: Or, Babies and the State', *Studies in Political Economy* 20, pp. 9-45.

Jenson, J., Hagen, E. and Reddy, C. (eds) (1988) *Feminization of the labor force: paradoxes and promises,* New York: Oxford University Press.

Jessop, B. (1982) *The Capitalist State,* Oxford: Robertson.

Johnson, C. and Savner, S. (1999) *Federal Funding Sources for Public Job Creation Initiatives,* Washington: Center On Budget And Policy Priorities.

Johnson, P. (1999) 'The Measurement of Social Security Convergence: The Case of European Public Pension Systems since 1950', *Journal of Social Policy* 28, pp. 595-618.

Join-Lambert, M.-T. (1997) *Politiques Sociales,* Paris: Dalloz (2d edition).

Kalisch, D., Aman, T. and Buchele, L.A. (1998), 'Social and Health Policies in OECD Countries: A Survey of Current Programmes and Recent Developments', *Labour Market and Social Policy Occasional Paper*, No.33, Paris: OECD.

Kamerman, S.B. (1986) 'Women, Children and Poverty: Public Policies and Female-Headed Families in Industrialized Countries.' in B. Gelpi, N. Hartsock, C. Novak, and M. Strober (eds) *Women and Poverty*, University of Chicago Press, pp. 41-63.

Kangas, O. (1997) 'Self-interest and the Common Good. The Impact of Norms, Selfishness and Context in Social Policy Opinions', *Journal of Socio-economics*, vol 26, no 5, pp 475-494.

Kangas, O. and Palme, J. (2000) 'Does social policy matter? Poverty cycles in OECD countries', *International Journal of Health Services*, vol 30, no. 2, pp. 335-352.

Katrougalos, G. (1996) 'The South European Welfare Model: The Greek Welfare State, in Search of an Identity', *Journal of European Social Policy*, vol. 6, no.1, pp. 40-60.

Kautto, M., Heikkilä, M., Hvinden, B., Marklund, S., and Ploug, N. (eds) (1999) *Nordic Social Policy. Changing Welfare States*, London: Routledge.

Kingdon, J. W. (1995) *Agendas, Alternatives, and Public Policies*, 2.ed., New York: Harper Collins.

Kluegel, J., Mason, D. and Wegener, B. (eds) (1995) *Social Justice and Political Change. Public Opinion in Capitalist and Post-communist States*, New York: De Gruyter.

Knijn, T. (1994) 'Fish without Bikes: Revision of the Dutch Welfare State and Its Consequences for the (In)dependence of Single Mothers', *Social Politics,* 1, pp. 83-105.

Knijn, T. and Kremer, M. (1997) 'Gender and the Caring Dimension of Welfare States: Toward Inclusive Citizenship', *Social Politics*, 4, pp. 328-61.

Kohl, J. (1981) 'Trends and Problems in Postwar Public Expenditure Development in Western Europe and North America', in P. Flora and A.J. Heidenheimer (eds) *The Development of Welfare States in Europe and America*, New Brunswick: Transaction Books, pp. 307-344.

Kolb, R. (1989) 'One hundred years of German pension insurance legislation', *International Social Security Review* 2, pp. 195-202.

Kolberg, J.E. (1991) *The Welfare State as Employer*, New York: M.E. Sharpe.

Korpi, W. (1985) 'Economic Growth and the Welfare system: Leaky Bucket or Irrigation System?', *European Sociological Review*, vol. 1, no. 2, pp. 97-118.

Korpi, W. and Palme, J. (1998) 'The Paradox of Redistribution and Strategies of Equality: welfare state institutions, inequality and poverty in the Western countries', *American Sociological Review*, 63, pp. 661-87.

Kötter, U. (1999), 'Health Care Systems between National Regulation and European Market', European Forum (Conference paper WS/41), Florence: European University Institute.

Kristensen, O.P. (1987) *Væksten i den offentlige sektor. Institutioner og politik.* Copenhagen: Jursit- og Økonomforbundets Forlag.

Krugman, P. (1996) *Pop Internationalism*. Cambridge, Mass: MIT Press.

Kuhnle, S. (ed.) (2000a) *Survival of the European Welfare State*, London: Routledge.

Kuhnle, S. (2000b) 'The Scandinavian Welfare State in the 1990's: Challenged but Viable', in *West European Politics* (Special Issue), vol. 23, no. 2, pp. 209-228.

Kvist, J. (1998) 'Complexities in assessing unemployment benefits and policies', *International Social Security Review,* vol. 51, no. 4, pp. 33-55.

Kvist, J. (1999) 'Welfare Reform in the Nordic Countries in the 1990s: Using Fuzzy-Set Theory to Assess Conformity to Ideal Types', *Journal of European Social Policy,* vol. 9, no. 3, pp. 231-52.

Kvist, J. (2000a) 'Idealtyper og fuzzy mængdelære i komparative studier – nordisk familiepolitik i 1990erne som eksempel' [Ideal types and fuzzy sets in comparative studies – Nordic family policy in the 1990s as example], *Dansk Sociologi*, vol. 11, no. 3, pp. 71-94.

Kvist, J. (2000b) 'Conceptualisation, Configuration, and Classification – Ideal Types and Fuzzy Sets in the Study of Welfare Reform Outcomes', paper presented at the COST A15 'Reforming Social Protection in Europe' meeting of WG2, Brussels 9-10 March.

Kvist, J. (2000c) 'Activating Welfare States. Scandinavian Experiences in the 1990s', *Working Paper*, no. 7, The Danish National Institute of Social Research.

Lake, M. (1992) 'Mission Impossible: How Men Gave Birth to the Australian Nation - Nationalism, Gender and Other Seminal Acts', *Gender and History*, 4, pp. 305-22.

Land, H. and Hilary, R. (1985) 'Compulsory Altruism for Some or an Altruistic Society for All?' in P. Bean, J. Ferris and D. Whynes (eds) *In Defense of Welfare*, London: Tavistock, pp. 74-96.

Larsen, F. and Stamhus, J. (2000) 'Active Labour Market Policy in Denmark: Labour Market Reform, Crucial Design Features and Problems of Implementation' *Working Paper*, Department of Economics, Politics and Public Administration, Aalborg University.

Lasch, C. (1978) *The Culture of Narcissism*, New York: Norton.

Leibfried, S. (1992) 'Towards a European Welfare State? On integrating Poverty Regimes into the European Community', in Z. Ferge and J. Kolberg (eds) *Social Policy in a Changing Europe*, Boulder, CO.: Westview.

Leibfried, S. (1993) 'Toward a European welfare state ?', in C. Jones (ed.) *New perspectives on the welfare state in Europe*, London: Routledge, pp.133-156.

Leibfried, S. (ed) (2000) 'Welfare State Futures', *European Review*, vol. 8, no.2.

Leira, A. (1992) *Welfare States and Working Mothers: The Scandinavian Experience.* New York: Cambridge University Press.

Leisering, L. and Leibfried, S. (1998) *Time, Life and Poverty. Social Assistance Dynamics in the German Welfare State*, Cambridge: Cambridge University Press.

Levy, J. (1999) 'Vice into virtue? Progressive Politics of Welfare reform in Continental Europe', *Politics and Society*, 27, pp. 239-273.

Levy, J. (2000) 'France: Directing Adjustment?' in F. Scharpf and V. Schmidt (eds) *Welfare and Work in the Open Economy*, vol. 2, Oxford: Oxford University Press, pp. 308-350.

Lewis, J. (1992) 'Gender and the Development of Welfare Regimes', *Journal of European Social Policy*, 3, pp. 159-73.

Lewis, J. (ed.) (1993) *Women and social policies in Europe: Work, Family and the State,* Aldershot: Edward Elgar.

Lewis, J. (1997a) 'Gender and Welfare Regimes: Further Thoughts', *Social Politics,* 4, pp.160-77.

Lewis, J. (ed.) (1997b) *Lone Mothers in European Welfare Regimes,* London: Jessica Kingsley.

Lindbeck, A. (1994) 'The Welfare State and the Employment Problem', *The American Economic Review,* vol.84, no. 2 , pp.71-75.

Lindbeck, A. (1994) 'Uncertainty under the Welfare State – Policy-induced Risk –', *The Geneva Papers on Risk and Insurance* 19, pp. 379-393.

Lindbeck, A. and Snower, D. (1988) *The Insider-Outsider Theory of Employment and Unemployment,* Cambridge, Mass.: MIT Press.

Lindenberg, S. (1990) 'Homo Socio-economicus. The Emergence of a General Model of Man in the Social Sciences', *Journal of Institutional and Theoretical Economics,* no 146, pp 727-748.

Lipsky, M. (1980) *Street-Level Bureaucracy: Dilemmas of the Individual in Public Services,* London: Harvester Wheatsheaf.

Lister, R. (1997) *Citizenship: Feminist Perspecitives.* London: Macmillan.

Liu, L. (1999) 'Retirement Income Security in the United Kingdom', *Social Security Bulletin,* vol. 62, no.1, pp. 23-46.

Lødemel, I. and Trickey, I. (eds) *An Offer You Can't Refuse,* Bristol: Policy Press.

Lolle, H. (1999) *Serviceudgifter og brugertilfredshed i danske kommuner,* Aalborg: Aalborg University Press.

Lonsdale, S. (1993) *'Invalidity benefit: an international comparison',* London: Department of Social Security.

Majone, G. (1991) 'Research Programmes and Action Programmes, Or Can Policy Research Learn from the Philosophy of Science?', in P. Wagner et al. (eds), *Social Sciences and Modern States,* Cambridge: Cambridge University Press, pp. 290-306.

Manow, P. and Seils, E. (2000) 'Adjusting Badly: The German Welfare State, Structural Change, and the Open Economy', in F. Scharpf and V. Schmidt (eds) *Welfare and Work in the Open Economy,* vol. 2, Oxford: Oxford University Press, pp.264-307.

Mansbridge, J. (1990) 'On the Relation of Altruism and Self-interest', in J. Mansbridge (ed) Bey*ond Self-interest,* Chicago: University of Chicago Press.

Mantel, J. and Thomsen, M. (2000) Pension Reform in France: A Missed Opportunity, Merrill Lynch and Co., Global Securities Research and Economics Group, London (mimeo.).

MAP (1997) Estudio sobre reparto del gasto público en 1997 entre los distintos niveles de administración, Madrid: Ministerio de Administraciones Públicas.

March, J.G. and Olsen, J.P. (1984) 'The New Institutionalism: Organizational Factors in Political Life', *American Political Science Review,* vol.78, no. 3, pp. 734-749.

Martin, J.P. (2000) 'What works among active labour market policies: evidence from OECD countries' experiences', *OECD Economic Studies* no. 30, Paris: OECD.

Mayhew, L. (1971) *Society. Institutions and Activity,* Illinois: Glenview Press.

McCarthy, S. (1998) 'Martin backs off seniors plan', *The Globe and Mail,* July 29, A1 and A4.

McDonald, P. (1997) 'Gender Equity, Social Institutions and the Future of Fertility',

Working Papers in Demography, Canberra: Research School of Social Sciences, no. 69, pp. 1-25.

McLaughlin E., Trewsdale J. and McCay, N. (2001) The Working Families Tax Credit: some issues and estimates, *Journal of Social Policy and Administration* (forthcoming).

Ministry of Finance (1996) *Finansredegørelse 1996*, Copenhagen: Ministry of Finance.

Ministry of Finance (1999) *Finansredegørelse 1998-99*, Copenhagen: Ministry of Finance.

Ministry of Finance (2000) *Finansredegørelse 2000*, Copenhagen: Ministry of Finance.

Ministry of Labour (2000) *Effekter af aktiveringsindsatsen*, Copenhagen: Ministry of Labour, March 2000.

Mishra, R. (1999) *Globalization and the Welfare State*, Cheltenham: Edward Elgar.

MISSOC (2000) *Social Protection in the EU Member States and the European Economic Area,* Luxembourg: Office for Official Publications of the European Communities.

Moghadam, V. (1993) *Social Protection and Women Workers in Asia*. Helsinki: WIDER; WIDER Working Paper No.110.

Moore, M.J. and Viscusi, W.K. (1990) *Wages, Workers' Compensation and Product Liability*, Princeton University Press, Princeton.

Moreno, L. (ed.) (1993) *Social Exchange and Welfare Development*. Madrid: CSIC.

Moreno, L. (1999) 'Local and Global: Mesogovernments and Territorial identities', *Nationalism and Ethnic Politics*, vol. 5, no. 3-4, pp. 61-75.

Moreno, L. (2000), 'The Spanish development of Southern welfare', in S. Kuhnle (ed.) *Survival of the European Welfare State*. London: Routledge.

Moreno, L. and Arriba, A. (1999) 'Welfare and Decentralization in Spain', EUI Working Paper EUF 99/8. Florence: European University Institute.

Morlino, L. (1998) *Democracy between Consolidation and Crisis: Parties, Groups and Citizens in Southern Europe*, Oxford : Oxford University Press.

Mouzelis, N. (1995) *Sociological Theory What Went Wrong? Diagnosis and Remedies*, London: Routledge.

MSZW (2000)   *Efforts to Reintegrate the Unemployed: An Overview*, Den Hague: Minsiterie van Sociale Zaken en Werkgelenheid.

Mueller, D. (1989) *Public Choice II,* Cambridge: Cambridge University Press.

Muffels, R., Nelissen, J. and Nuyens, W. (1986) *Social Security and Income Inequality. A Comparative Study, Series on Social Security Studies*, Tilburg: Tilburg University Press.

Müller, K. (2000) 'Die Reform der Alterssicherung in den östlichen Transformationsländern: eine Zwischenbilanz', *Deutsche Rentenversicherung* no. 5, pp. 280-293.

Myles, J. and Pierson, P. (1997) 'Friedman's revenge: The reform of 'liberal' welfare states in Canada and the United States', *Politics and Society*, 25, pp. 443-72.

Myles, J. and Pierson, P. (2001) 'The Comparative Political Economy of Pension Reform', in P. Pierson (ed.) *The New Politics of the Welfare State,* Oxford: Oxford University Press.

Myles, J. and Quadagno, J. (1997) 'Recent Trends in Public Pension Reform: A Comparative View'. in K.G. Banting and R. Boardway (eds) *Reform of Retirement*

Income Policy: International and Canadian Perspectives, School of Policy Studies, Queen's University, Kingston, Ontario.

Nussbaum, M. and Sen, A. (eds) (1993) *The quality of life*, Oxford: Oxford University Press.

Nye, R. (1996) *Welfare to Work: The America Works Experience*, London: Social Market Foundation.

O'Connor, J., Orloff, A. and Shaver, S. (1999) *States, Markets, Families: Gender, Liberalism and Social Policy in Australia, Canada, Great Britain and the United States, Princeton*, N.J.: Princeton University Press.

O'Connor, J. (1993) 'Gender, Class and Citizenship in the Comparative Analysis of Welfare State Regimes: Theoretical and Methodological Issues', *British Journal of Sociology*, 44, pp. 501-18.

OECD (1985) *Social Expenditures 1960-1990: Problems of Growth and Control*, Paris.

OECD (1993) *OECD Health Systems*, Paris, Vol. I.

OECD (1994a) *New Orientations for Social Policy*, Social Policy Studies, No. 12, Paris.

OECD (1994b) *The OECD Jobs Study. Evidence and Explanations 1-2*, Paris: OECD.

OECD (1995) *Employment Outlook*, Paris: OECD.

OECD (1996a) *Ageing in OECD Countries: A Critical Policy Challenge*, Social Policy Studies, No. 20, Paris.

OECD (1996b) *The Public Employment Service Austria, Germany Sweden*, Paris: OECD.

OECD (1997a) *Historical Statistics*, Paris: OECD.

OECD (1997b) *Japan*, Economic Surveys, 1996-1997, Paris: OECD.

OECD (1997c) *Family, Market and Community: Equity and Efficiency in Social Policy*, Paris: OECD.

OECD (1997d) *Implementing the OECD Jobs Strategy*, Paris: OECD.

OECD (1998a) *Economic Outlook*, Paris.

OECD (1998b) *Maintaining Prosperity in an Ageing Society*, Paris: OECD.

OECD (1998c) *National accounts; Main aggregates*, volume I, Paris: OECD.

OECD (1999a) *Employment Outlook*, Paris: OECD.

OECD (1999b) *The Public Employment Service in the United States*, Paris: OECD.

OECD (2000a) *Education at a Glance*, Paris: OECD.

OECD (2000b) *Reforms for an Ageing Society*, Paris: OECD.

Offe, C. (1988) 'Democracy against the Welfare State', in J. Moon (ed), *Responsibility, Rights and Welfare*, Boulder: Westview Press.

Offe, C. (1996) 'Full Employment: Asking the Wrong Question?', in E. Oddvar Eriksen and J. Loftager (eds), *The Rationality of the Welfare State*, Oslo: Scandinavian University Press.

Official Journal of the European Communities (2000) 'Council Directive 2000/78/EC of 27 November establishing a general framework for equal treatment in employment and occupation', Luxembourg: Office for Official Publications of the European Communities.

Ogus, A.I. and Wikeley, N.J. (eds) (1995) *The Law of Social Security*, Fourth Edition, London: Butterworths

Okun, A. (1975) *Equality and Efficiency: The Big Trade-Off*, Washington DC: MIT Press.

Oliver, M. (1983) *Social Work with Disabled People*, London: Macmillan

Oliver, M. and Barnes, C. (1990) 'Disability, discrimination and welfare: from needs to rights' in I. Bynoe, M. Oliver and C. Barnes, *Equal rights for disabled people: the case for a new law,* London: Institute for Public Policy Research.

Olson, M. (1977) *The Logic of Collective Action. Public Goods and the Theory of Groups,* Cambridge: Harvard University Press.

Orloff, A. S. (1993) 'Gender and the Social Rights of Citizenship: The Comparative Analysis of Gender Relations and Welfare States,' *American Sociological Review* 58, pp. 3-28.

Orloff, A. S. (1997) 'On Jane Lewis's Male Breadwinner Regime Typology', *Social Politics,* vol. 4, no. 2, pp. 188-202.

Orloff, A. S. (2001) 'Ending the Entitlements of Poor Single Mothers: Changing Social Policies, Women's Employment Caregiving', in N. Hirschmann and U. Liebert (eds) *Women and Welfare: Theory and Practice in the United States and Europe,* New Brunswick: Rutgers University Press.

Ostner, I. (1993) 'Slow Motion: Women, Work and the Family in Germany.' in J. Lewis (ed) *Women and Social Policies in Europe. Work, Family, and the State,* Hants: Edward Elgar, pp. 92-115.

Ostner, I. (1997)'Lone Mothers in Germany Before and After Unification,' in J. Lewis (ed.) *Lone Mothers in European Welfare Regimes,* London: Jessica Kingsley, pp. 92-115.

Ostner, I. and Lewis, J. (1995) 'Gender and the Evolution of European Social Policies,' in S. Leibfried and P. Pierson (eds) *European Social Policy: Between Fragmentation and Integration,* Washington DC: Brookings, pp.159-93.

Overbye, E. (1994) 'Convergence in Policy Outcomes: Social Security Systems in Perspective', *Journal of Public Policy* 14, pp. 147-74.

Overbye, E. (1997) 'Mainstream pattern, deviant cases: The New Zealand and Danish pension systems in an international context', *Journal of European Social Policy,* vol.7, no. 2 , pp. 101-117.

Overbye, E. (1998) 'Risk and welfare. Explaining stability and change in "welfare" policies', Oslo: Norwegian Social Research.

Palier, B. (2000) '"Defrosting" the French Welfare State', *West European Politics.* vol. 23, no.2, pp. 113-136.

Palier, B. (2001) 'Reshaping The Social Policy Making Framework: France from the 1980s to 2000 ', in P. Taylor-Gooby (ed.) *Welfare states under pressure,* London, Sage: forthcoming.

Palmer, E. (2000) 'The Swedish Pension Reform Model – Framework and Issues, World Bank', Social Protection Discussion Paper no. 0012, Washington, D.C.

Pampel, F. C. and Williamson, J. B. (1989) *Age, class, politics, and the welfare state,* Cambridge: Cambridge University Press.

Papadakis, E. and Bean, C. (1993), 'Popular Support for the Welfare State. A Comparison between Institutional Regimes', Jou*rnal of Public Policy,* vol 13, no 3, pp 227-254.

Parsons, T. (1951) *The Social System,* London: Routledge & Kegan Paul.

Pearce, D. (1978) 'The Feminization of Poverty: Women, Work and Welfare', *Urban and Social Change Review* 11, pp. 28-36.

Pedersen, A.W. (1999) 'The taming of inequality in retirement. A comparative study of pension policy outcomes', Oslo: FAFO. Report 317.

Pedersen, S. (1993) *Family, Dependence, and the Origins of the Welfare State: Britain and France, 1914-1945.* New York: Cambridge University Press.

Peillon, M. (1995) 'Support for Welfare in Ireland: Legitimacy and Interest' *Administration,* vol 43, no 3, pp 3-21.

Pettersen, P. (1995) 'The Welfare State. The Security Dimension', in O. Borre and E. Scarbrough (eds) *The Scope of Government,* Oxford: Oxford University Press.

Pierson, C. (1991) *Beyond the Welfare State?,* Cambridge: Polity Press.

Pierson, P. (1994) *Dismantling the Welfare State? Reagan, Thatcher and The Politics of Retrenchment,* Cambridge: Cambridge University Press.

Pierson, P. (1996) 'The New Politics of the Welfare State', *World Politics* 48, pp. 143-179.

Pierson, P. (1998) 'Irresistible Forces, Immovable Objects: Post-industrial Welfare States Confront Permanent Austerity', *Journal of European Public Policy* 5/4, pp. 539-60.

Pierson, P. (ed) (2001a) *The New Politics of the Welfare State,* Oxford: Oxford University Press.

Pierson, P. (2001b) 'Coping with permanent austerity: welfare state restructuring in affluent democracies', in P. Pierson (ed) (2001) *The New Politics of the Welfare State,* Oxford: Oxford University Press.

Platenga, J. (1998) 'Double Lives: Labour market participation, citizenship and gender,' in J. Bussemaker and R. Voet (eds) *Gender, Participation and Citizenship in the Netherlands,* Aldershot, England: Ashgate, pp.51-64.

Ploug, N. (1996) The Welfare State. Consistent Attitudes in a Changing World, Paper presented at the ISA RC 19 Annual Meeting, 19-23 August, Canberra.

Ploug, N. and Kvist, J. (eds) (1994) *Recent Trends in Cash Benefits in Europe,* Copenhagen: Danish National Institute of Social Research.

Priestley, M. (2000) 'Adults only: disability, social policy and the life course', *Journal of Social Policy,* vol. 29, no. 3, pp. 421-439.

Prottas, J., M. (1979) *People-processing: The Street-Level Bureaucrat in Public Service Bureaucracies,* Massachusetts: Lexington Books.

Quadagno, J. (1999) 'Creating a Capital Investment Welfare State: The New American Exceptionalism', *American Sociological Review,* 64, pp. 1-11.

Rainwater, L. and Smeeding, T. (1995) 'Doing poorly: The real income of American children in a comparative perspective', Luxembourg Income Study: *Working Paper* no. 127.

Rawls, J. (1972) *A Theory of Justice,* Oxford: Oxford University Press.

Rawls, J. (1996) *Political liberalism,* New York: Columbia University Press.

Rayner, E. et al (2000*) Evaluating Jobseeker's Allowance: A summary of the research findings.* DSS Research Report No 116, Leeds: Corporate Document Services.

Rhodes, M. (1996) 'Southern European Welfare States: Identity, Problems and Prospects for Reform', *South European Society and Politics,* vol. 1, no. 3, pp. 1-22.

Ringen, S. (1987) *The Possibility of Politics. A Study in the Political Economy of the Welfare State*, Oxford: Clarendon Press.

Room, G. (1994) 'Poverty studies in the European Union: retrospect and prospect', paper for conference on *Understanding Social Exclusion in Europe*, London: Policy Studies Institute, November.

Rose, R. and Peters, B. (1978) *Can Government Go Bankrupt?*, New York: Basic Books.

Roseveare, D., Leibfritz, W., Fore, D. and Wurzel, E. (1996) *Ageing Populations, Pension Systems and Government Budgets: Simulations for 20 OECD Countries*, Economics Department Working Papers, No. 168, Paris.

Ross, F. (1997) 'Cutting Public Expenditures in Advanced Industrial Democracies: The Importance of Avoiding Blame', *Governance* 10, pp. 175-200.

Ross, F. (2000) 'Interests and Choice in the 'Not Quite so New' Politics of Welfare', *West European Politics*, vol. 23, no. 2, pp.11-34.

Ruggie, M. (1988) 'Gender, Work, and Social Progress: Some Consequences of Interest Aggregation in Sweden', in J. Jenson, E. Hagen and C. Ready (eds) *Feminization of the Labour Force,* New York: Oxford University Press, pp. 172-88.

Ruggie, M. 1984)*The State and Working Women.* Princeton: Princeton University Press.

Sandmo, A. (1991) 'Presidential Address: Economists and the Welfare State', *European Economic Review,* vol.35, no. 2-3, pp. 213-39.

Saraceno, C. (1994) 'The Ambivalent Familism of the Italian Welfare State', *Social Politics*, 1, pp. 60-82.

Saunders, P. (1994) *Welfare and Inequality. National and international perspectives on the Australian Welfare State*, Cambridge: Cambridge University Press.

Scharpf, F. (2000) 'Institutions in Comparative Policy Research', *MPIfG working paper 00/3*, Cologne: Max Planck Institut für Gesellschaftsforschung.

Scharpf, F.W. and Schmidt, V.A. (eds) (2000) *From Vulnerability to competitiveness: Welfare and Work in the Open Economy,* Oxford: Oxford University Press (2 volumes).

Scherman, K.G. (1999) 'The Swedish Pension Reform', International Labour Office, Social Scurity Department, Issues in Social Protection, Discussion Paper No. 7, Geneva: ILO.

Schmidt, M. (1993) 'Gendered Labor Force Participation.' in F.G. Castles (ed) *Families of Nations*, Aldershot: Dartmouth, pp. 179-237.

SCP (1994) *Profijt van de overheid III* (Profiting from the Government III), Rijswijk: Social and Cultural Planning Office.

Sen, A. (1990)'Gender and Cooperative Conflicts,' in I. Tinker (ed) *Persistent Inequalities,* New York: Oxford University Press.

Sen, A. (1999) *Development as Freedom*, Oxford: Oxford University Press.

Shin, D-M. (2000) 'Financial Crisis and Social Security: The Paradox of the Republic of Korea', *International Social Security Review*, vol. 53, no. 3, pp. 83-108.

Siim, B. (1997) 'Dilemmas of Citizenship in Denmark: Lone Mothers Between Work and Care,' in J. Lewis (ed.) *Lone Mothers in European Welfare Regimes*, London: Jessica Kingsley, pp. 140-71.

Simon, H.A. (1985) 'Human Nature in Politics: The Dialogue of Psychology with Political Science', *American Political Science Review,* vol. 79, pp. 293-304.

Sinfield, A. (1997) 'Blaming the Benefit: The costs of the distinction between active and passive programmes', in J. Holmer and J. Karlsson (eds) *Work - Quo Vadis?*, Aldershot: Avebury.

Sinn, H.W. (1995) 'A Theory of the Welfare State', *Scandinavian Journal of Economics*, vol. 97, pp. 495-526.

Smitdtz, D. (1998) 'Taking responsibility', in D. Schmidtz and R.E. Goodin (eds) *Social welfare and individual responsibility*, Cambridge: Cambridge University Press, pp. 3-96.

Søndergaard, J. (1999) 'The Welfare State and Economic Incentives', in T. Andersen (et al) (eds) *Macroeconomic perspectives on the Danish economy*, London: Macmillan.

Sozialbeirat (1998) 'Gutachten des Sozialbeirats zum Rentenversicherungsbericht 1998 und Stellungnahme zu einigen weiteren Berichten zur Alterssicherung', in Bundesregierung, *Rentenversicherungsbericht 1998*, Deutscher Bundestag, Drucksache 13/11290 (v. 17.07.98), Bonn, pp. 239-251.

Standing, G. (1990) 'The Road to Workfare: Alternative to Welfare or Threat to Occupation?', *International Labour Review*, vol. 129, no. 6, pp. 677-91.

Standing, G. (1996) 'Social Protection in Central and Eastern Europe: a Tale of Slipping Anchors and Torn Safety Nets,' in G. Esping-Andersen (ed) *Welfare States in Transition: National Adaptations in Global Economies*, London: Sage, pp. 225-55.

Statistiches Bundesamt (1999) Ergebnisse der Sozialhilfe- und Asylbewerberleistungsstatistik 1997, *Wirtschaft und Statistik* 2, pp. 96-110.

Stevens, F. and Diederiks, J. (1995) 'Health Culture in Europe', in G. Lueschen et al. (eds) *Health Systems in the European Union*, Munich: Oldenburg Verlag.

Stinchcombe, A.L. (1968) *Constructing Social Theories*, New York: Harcourt, Brace & World.

Stone, D. (1985) *The Disabled State*, Philadelphia PA: Temple University

Svallfors, S. (1989) *Vem aelsker Vaelfaerdstaten?*, Lund: Arkiv.

Svallfors, S. (1996) *Välfärdsstatens moraliska ekonomi*. Umeå: Borea.

Svallfors, S. (2000) 'Political Trust and Support for State Intervention in Different Policy Regimes', paper presented at the Annual Meeting of the International Social Survey Program, Lisbon May 7, 2000.

Swartz, R. et al. (1999) *Where did Families go when AFDC ended in Milwaukee?* Indianapolis: The Hudson Institute.

Tálos, E. and Kittel, B. (1999) 'Sozialpartnerschaft und Sozialpolitik', in F. Karlhofer and E. Tálos (eds) *Zukunft der Sozialpartnerschaft. Veränderungsdynamik und Reformbedarf*, Wien: Signum, pp. 137-164.

Taylor-Gooby, P. (1983) 'Legitimation Deficit, Public Opinion and the Welfare State', *Sociology*, no 17, pp 165-184.

Taylor-Gooby, P. (1985) *Public Opinion, Ideology and State Welfare*, London: Routledge.

Taylor-Gooby, P. (1999) 'Markets and Motives', *Journal of Social Policy*, vol 28, no 1, pp 97-114.

Ter Bogt, T. and Van Praag, C. (1992) *Jongeren op de drempel van de jaren negentig* (Young People on the Threshold of the Nineties), Rijswijk: Social and Cultural Planning Office.

Bibliography

Thomson, D. (1991) Selfish Generations? The Ageing of New Zealand's Welfare State, Wellington: Bridget Williams.

Titmuss, R.M. (1968) *Commitment to Welfare*, London: Allen and Unwin

Titmuss, R.M. (1976) 'Pension Systems and Population Change', in *Essays on 'The Welfare State'*, 3rd ed., London: George Allen and Unwin Ltd., pp. 56-74.

Torp, H. (1999) 'Dagpengesystemerne i Norden', in Nordisk Ministerråd, Dagpengesystemerne i Norden og tilpasning på arbeidsmarkedet, *TemaNord Arbeidsmarked*, Copenhagen: Nordic Council of Ministers.

Tullock, G. (1987) *Autocracy,* Dordrecht: Kluwer Academic Publishers

Udredningsudvalget (1992) 'Rapport fra udredningsudvalget om arbejdsmarkedets strukturproblemer', Copenhagen: Udredningsudvalget.

UK (1920a) First and Second Reports of the Select Committee on Pensions, HC 149 and 247, London: HMSO.

UK (1920b) First and Second Reports of the Select Committee on Pensions, Minutes of Evidence, Q 2078, London: HMSO.

UK (1975) Social Security Act 1975, S 17 (I) (a).

UK (1998) Secretary of State for Social Security, *A New Contract for Welfare: Support for Disabled People,* Cm 4103, London: Stationery Office.

UK (1999a) 'Incapacity benefit and severe disablement allowance: quarterly summary of statistics', Department of Social Security, November.

UK (1999b) 'Health statistics quarterly', Office for National Statistics.

UNEDIC (2000) *Annual Report 1999*, Paris.

UPIAS (1976) *Fundamental Principles of Disability,* London: Union of the Physically Impaired against Segregation.

US Department of Commerce (2000) *Statistical Abstract of the United States 120th edition*, Washington: USDC.

US Social Security Administration (1998) *Social Security Bulletin Annual Statistical Supplement,* Washington: SSA.

Uusitalo, H. (1999) 'Changes in income distribution during a deep recession and after', (mimeo) Stakes: Helsinki.

Van Deth, J. (1984) *Politieke waarden* (Political Values), Amsterdam: CT Press.

Van Kersbergen, K. (1995) *Social Capitalism. A study of Christian democracy and the welfare state*, London: Routledge.

Van Kersbergen, K. (2000) 'The declining resistance of welfare states to change?', in S. Kuhnle (ed.) *Survival of the European Welfare State*. London: Routledge.

Van Oorschot, W. (1997) The Common Good, Nearness and Dependence. On Solidarity and its Motives, *AWSB Working Papers* 97/12.

Van Oorschot, W. (1998) *Dutch Public Opinion on Social Security*, Loughborough: CRSP Series, Centre for Research in Social Policy.

Van Oorschot, W. (1999a) Work, Work, Work. Labour Market Policies in the Netherlands 1970-2000, paper presented at the RC19 annual conference, Prague.

Van Oorschot, W. (1999b) *The Legitimacy of Welfare. A Sociological Analysis of Motivations to Contribute to Welfare*, Tilburg: WORC paper, Tilburg University.

Van Oorschot, W. (2001) 'Who Should Get What and Why?', *Policy and Politics*, (forthcoming).

Van Oorschot, W. and Engelfriet, R. (1999) Work, work, work: Dutch labour market policies 1970-2000, *Working Paper*, Florence: European University Institute.

Oorschot, W. van and Boos, C. (1999) 'Dutch Pension Policy and the Ageing of the Population', *European Journal of Social Security* 1, pp. 295-311.

Vesterø-Jensen, C. (1985) *Det tvedelte pensionssystem*, Roskilde: Forlaget Samfundsøkonomi og Planlægning.

Visser, J. and Hemerijck, A. (1997) *A Dutch miracle', Job Growth, Welfare Reform and Corporatism in the Netherlands,* Amsterdam: Amsterdam University Press.

Voges, W., Jacobs, H. and Trickey, H (2001) 'Uneven Development: Local Authorities and Workfare in Germany', in I. Lødemel and H. Trickey (eds) *An Offer You Can't Refuse,* Bristol: Policy Press.

Von Rhein-Kress, G. (1993) 'Coping with Economic Crisis: Labour Supply as a Policy Instrument'. In F.G. Castles (ed) (1993) *Families of Nations: Patterns of Public Policy in Western Democracies,* Aldershot: Dartmouth, pp. 131-78.

Waernes, K. (1987) 'On the Rationality of Caring', in A. Showstach (ed) *Women and the State,* London: Hutchinson.

Walker, R. (1998) The Americanisation of British Welfare: A case-study of Policy Transfer, *Focus,* vol. 19, no. 3, pp. 32-40.

Wasserman, D. (1998) 'Distributive Justice', in A. Silvers, D. Wasserman and M. Mahowald, *Disability, Difference, Discrimination: Perspectives on Justice in Bioethics and Public Policy,* Lanham MD: Rowman and Littlefield.

Weatherley, R. (1979) *Reforming Special Education: Policy Implementation from State Level to Street Level,* Cambridge Mass.: MIT Press.

Weatherley, R. and Lipsky, M. (1977) 'Street-Level Bureaucrats and Institutional Innovation: Implementing Special-Education Reform', *Harvard Educational Review,* vol. 47, no. 2/May, pp. 171-197.

Weaver, R.K. (1986) 'The Politics of Blame Avoidance', *Journal of Public Policy* 6, pp. 371-398.

Weaver, R.K. (1998) 'The Politics of Pensions: Lessons from Abroad', in R.D. Arnold et al. (eds), *Framing the Social Security Debate,* Washington, D.C.: Brookings Institution Press, pp. 183-229.

Weir, M., Orloff, A.and Skocpol, T (1988) 'The Future of Social Policy in the United States. Constraints and Possibilities', in M. Weir, A. Orloff and T. Skocpol (eds) *The Politics of Social Policy in the United States,* Princeton: Princeton University Press.

Welfare Commission (1995) *Kommissionen om fremtidens beskæftigelses- og erhvervsmuligheder: Velstand og Velfærd,* Copenhagen: Statens Information.

Whiteley, P. (1981) 'Public Opinion and the Demand for Welfare in Britain', *Journal of Social Policy,* vol 10, pp 453-476.

Wiesenthal, H. (2000) 'Die politische Organisation des Unwahrscheinlichen', in K. Hinrichs et al. (eds), *Kontingenz und Krise. Institutionenpolitik in kapitalistischen und postsozialistischen Gesellschaften,* Frankfurt/New York: Campus, pp. 189-217.

Wikeley, N. (2000) 'Social Security and Disability' in N. Harris, *Social Security Law in Context,* Oxford: Oxford University Press.

Wilensky, H. (1975) *The Welfare State and Equality. Structural and Ideological Roots of Public Expenditure,* Berkeley: University of California Press.

Wilensky, H. L. (1975) *The Welfare State and Equality,* Berkeley, California:

University of California Press.

Wilson, J.J., Mulgan, G., Hills, J. and Piachaud, D. (1998) 'Welfare Reform: Learning from American Mistakes?', CASEreport 4, London, Centre for Analysis of Social Exclusion, London School of Economics.

World Bank (1994) *Averting the Old Age Crisis: Policies to Protect the Old and Promote Growth*, New York: Oxford University Press.

World Health Organisation (2000) 'International Classification of Functioning, Disability and Health, pre-final draft, full version' Classification, Assessment and Terminology Team, Geneva.

Worrall, J.D. and Butler, R.J. (1988) 'Experience Rating Matters' in P.S. Borba and D. Appel (eds) Workers' Compensation Insurance Pricing: Current Programs and Proposed Reforms, Kluwer, Boston.

Zacher, H.F. (1987) 'Grundtypen des Sozialrechts', in W. Fürst et al. (eds), *Festschrift für Wolfgang Zeidler*, Bd. 1, Berlin: Walter de Gruyter, pp. 571-595.

Zedlewski, S. and Brauner, S. (1999) *Are The Steep Declines in Food Stamp Participation Linked to Falling Welfare Caseloads?*, Washington: Urban Institute.

Zhongli, L. (2000) 'The methodology for reforming China's social security system and its developmen', paper presented at Conference on restructuring China's social security system: Funding, operations and governance. Beijing, 19-20 August.

Zijderveld, A. (1979) 'Het ethos van de verzorgingsstaat', *Sociale Wetenschappen*, vol 22, no 3, pp 179-203.